T0368917

Michael Joseph
an imprint of
Penguin Books

———

the whole vegetable

sophie gordon

Photography by
Issy Croker

Illustrations by
Holly Ovenden

introduction p.4   getting organized p.13

spring has sprung p.23

early summer p.71

height of summer p.121

autumn p.175

winter begins p.241

depths of winter p.303

the basics p.351   thanks p.374   index p.375

introduction

I'm commonly known among friends for being an obsessive vegetable hoarder. A quarter of a pepper sitting in the fridge, carrots in a jar of water, leaves trimmed and bagged: you'll find me roasting up some cauliflower leaves with chilli flakes, salt and lemon juice, or using those 'inedible' onion skins or vegetable peelings for a trusty homemade stock. Wherever I am, I'm pretty good at whipping something up based on what's in the fridge or cupboard, to make delicious nourishing recipes from what seems like nothing.

We've become fixated on using multiple ingredients in our meals – from a ready meal with an ingredients list too long to read, to the belief that a dinner party means buying 30 new items from a supermarket. I'm here to show you that using fewer ingredients doesn't mean compromising on taste; in fact, by eating seasonally, you will create dishes that are vibrant and full of flavour – because the produce is at its peak!

Every recipe in this book has been created with the idea of making use of the whole vegetable. I encourage you to not throw away what you might normally, saving those scraps to be re-worked into another dish or put into your stock box for later. What doesn't get used can then of course be composted. There are lots of ways you can adapt the recipes to suit your style or taste, as well as where you are in the world, making use of what's in season or what the weather may be like.

This approach sums up my way of cooking to a tee. I'm passionate about (and slightly obsessed with) the minimization of waste,

taking the not-so-ordinary or usually
discarded parts of a fruit or vegetable and
using them to their full potential – and
even to our advantage. Homemade stocks,
vegetable-top pestos, broccoli chops, salty
roasted leaves, the works. I believe fruit
and vegetables should be celebrated,
enjoyed with minimal preparation or fuss
and simply enhanced with little more than
a pinch of salt, a grind of pepper, a drizzle
of olive oil or a glug of balsamic vinegar.
Making vegetables the star feature of a
recipe brings them to life, paired perfectly
with wholegrains, healthy fats and good-
quality oils, sweet and savoury vinegars,
natural sugars, fresh herbs and other
seasonings. I aim to balance textures,
tastes and nutrients through my cooking,
inspiring a simpler way to go about eating,
lower your overall waste and improve your
general attitude towards food.

Cooking and eating seasonally

I am a true fanatic when it comes to fresh ingredients, a sucker for using the best 'in season' produce. Of course, it has to be achievable, and the best way to eat seasonally is to shop local, supporting smaller businesses, farms, markets and so on, where you'll find everything from vibrant freshly picked cherries to carrots with their tops and kohlrabi with their shoots, and even olive oil with just a simple slinky label, made locally at its best.

Eating seasonally makes us more connected to what we eat: foods are fresher and tastier when picked just at the right moment to make that perfect summer salad or that warming winter crumble. In the summer, our bodies crave fresh foods with higher water content, such as cucumbers or tomatoes, while in the winter we crave more starchy, rich and grounding foods like potatoes, pumpkins and beetroots. Cooking seasonally also means better flavours – the peas in April always taste a little sweeter and the sweetcorn in July is the most naturally buttery thing going – and you soon start to associate these tastes with the time of the year.

As well as eating produce seasonally for its enhanced and superior flavour, doing so can help us support the planet. It takes resources to grow food; a lot of maintenance goes into growing and tending to crops. Seasonal eating helps to lower greenhouse gas emissions, in turn reducing our carbon footprint. We've all experienced those tasteless tomatoes, stringy avocados, bitter courgettes or sugar snap peas that are far from sweet. It's not uncommon for produce to taste different when it's been through environmental stress like high temperatures, drought, floods, dubious practices or even just simply been picked

before it was ready, for importing purposes. The more seasonally we eat and the more support we give to local producers, the more efficient things will be in the long run as demands change, chains shorten, and that extra £1 is knocked off those juicy berries we so fondly love, when buying them in season. Seeing the same produce 365 days of the year shouldn't be normal, whereas shopping locally and eating seasonally should be normal, and indeed it once was, so let's bring it back again. A lot of love goes into the process from local farmers and growers, so we should celebrate and relish the natural flavours, textures and sizes of produce in its prime.

I am forever dreaming about one day having my own vegetable garden, growing almost all of what I eat, seasonally. But for now, taking the time to shop at markets and local grocers, and to grow my own herbs (with a little rogue foraging here and there – I'm a sucker for wild garlic and elderflower) is the next best thing. As for the rest, I either buy in bulk or from zero-waste stores, filling up on what I need when I need it. Because I travel often for my job, I like to buy local oils or sauces to bring back, not only as a memento, but also to help support the local businesses in the places I visit.

Knowing when certain fruits and vegetables come into season is like second nature to me now, so when I see the first chestnuts of the year, or kale showing off a beautiful shade of purple, my excitement is second to none. Naturally, buying and eating seasonally will also save you money, which in this current world is not a bad thing. Produce in season is more abundant, it travels less, therefore there are fewer expenses to meet the demands of supplying a particular ingredient, ultimately saving you some pennies.

Introducing my six seasons

We typically know the seasons as the traditional four – autumn, winter, spring and summer – but as you'll discover in this book, there is a huge amount of overlap between these when it comes to fresh produce, and what's going on at the farms or in the fields isn't always matched in a super-market, with countless fruits and vegetables being imported. By introducing the idea of six seasons, with the crossover of certain fruits and vegetables between them, I've found a way to embrace what's on offer throughout the year, while focusing in on the detail of what is actually growing when, and how availability can change in just a few subtle weeks.

Getting to grips with six seasons is a whole lot easier than you might think. Produce varies dramatically from the start of winter to the end, or from the beginning of summer through to its height. Typically, spring and summer are where an awful lot goes on crop-wise, and with the weather being warmer and sometimes wetter (especially here in the UK) you may see strawberries appearing earlier, sweetcorn around for longer, broad beans a preference over peas. Just as the produce changes, our needs change, aligning a little more with the weather. In winter, we're more likely to want those warming recipes making the most of hearty produce, whereas in summer we crave light ingredients to create a refreshing salad . . . it all makes perfect sense.

Of course, seasons vary around the world, but traditionally the produce we get in the warmer months or the colder ones is the same, making the recipes in this book and the seasons relatable, no matter where you are.

What's the deal with waste?

The numbers and the facts about waste are just as significant as seasonality: over 50% of household waste is from food, most of this being 'avoidable' waste that was edible at some point. We waste food for many reasons – lack of planning, throwing away less aesthetically pleasing produce, buying too much, confusion about 'use-by' dates, not storing food correctly or sensibly, perhaps in ways that are not so pleasing to the eye, and even just incorrect portioning at mealtimes. Food waste is on the rise, despite more of us becoming truly concerned about our impact on the planet. Many of us hugely overspend on food, a lot of the time because we are buying out-of-season produce that in turn is more expensive and wrapped in plastic, versus food that is fresh from a market and was picked as recently as the day before or perhaps even that morning.

All of us, no matter our diet or eating habits, by now can accept that vegetables are key to staying healthy and feeling great. Unfortunately, vegetables in plastic packaging make up a huge amount of waste – who hasn't had to empty a pile of rotting pulp from their fridge drawer?

So, my core aim with this book is to challenge the idea that eating seasonally, with a less-waste approach, is complicated or involves too much time and planning. Focusing on the use of the whole vegetable is a big step towards preventing food waste.

Why do I cook like this?

My love and passion for cooking started at a young age. I would spend weekends repeatedly making butterfly or angel cakes, and I was always keen to get involved with what my parents were cooking, pulling up a stool and watching in awe, reaching my little hands over the counter, grabbing what I could, or dipping a finger in a simmering sauce. It's pretty lucky I didn't have any of my fingers sliced off, or scalded! My parents had a mighty recipe book collection, and would spend time selecting recipes that my brother and I might enjoy with our amateur taste buds, such as a hearty veggie-heavy bulgur wheat bake from Mum and a made-from-scratch pizza from Dad, with a rich Italian tomato sauce and every topping imaginable. Food quickly became a big love in my life and I always had a keen interest in what I was eating and where it came from. I was encouraged to experiment with the foods I ate, and often played around with different cuisines, spices and ingredients. Growing up in Devon played a huge part in shaping my philosophy towards eating and cooking through the seasons – a key and obvious part of eating well for ourselves and for the planet. We were immersed in nature a lot of the time; country walks, village strolls and weekend trips to family friends' farms. We were encouraged to spend as much time outside as we could, which meant witnessing the ever-changing seasons through the weather. And along with the weather, of course, came the different foods we'd encounter and the meals my parents cooked. Devon is known for the rugged beauty of its moors and the wildlife along the coastline. Local farmers had easy access to some of the greatest and freshest produce, and we became

a part of that, shopping from them, seeing their passion and learning exactly where our apples for our crumble were coming from, or why the garlic was a shade of purple, with fresh leaves accompanying it. With our father a keen chef, his food adventures inevitably became ours.

This desire to eat fresh foods grew even stronger when I lived in Australia, where I really began to understand and appreciate seasonal food. Fresh produce is a lot more accessible there because of the climate, so I was able to create more recipes with a wider range of ingredients. I stayed with some family friends for my first few weeks there, who also contributed massively to my journey. They were food enthusiasts and I'd always be over for dinner, knowing that Debbie would have cooked up a storm with her farmers' market finds or new herb-based sauce, a true inspiration. Upon coming back to London, I realized just how lucky I had been. Picking up an avocado in the middle of winter felt abnormal, not to mention its watery taste and paler flesh.

I spent just under two years in Australia, but it was probably the most valuable time of my life in terms of the way I cook today. After a few weeks back in the UK I couldn't stop thinking about the Australian approach to food. Sure, a lot was down to the climate, but the quality of ingredients and produce was pretty special. Upon arriving back in the UK, as well as founding a food business called Dust Granola (named after the time someone asked me if as a vegan all I ate was dust), my initial plans were simply to suss out where I belonged in the London food scene and explore different avenues, while using it as a chance to cook for others. Regular brunches turned into suppers and events for all occasions. I'm a people person

by nature and I love nothing more than sharing what I love with others, rustling up a collection of dishes and serving them to people, satisfying their hungry bellies. Doing so involves prepping menus, finding venues, shopping for ingredients, gathering friends or inviting guests, creating a scene and setting the tables . . . and I can wholeheartedly say I'd happily do it any day, every day. My love for food and cooking has pretty much become the entire focus of my life. I embrace every part. Watching people's expressions when they tuck into a spread is really quite special, my cup well and truly filled, from the adrenaline of the event, and most importantly, from the fact that I'm giving to others in the best way I know how.

The adventure is ongoing and I'm lucky enough to use my passion and obsession for detail and good produce as a means to make a living. It brings me to life. I thrive when stumbling upon locally grown ingredients or the season's finest at a weekend market, before heading home to have a bit of fun in the kitchen. More often than not, my casual market purchases turn into some of my most favoured dishes that will get tested on several different friends – or sometimes the same friends multiple times! – before making their way, ever so humbly, on to a retreat or supper club menu.

About my recipes

I'm pretty laid back in the kitchen, and truly believe cooking should be a fun pastime, not a chore or task, so gaining enough confidence to actually relax into it is something I think is very valuable. I don't mind making mistakes and am happy to attempt something new because personally I find it always leads to something great, whether it's the end result that time or after a few more tries. I cook for happiness, a little clichéd, but it is my meditation. It slows me down, gives me a focus, and most importantly, brings people together.

When it comes to creating recipes, I let my taste buds guide me, my travels inspire me, and my adventurous attitude help me to explore. I love to play about in the kitchen, combining hearty flavours with fresh produce to create appetizing dishes, and making use of the robust textures of seasonal grains. I find pleasure in both the simplest of dishes and the more involved ones.

I love texture, there's a reason why I can't just have a soup as a meal! Loading it with broad bean croutons or pairing it with fresh bread and tossing in some extra greens is a must for me. I'm pretty consistent when it comes to cooking, and you'll notice I'm big on the use of oils and vinegars as seasoning rather than overloading a dish with them. I believe it's important to always have a balance, seasoning enough but not too much, whether that be with salt and pepper or with herbs and lemon zest, something I'm a huge fan of. From my many years of cooking, I've learnt that the right seasoning is just as important as the right balance of ingredients.

I rely heavily on the produce that's in season depending on where I am. Because of the uncertainty of produce when I'm catering abroad, I've developed many techniques to help me quickly adapt a particular recipe or dish, by substituting different vegetables, grains and so on. I don't always realize it at the time, but my frequent travelling has helped me develop a variety of transferable skills, from the way that I cook the food to the choices about what dish I'm actually cooking. Naturally these skills and techniques don't just apply when I'm cooking on a job, or just to myself for that matter. So I've shared them all in this book. As you make your way through the recipes, you'll notice lots of options and suggestions for substitutions or alternative ingredients to achieve a similar end result, as well as numerous little 'waste tips' to make your veg go further.

One last thing I should add, and something that you'll start to discover as you read on, is that I'm a BIG fan of condiments. Dips, sauces, chutneys, pickles, pestos and all types of mustards are always in my fridge, whether for a particular recipe or simply to serve on the side. My friends will vouch for me when I say I'm obsessed!

That all being said, my recipes offer something for any and every taste bud. Sharp, sweet, citrus or just something a little fancier, the recipes are yours just as much as the dish you are about to eat from is, so make them your own.

How to use this book

All the recipes in the book are organized by my six seasons, so you'll quickly be able to flick to a certain chapter, checking what is available at that time of year in terms of fresh produce and which grains/legumes you might choose. For each of the seasons you'll find there are 5 core ingredients as the focus of all the recipes, typically four vegetables and one fruit. For each core ingredient I give general advice on how to reduce and re-use your waste, plus I give a more specific 'waste tip' at the end of each separate recipe. This is to help you make use of the whole of every vegetable with ideas on how to store them, how you could make use of the recipe as a leftover (a dal transformed into curried hummus is one of my personal favourites!), or what else you could substitute if you happen to be cooking in another season or another part of the world, if you just don't have something in, or if you want to adapt the recipes to suit your style or taste. For example, you may be some-where where squash is available much more frequently, or where tomatoes are more abundant slightly later or earlier than suggested, so you can use it as a rough guide and make it your own.

The recipes vary in serving sizes, being for 2, 4, 6 and so on. Each recipe will easily divide in half, or thirds, etc., if you need to tailor it for a different amount. If you want to make something for just yourself, you can adapt the recipe to suit your needs, or equally cook a bigger quantity in order to have leftovers. The majority of the condiments or sauces within the main recipes and in the 'basics' section (page 351) will make a batch, the size of which is usually stated. Occasionally it will be just

enough for that recipe but making a bigger batch of pesto or cashew-based cheese is never a bad thing. Everything keeps in the fridge and this is stated in the 'waste tips' provided.

There is also a section of the book that will help you get to grips with being a little more organized (page 13), from shopping smartly and getting ahead of the game with a little bit of planning, to cooking and buying in bulk, and the best way to store fresh produce and cupboard ingredients.

And at the back of the book you will find the 'basics' recipe section (see page 351). This includes many of the staples I use throughout the book, such as a pesto base, harissa or hummus, plus some additional core staples such as homemade stocks and dressings. There are a few extras thrown into the mix too, with pancake bases, my go-to vegan cheese recipe and another personal favourite, granola. You can refer to this section at any time and there are references or prompts included as to when it might be useful to do so.

Above all, this book should help to inspire you in the kitchen while using easy tools and tips to reduce your waste at the same time. I want you to get excited, cook for yourself, cook for others, have fun, make mistakes, season to your taste, and appreciate both the simple and the complex. There is something for everyone.

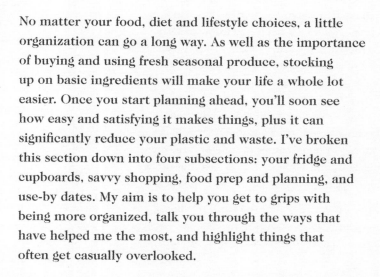

getting organized

No matter your food, diet and lifestyle choices, a little organization can go a long way. As well as the importance of buying and using fresh seasonal produce, stocking up on basic ingredients will make your life a whole lot easier. Once you start planning ahead, you'll soon see how easy and satisfying it makes things, plus it can significantly reduce your plastic and waste. I've broken this section down into four subsections: your fridge and cupboards, savvy shopping, food prep and planning, and use-by dates. My aim is to help you get to grips with being more organized, talk you through the ways that have helped me the most, and highlight things that often get casually overlooked.

Your fridge and cupboards

You know those times when you want to cook something, you've bought all your fresh ingredients, but you get to your cupboards and that potentially crucial bottle of soy sauce or vinegar has nothing more than a dribble in it? Occasionally, you can substitute other ingredients, using different grains or legumes, or swapping one cruciferous vegetable for another, but when you've got your heart set on a dish, there is nothing worse than a sad-looking fridge or empty cupboard. So having ingredients in that you can reach for at any time means you'll always be able to whip up a dressing, add crunch to a salad, mix your own spice/herb blends, or create a quick meal using leftover vegetables.

Let's start with your fridge. As simple as it sounds, condiments are a great place to begin when organizing it. Mine has a whole shelf dedicated just to condiments, from mustards to miso paste, homemade harissa to fresh hummus, which enables me to know exactly where they are and leaves plenty of room in the rest of the fridge for fresh produce. Typically, condiments sit on the top shelf as well as in those handy shelves in the fridge door. I like to keep anything that's opened or needs using first at the front, but if you like you could put older things on the left, newer on the right, and your 'go-tos' or 'use-me-nows' in the fridge door.

Making your way down to the fresh produce shelves and bottom drawers, my number-one tip here is to keep things clutter free. When you can clearly see and easily access everything, you'll be able to take note of what you do and don't have, helping you to write appropriate shopping lists with less stress and fuss. Again,

separate your old and new produce and perhaps even write a quick inventory. It may take a little bit of time initially, but it will reap rewards. When it comes to organizing your produce, try to group your fruits and vegetables. Foods that rot or wilt more quickly are better placed together so you know where they are, and to prevent some of your fresher produce doing the same. I like to keep my greens together, with older ones on top; herbs delicately placed on a shelf; harder fruits together; and so on. Nobody wants gunky greens wilting at the back of the fridge, so organizing and storing properly is key.

On the subject of wilting greens, let's talk about appropriate storage. Containers, tea towels and food/stasher bags are your best friends. One of the most useful things I've found for keeping my fridge nice and organized is investing in containers/mason-type jars; or better yet, saving old jars, no matter how big or small. Trust me when I say they will come in handy. You don't have to buy the most expensive containers or Tupperware, but bear in mind that you will re-use them often. Re-usable food bags vary in price and come in various sizes, making it easy to store snacks, frozen fruit, bread and even prepped and chopped vegetables. Just make sure they are 100% silicone, to ensure they are plastic- and toxin-free (vs some that are mixed material). When it comes to allocating your containers or food bags, you could save particular ones for leftover dishes or for storing fresh produce, making sure you wash them thoroughly first. Jars and small containers are a perfect, easy-to-access way to store homemade sauces or condiments, like pesto, harissa and salad dressings. As a little bonus, a jar of any of these makes a great gift for giving out to friends.

Back to those greens I was drumming on about: the best tip for storing leaves and fresh herbs is in fact within a damp tea towel or cloth. Wash them thoroughly before loosely rolling up. More robust kale types, such as cavolo nero, will keep well in a jar filled with water, then propped upright in the fridge. Fruits and berries do well if they are washed and patted dry, then kept on a damp cloth in a bowl with another cloth loosely placed over the top. This extends their shelf life, and prevents that early mould, which by the way, if it does occur, is totally OK and natural. You don't have to discard fruits that grow a few fluffy bits, it's spores or sprouting that you want to look out for, so you can just carefully remove those and keep the rest of the fruit. Of course, if the entire fruit looks less like it should do and more like mould, it's probably time to compost it. Keeping the ends on your vegetables will prevent them from rotting, and you can just compost those bits as and when you use the ingredients. Vegetables such as carrots, celery and radishes can be submerged in water, either the whole vegetable or just the roots depending on when you are going to use them.

A lot of vegetables can also be stored outside of the fridge. If, like me, you like a cold, crisp apple, only pop it into the fridge a few hours before eating, as they actually prefer to be out of the fridge, as does their good friend the potato. It's a common belief that potatoes should be kept away from other produce, but they can actually be placed with harder fruits such as apples and pears. Bananas are great to keep close to avocados, as they help with ripening, and if you've got some harder lemons that you know are not yet juicy enough, they can sit next to the bananas before later putting them into the fridge should you wish, as they do well both in and out. Most root vegetables, onions and garlic can also be kept out of the fridge. You can store them in linen tote bags but they do like a little bit of light, so roll the top down and keep it on the counter. Of course, when ingredients start to look a little limp, pop them into the fridge and use within a few days, making sure to compost any scraps or put them into your stock box for later – don't worry, we'll get to that.

Good organization applies to your cupboards too. Storing pantry and dried goods in jars is not only aesthetically pleasing but will help keep them fresher for longer, so long as they have airtight lids. Depending on the space you have, you can line them up, creating different sections. I like to group my grains together, placing my most frequently used ones at the front with the others behind. The same goes for oats, legumes, nuts, seeds, dried fruit, etc. (Occasionally, I'll combine a variety of nuts, seeds and dried fruits in a jar for a homemade trail mix, or pair that with about 70% oats for a homemade muesli.) Take advantage of smaller spaces by stacking, especially if you have similar jars that will stack neatly, then you can see what you have from pretty much just a glance. Just like I suggested for your fridge, you can quickly put together an inventory, making note of what you have on a piece of paper and sticking it to the back of the cupboard door. I find this really helps me when planning meals and helps to avoid buying things I don't need.

Most dried spices and herbs these days come in jars, which make it easier when organizing. If you do decide to write an inventory, spices should sit at the top of that in terms of priority. More often than not we have three jars of dried cumin or an overspilling paper bag of oregano waiting for a home. Most zero-waste stores have these dried delights on offer to refill, something I will get to in the next section.

Below I have listed a variety of ingredients (condiments and cupboard items) that you are likely to stumble across throughout the book. These are all widely available and definite staples in my house. It is of course not essential that you have all of these in at all times, so tailor the list to your needs or perhaps a bundle of recipes you want to try. I buy my legumes dried; this is a personal preference, but feel free to substitute for tinned – the washed-out tins make great containers to store raw veggies in at a later point, or kitchen utensils that you regularly use.

Grains/legumes: chickpeas, butter beans/ variety of white beans, lentils (orange or yellow), split peas, millet, rice (risotto, long and short grain, wild rice), pasta

——

Fats/oils: tahini, olive oil, coconut oil, sesame oil, nuts (variety), seeds (variety, including sesame seeds), coconut (sometimes flakes, sometimes desiccated, coconut milks)

——

Flours/baking: plain white, wholemeal, buckwheat, spelt, any other gluten-free alternatives of choice, baking powder, arrowroot, bicarbonate of soda

——

Vinegars: apple cider vinegar, red and white vinegar, balsamic/balsamic glaze, mirin and/or rice vinegar (both great for Asian-type dishes), liquid aminos

——

Dried fruits: dates, figs, sultanas

Herbs/spices: oregano, dried chilli flakes, cayenne pepper, cumin (ground and seeds), fennel seeds, coriander (ground and seeds), mint, thyme, rosemary, cinnamon, nutmeg, mixed spice, cardamom, clove, salt, pepper

Other: soy/tamari sauce, nutritional yeast, miso pasta, Dijon mustard, wholegrain mustard, maple syrup or other of choice, dried mushrooms, silken tofu, cacao powder, natural sugars (coconut sugar, pure cane, palm sugar), tomato paste, vanilla extract

A note on cooking beans/legumes/pulses:

Soak them first, ideally overnight if possible, and make sure you rinse them well. When it comes to cooking, make sure you add salt when they are al dente rather than straight away, but make sure not to salt too late, and cook until tender. This can vary from 45 minutes to 2 hours, depending on the size. Typically, you'll have double the weight of dried to cooked, for example 125g dried chickpeas to 250g once cooked. You can store them in the fridge with a bit of water for freshness (rinsing before use) or in the freezer for longer.

Savvy shopping

I know going to the supermarket isn't everyone's idea of fun – traipsing around the aisles can be laborious – but it can definitely be turned into something to enjoy. First things first, plan ahead, that way you can buy less to save more. The best way to start planning your shopping is by keeping a notebook in your kitchen. Every time you run out of an item, pop it on to the list. I tend to split mine into two columns, one for the 'urgent' things, the other for less important ingredients that I want to get at some point. Of course, if you are keeping an inventory for your fridge or cupboards, you can just refer to this to know exactly what you need. There are a few exceptions to the rule. For example, if I'm prepping for a dinner party, I'll check my cupboards and fridge for everything I need and then make a separate list to go shopping with. Occasionally there will be leftovers from this, whether that's a complete dish or just the vegetables, in which case I'll then do a bit of meal planning with what's left over and go from there. Another thing to think about when it comes to planning and writing lists is to make sure you take into account the days you won't be at home. You don't have to do it day by day, but if you know you'll be out two days of the week, just plan for the other five. Depending on how frequently you like to shop and where you live, you can also do what I like to call 'buy to make'. This involves a little more effort and time in terms of going out to get produce more frequently, but it can be a great way to avoid waste, especially if you're unsure of how the week might unfold. Essentially it means shopping for a specific recipe or dish, planning exactly what you need and buying the precise amount of ingredients for that dish. Often you'll have the cupboard ingredients in already but will need to get the fresh bits. When you're buying for a specific recipe, shopping at a grocer's or market tends to be the best option, as they usually let you buy produce according to the exact quantity you need.

Now for the actual shopping trip . . . After you've got your list prepared, make sure you have plenty of bags and/or boxes to bring home your produce in. These don't have to be fancy or expensive, especially if you are re-using what you already have, but with fabric bags it's a good idea to use ones that can be easily washed, as you'll tend to get bits of soil or dirt left over from the produce. You could use cotton tote bags, old 'bags for life', boxes, picnic-style bags or baskets, it's up to you. If you are thinking of purchasing something new, I suggest getting some reusable bags, preferably with a drawstring. You can get these in a variety of materials, from canvas to mesh or cotton and in a variety of sizes. Taking your own bags and boxes is the easiest way to avoid single-use plastic when shopping. A lot of markets and grocers tend to automatically put the produce you've picked up into a plastic bag, or sometimes paper (which is better than plastic and you can easily re-use these), but taking your own totally avoids this happening. It doesn't just stop at bags and boxes; if you are able to, taking jars is also handy for filling up your dried goods there and then.

This conveniently leads me on to talking about zero-waste and bulk-buy stores. If you live close to one of these, you'll probably never want to leave . . . or maybe that's just me. There are more and more of these kinds of stores popping up and it's worth doing a bit of research to see where your closest one is. You don't have to buy everything from there, but more often than not they will have everything you need. From dried pastas to rice, nuts and seeds, oils, vinegars, crisps even . . . and a personal favourite, dried mango . . . a chocolate-covered almond also never goes amiss. The beauty of these stores is that you can buy as much or as little as you like. It really is as simple as that: weigh and pay.

Once you've got your grains sorted, let's talk produce. As I've mentioned a handful of times, one of the greatest ways you can minimize your waste and eat seasonally is to get your fresh goods from places like markets. Usually, with minimal research you'll be able to see where your closest market is, or perhaps there is one you've wanted to go to for a while and can make a day of it. Markets tend to be on a weekend, but depending on where you are, there are some-times mid-week ones in villages. You'll want to get there nice and early to avoid any crowds, and if you are wanting to shop relatively quickly, you'll naturally avoid any loiterers by getting there for opening. In the summer there are lots of outdoor markets so it's a great opportunity to shop somewhere different. Produce at markets tends to be naked with minimal packaging, it's fresh, at eye level and the majority of the time is grown by farmers who take pride in their produce. When it comes to planning, the same rules apply: have your list ready before you head down, and buy only what you need, though maybe leave a little room for something newly 'in season' or that on-the-way-home snack. It's easy to get carried away when there is an abundance of fresh produce. Occasionally I'll pick up a bunch of grapes or strawberries in the summer that weren't on my list but will always get eaten no matter what. Make sure to take your bags for your produce and perhaps have a box in the car to easily transfer into the house. One last tip when it comes to going to a market is to have a walk-through first, if time allows. Scout the vendors and see what they have to offer – this allows you to compare the quality of the produce as well as the prices if you're trying to stick to a budget. It's also a great way to see what is available in general, and maybe for spotting that little something extra to add to the list, if it tickles your fancy.

Of course, going to a market is not something that everyone can do, or has time for. If you want to make it more achievable, you could perhaps tie it in with a catch-up with a friend, or take your kids, enabling them to see fresh produce at its finest, educating them subtly – in the best possible way, in my opinion. If you can't get yourself to a market, another great alternative is to sign up to fresh veg boxes. There are so many on offer these days, varying from just fresh produce to guided recipe boxes. These are great whether for just one person or for more if you have a family to feed. Depending on which box you go for, the produce tends to come from areas across the UK and occasionally slightly further, but you can choose. Companies like Abel & Cole and Riverford are great when it comes to how much plastic or packaging they use, with most of it being returnable or compostable. The produce is always seasonal and freshly delivered to your door. Something to make a note of when shopping at markets or buying food boxes is that you'll notice a huge variation in what the produce looks like. With fewer or no pesticides, the ingredients have a chance to grow in their own way, just how they should. This might mean they look more knobbly, bobbly, longer, shorter than the norm, but they shouldn't be given a hard time or not picked because they don't fit into the 'normal' constraints of what a fruit or vegetable is thought to look like. If anything, this veg makes for a more interesting dish, will probably taste better, and these days is often cheaper than perfect-looking ones.

If you are shopping in a supermarket or buying something in packaging, make it worth your while. Supermarkets are in convenient places for a reason, drawing us in because of their ease. Don't get me wrong, the produce can be just as good, and we all pop into one when we need something urgently, but try to be a little more aware of the packaging and buy as little in plastic as possible. If you do need to buy something in packaging, check for composting and recycling symbols, re-use what you can, and try to offset it if possible, by getting yourself to a market or bulk-buy store for other items.

It's not always possible to keep your entire shop plastic free, but doing your best, bit by bit, is what is important. It's a phrase you will have heard many a time, but every little bit really does count. Doing something consistently to help prioritize how you eat and what you waste, no matter how big or small, makes a difference. Celebrate the victories you make while shopping, forge new routines and get excited about them and the produce you bring home!

One final word on produce: I'm sure I'm not the only one who dreams of having my own vegetable garden. While we're not all able to do this, because of lack of outside space or other limitations, starting small is just as great. Herbs grow easily on windowsills, and some plants will survive inside. No matter what you choose to grow, have fun with it and take care of it. There are lots of DIY ways to create plant pots for seeds – an old milk carton cut open at the top, filled with soil and then some seeds is just one of many ideas. You can conveniently keep this in your kitchen, watching the little seeds sprout. If you do have a space or an opportunity to have your own vegetable garden, no matter how big or small, I really urge you to do this – it's a great hobby and is great for the planet.

Food prep and planning

As I'm sure you'll know by now, I'm big on prepping and getting ahead of the game. As you make your way through this book, you'll be able to collect my tips for prepping meals in advance. Throughout the recipes, I'll warn you if anything needs soaking or prepping in a certain way beforehand. Following my tips, you'll soon get to grips with the preparation of certain ingredients such as beans or pulses. At the back of the book you'll find a variety of 'basic' recipes, a lot of which are bases or foundations and condiments that you can make in a batch and store in the fridge. You can easily flick to and from this section whenever you need, making things as you go, prepping for the week ahead. Making your own condiments is simple and easy, and if you can do this versus buying them from the shops, it will naturally contribute to keeping your waste down and avoiding over-buying.

You can't plan for every eventuality, but you can get better at looking at all the meals for a week and thinking about what you really need, rather than guessing and overbuying. As I said before: plan to buy! Get out of the habit of thinking each meal requires a raft of new ingredients, and focus on one or two key items which can make many different meals; this is an easy but conscious shift that can make a real difference. For example, buying a few cauliflowers or a big bag of potatoes or mushrooms – stored properly, these last a long time despite being fresh, and can be used to make so many different meals.

I want to encourage everyone to make a 'fridge dinner' into a weekly habit. So, you open your fridge, you see some limp lettuce, a bunch of condiments, and a few other unappealing scraps of produce in the trays. Normally, you'd panic, and perhaps order a takeaway (full of processed ingredients, packed in lots of plastic) – well, this is all about to change. By simply having useful condiments, plus a well-stocked and organized cupboard, fridge and freezer, that limp lettuce can be turned into the best salad you've ever made. Perhaps you slice up some potatoes to roast in oregano, paprika and nutritional yeast, cook some lentils in stock, drain a tin of chickpeas, sauté the rest of the vegetables in a little soy sauce, toss in some crushed nuts and seeds for a bit of crunch, then top it with an unforgettable creamy tahini dressing. Or maybe you made a batch of pesto a few days ago, so just add a little more lemon juice or a plant-based milk and you're good to go. A 'limp lettuce' salad turns into an appealing and delicious meal. It doesn't have to be just a salad either . . . one-pot recipes are great for using up produce and legumes; most hearty stews are born this way and also make great stocks if you don't manage to finish up.

Lastly, on the subject of prepping, let's talk grains and legumes. You may not know exactly what meal you plan to make, but it's always an idea to batch-cook legumes and grains where possible. My go-tos are chickpeas, lentils, rice and millet. More often than not I'll whip up a batch of hummus for the week, varying it with different flavours, and I tend to make sure I have one or two of my favoured grains cooked and kept in the fridge. Legumes that are bulk bought/dried do need a bit of prepping, as you have to soak them before cooking. It is of course easier (and more usual) to reach for a tin of chickpeas instead, but with dried you can tailor the amount to your needs, wasting less, or, if you have leftovers, using them to make something else as well. If you want to cook a recipe with beans/legumes done from scratch, just ensure you get them soaking beforehand.

Use-by dates

Typically, most foods that come in some form of packaging have a 'use-by' date. There is a big misconception when it comes to this 'date', especially with regard to fresh produce. They can occasionally be called expiration dates, and that (I'm sure you've guessed where I'm going) inevitably leads to a huge amount of food waste. We have started to take this phrase very literally, and while in some cases this may be necessary – with meats, fish, dairy products – for fruit and vegetables it is a little different. Use-by dates should be treated as a rough guide: the reason they are there is to prevent any foods that may be risky to eat from causing foodborne-related illnesses or poisoning. Meanwhile, a 'best-before' date tends to be more about quality rather than safety. Best-before dates are usually found on cupboard items rather than fresh ingredients; however, if they are on something fresh, it'll simply mean that the item will taste better, look better, etc., before the date given.

The fresher the produce, with minimal or no pesticides and especially if organically grown, the higher the quality of the food, and the better it will be in terms of flavour and/or texture. For example, a fruit or vegetable that has been messed about with a little more may have less flavour, a watery texture, or be far away from what it should be like. It isn't always possible to get produce in this way of course, especially with the high demand, but when buying fruits and vegetables you can easily take a mental note of when you bought them, where they came from, whether they are organic or not . . . this will give you an indication as to how long they might last, which is frequently much longer than the suggested 'use-by' date. Small 'mould' sightings on berries is normal, just like the minor bruises you may find on an apple or the thin hairs on a carrot. Simply wash your produce well, scrubbing any excess dirt off and storing correctly. Sure, if something is growing full-on spores or sprouts, then re-think things, but don't just chuck something away when a simple rinse before storing will suffice.

Finally, if you are disposing of fresh produce, compost it. It's one of the greatest ways to help reduce our landfill, plus give back to the earth's soil. These days compost bins are very frequently given out by local councils, but if yours doesn't, they are inexpensive and will change your life (it may sound dramatic, but it's true!). You can just keep it in your kitchen, and you'll be surprised at the amount of stuff you'd usually throw into the normal bin. I compost as much as I can, and when not composting, I have a 'stock box' in my freezer. If I have any larger pieces of vegetable left, or onions/garlic, etc., these go in there. If the vegetable is still edible in its raw form, I simply put it into a Tupperware and store it in the freezer. Once it's full, I use it to make a homemade stock (see recipes on page 352 of the basics section). It's a real game-changer, and once you start to get to grips with the real shelf life of produce, plus getting yourself a compost bin, you'll dramatically lower your food waste and (in my opinion the best part) find new ways to use those so-called scraps.

spring
has sprung

Ah, spring! So clean, fresh, light . . . calling out for simplicity when dining. That being said, it's a time that signifies newness, so it's also a great opportunity to get creative, using produce in different and innovative ways. Spring tends to be when we start to think a little more about seasonal produce, as we notice the fresh ingredients that surface after the depths of winter. The asparagus spear was made for spring, and an abundance of fresh light greens appear, showing off how wildly they can grow!

Spring also brings one of my favourite fruits: rhubarb. When I was growing up, my grandparents lived in Cornwall, not far from where we lived at the time in Devon (I'm a country bumpkin at heart!). Their house had a big, beautiful garden where my brother and I spent many hours, and my grandad had quite the setup for growing rhubarb, which crowned at the beginning of spring. He had more than he knew what to do with, and would hand it out to neighbours and visitors, as well as rustling up a smooth, sweet, but ever-so-sour stewed concoction. When we were young, our favourite way to enjoy this was naturally with an enormous scoop of vanilla ice cream, always Cornish, with second helpings. My grandad took great pride in growing this ever-abundant spring delight, grooming it throughout the year, and giving us monthly updates on it. So often, my favourite recipes are those with a story or sense of nostalgia behind them, and stewed rhubarb is one of these. I can usually be found spoon-feeding myself while it's simmering away, adding a little grated ginger for a fiery kick and just a pinch of salt, which is my secret ingredient, to lift the sweetness and cut through the sourness along with sugar.

Some may say I get a little carried away at the local markets on spring weekends, but it's always all used, every last bit . . . and those who know me know how much I enjoy chopping up and nibbling on broccoli or cauliflower stalks while I prepare food, usually dipped in some form of mustard or chutney . . . trust me, don't knock it until you try it.

star produce

Broccoli

———

Cauliflower

———

Broad beans

———

Rhubarb

———

Asparagus

———

Other seasonal produce: Broccoli varieties (Tenderstem, purple sprouting), new potatoes, leeks (ramp, wild and wood variety), rocket, watercress, spring onions, spinach, marrow, elderflower, chillies (a variety), spring radishes, aubergine, artichoke, morel mushrooms, dill, mint, stone fruit, wild garlic.

———

You will of course notice some of these vegetables in other seasons as well. There is a big overlap these days because of the climate and average temperatures we experience, regardless of where we are.

———

Grains harvested at this time of the year: Wheat/spring/young wheat, buckwheat, millet, oats, micro sprouts/alfalfa.

———

broccoli

One of my all-time favourite vegetables to eat, even when I was young. It would have been a rare occasion that I didn't ask for a second large helping of the great green vegetable. Broccoli varies in seasons depending on where in the world you are, often appearing towards the end of summer and into early autumn, but across Europe and the UK it's most commonly a plentiful springtime vegetable. It's so versatile: roasted, grilled, sautéd, steamed . . . served with a pinch of salt and a squeeze of lemon or a drizzle of olive oil, you can't really go wrong. Its vibrant colour and distinctive taste are, in my opinion, what really make it complement most dishes or mains. When in its usual form, broccoli looks very robust, but when chopped, its delicate florets can be shown off in many ways. As I've mentioned, the stalk is one of my favourite parts, and slicing it lengthways to create a longer, more leggy cross-section allows you to appreciate the whole vegetable just in the slice. Romanesco, broccolini/Tenderstem, Chinese, Destiny, raab: there are many types of this wonder veg, all serving a purpose, and each as showstopping as the next.

Waste tips

Three times a charm, hey, that flavourful stalk I keep drumming on about, use it. Slice it up and add it to stir-fries, steam it with the rest of the florets, roast it, save it to chuck into a smoothie, it's just as nutritious with an amazing crunch and an almost creamy texture when roasted. Often if I want to use just the florets in a recipe, I'll finely chop the stalk, put it into a pan with a little olive oil, some salt and pepper and a dash of chilli, maybe even some cumin, and sauté it into little crispy 'croutons'. You could serve these with what you are making, or pop them into a jar and keep them in the fridge for a few days, adding them when desired.

One of my favourite springtime recipes! Risotto is a dish that keeps on giving, as it can be enjoyed all year round but tailored to the season. This recipe in particular is a great transition dish, giving you the warming comfort you need when it's still a little fresh outside but incorporating the season's finest greens, and finished off with an earthy, vibrant broccoli pesto.

GREEN RISOTTO

First make your broccoli pesto using the method on page 360. You can do this in advance if you want, as it will keep in a jar in the fridge for about a week, especially if you've drizzled some olive oil on the top to help keep it moist.

For the risotto, heat your oil in a pan and fry the onion/shallot and leek until they start to brown. You will notice that the pan starts to dry up, so add up to 4 tablespoons of water here if it is too dry. Add the garlic and continue to cook until soft.

Add the rice and stir well. You want to lightly cook this before adding liquid – you will notice the outside of the rice start to go slightly translucent.

Start adding the stock, a ladle at a time, stirring often to prevent the rice from sticking to the bottom of the pan. Season with salt and pepper. Continue until you have added all the stock and the risotto is simmering nicely.

In a small pan, dry fry your nuts if they are not already toasted. I'd recommend keeping them whole for the frying and crushing them afterwards. Saves any smaller bits burning when frying. Place to one side.

Add the nutritional yeast and continue to stir. After about 10–12 minutes, add the spinach and broad beans. Stir and cook for another couple of minutes, until the broad beans are soft and the spinach has wilted. You don't want the rice to have any bite, so be sure to test this too.

1 batch of broccoli pesto (see page 360)

1 tbsp olive oil + 4 tbsp water

1 large brown onion or 2 shallots, finely chopped

1 leek, chopped lengthways, washed, roughly chopped

3 cloves of garlic, crushed or finely chopped

500g risotto rice

approx. 1.5 litres vegetable stock (plus more hot water if needed)

salt and pepper

a handful of nuts, lightly toasted and crushed

30g nutritional yeast

200g fresh spinach, washed, roughly chopped

240g podded broad beans, fresh or frozen

To serve

fresh herbs or chilli flakes

Stir in your broccoli pesto, as much or as little as you want. You'll notice the rice turning slightly green from the spinach and pesto. Season with salt and pepper to taste.

Ladle into bowls and serve warm, sprinkled with toasted crushed nuts and fresh herbs or chilli flakes if you like.

Waste tips:

You can substitute the broccoli pesto with kale pesto here (see page 359 for a kale pesto recipe). Either type of pesto can also be easily turned into a creamy pasta sauce. Leftover risotto makes the best arancini balls. For a healthier, vegan take on the usual deep-fried, cheese-filled variety, place your leftover risotto in a mixing bowl and add enough nutritional yeast to thicken it up and bind it; I recommend adding a tablespoon at a time. Salt, pepper and dried herbs are also great additions. Blitz some bread into crumbs (stale bread is ideal) and add to the mix. You want it thick enough to form balls when you take a clump. Use your hands to roll the arancini, then lightly fry them or bake them in the oven until they crisp up and brown all over.

Roasting broccoli is a revelation and I think it's one of the
greatest ways to cook it, charred beautifully with irresistible
crispy tips. It makes the perfect star vegetable for this salad,
paired with toasted cumin seeds and almonds for a slightly
Middle Eastern feel, but still fresh and spring-like with the
other salad components. Great on its own or part of a spring
spread, it's a salad that keeps on giving.

Serves 4 as a
side, 2 as a main

BROCCOLI CHOP SALAD

Preheat your oven to 180°C fan. Roughly chop your
broccoli and put it on a baking tray. I often don't put the
oil on here as I find it chars better without, but you can
go ahead and add a small amount if you like, using your
hands to coat the broccoli. Roast for about 12–15 minutes.

Take the broccoli out of the oven and add the garlic to
the tray. Season with salt and pepper and pop it back into
the oven for a further 10 minutes to cook through. You
will notice some of the broccoli starting to brown/char
quicker than the rest.

While your broccoli is roasting, make the dressing. Either
whisk all the ingredients together in a bowl or put them
into a blender and blitz. Season with salt and pepper to
taste and pop to one side.

Put the leek and spinach into a bowl. Pour over a small
amount of the dressing, then, using your hands, begin
to massage a little to soften the leek and spinach.

Add the parsley, chopped apple/pear, toasted almonds
and toasted cumin seeds and mix well.

Remove the broccoli from the oven and let it cool to room
temperature. You could let it cool entirely if you'd prefer
the salad to be cold. Add to the bowl with the rest of the
dressing. Mix well to combine, then serve and enjoy.

For the salad

approx. 750g
broccoli (I like
to use half
normal broccoli
and half
broccolini/
Tenderstem/
purple
sprouting),
roughly
chopped,
lengthways

1–2 tbsp olive oil

3 cloves of garlic,
crushed or finely
chopped

salt and pepper

1 large leek, cut in
half lengthways,
finely diced

approx. 100g fresh
spinach, roughly
chopped

a large handful of
fresh parsley,
finely chopped

1 apple or pear,
chopped, seeds
discarded

50g almonds,
toasted, then
crushed

1 heaped tsp
cumin seeds,
toasted

For the dressing

3 tbsp olive oil

1 large lemon,
juice and zest

1 tbsp mustard
(Dijon or
wholegrain)

2 tsp apple cider
or white wine
vinegar

2 tsp pure maple
syrup, or any
other sweetener
you have

salt and pepper

Waste tips:

If you are having this as a main, I'd recommend adding some sort of grain to bulk it out a little and keep you fuller for longer. Brown rice, pearl barley and orzo are great options, as they all have a bit of bite to them. I also often sub the spinach with cauliflower leaves – blanch them in water to soften them, and add as you would the spinach.

cauliflower

Much like broccoli, the cauliflower is a superstar vegetable, if you ask me. It's my go-to. It bears magnificent rounded leaves, and despite its clustered middle is unusually fine and delicate. Its abstract appearance is what makes it so remarkable. Roasted whole, turned into a mash, puréed into a pâté, blitzed to a couscous texture, pickled . . . and better yet, those leaves, roasted with a good drizzle of soy sauce, some pepper and a dash of chilli, my oh my – salty, charred and crunchy topping dreams. My friends and I cook together regularly, often using cauliflower, especially at this time of the year and over the course of the summer. It's usually at its best between spring and summer, but as you'll have learnt, there is a lot of overlap with produce. A favourite recipe among us is a whole baked cauliflower, smothered in homemade harissa, stalks beautifully charred, served with freshly chopped herbs and a drizzle of tahini. It's the perfect main to a refreshing and crisp salad. I have to confess, and as you may have started to grasp, I'm pretty fascinated by the cauliflower, it's a total love affair and features in some of my favourite dishes to date.

Waste tips:

Those leaves and that stalk – if you're a stranger to using them, this is your chance to change that. The leaves are not only great roasted but add a beautiful texture when chopped into most dishes, whether they're raw and chopped into a salad, lightly sautéd and added to a savoury snack, or bunged into a soup/stew for a colder day. Often, when storing it in the fridge, I'll chop off the base of the cauliflower, removing the leaves but leaving them still attached to a small part of the stalk. It keeps a little better like this, as the centre has space to breathe. The leaves will then keep well in a damp towel, simply folded around and placed in the fridge.

So simple, but so effective, I commonly refer to these as 'veggie bombs'. Cooking in foil parcels creates soft, succulent veggies in a luscious 'jus', and turns the garlic into nuggets of goodness, while the subtle tang from the tofu cream helps all the flavours pop. This recipe uses the oven but these are also a great veggie side for the barbecue. Perfect if you're feeling a little lazy and have leftover cruciferous veg to use up.

Serves 4 as a side

CHARRED CAULIFLOWER AND BROCCOLINI

w/ sesame seeds, tofu cream

Preheat your oven to 220°C fan. Tear 4 pieces of foil, each about A4 size, and put to one side. (If reusing foil, don't panic too much about size, this is approximate.)

Put the chopped cauliflower and broccoli into a mixing bowl. Add the lemon juice and zest, shallot and garlic. Drizzle with olive oil to coat and mix well. Season with salt and pepper to taste.

Lay the foil out in front of you. Put a quarter of the mix into the middle of each piece of foil. Season with salt and pepper again, then fold in the foil to form small parcels and place in the oven on a rack at the top. Cook for about 30 minutes – you want the vegetables to char, so that some are darker than others and all lovely and tender.

While the vegetables are in the oven, make your tofu cream. Put the silken tofu into a blender along with the apple cider vinegar, mustard, garlic, lemon juice and zest, oregano, salt and pepper. Blend until you have a smooth creamy texture, then place to one side or in the fridge.

Remove your parcels from the oven, checking they are cooked through and charred nicely. You can pop them back in for further charring with the foil folded back if you wish to add a little more crispness on top.

To serve, either plate up or eat straight from the foil, with a drizzle of tofu cream and a sprinkle of sesame seeds.

For the charred vegetables

1 small cauliflower, leaves included, roughly chopped

1 small bunch of broccolini/ Tenderstem (or an additional small regular broccoli)

1 small broccoli, roughly chopped

1 small lemon, juice and zest

1 shallot, finely chopped

5 cloves of garlic, crushed with the back of a spoon or knife, skin removed, chopped into rough quarters

olive oil, to drizzle

salt and pepper

4 tbsp sesame seeds, lightly toasted

For the tofu cream (makes one small jar, approx. 580ml)

300g silken tofu, drained

1½ tsp apple cider vinegar

2 tsp Dijon mustard

1 clove of garlic, crushed or finely chopped

1 small lemon, juiced, plus a dash of zest

2 tsp dried oregano

salt and pepper

34   the whole vegetable

Waste tips:

If you can get your hands on some recyclable foil (it is slightly different) or have baking sheets/mats already, this is a great alternative to reduce your waste. I often rinse my foil and re-use it. The reusable/recyclable one has a slightly different inner film which allows you to do this. This recipe is great for barbecues or fires. If you have access to a garden and can light a fire/fire pit or a barbecue, follow the same instructions but place the parcels on the fire. My friend likes to call these veggie bombs, and we often do this with leftover vegetables in the fridge, potatoes, onions – you know, the things you always seem to have left over. They're great for group dinners too, easy and quick, with hardly any prep work. I like them as an addition to tacos, salads, or just a snack from the fridge too. A great way to use leftover cruciferous vegetables!

Cauliflower, blended into a creamy sauce, is a great alternative to the usual cheese-based carbonara recipe. This dish makes a regular appearance in my kitchen at the start of spring, when the abundance of cauliflowers instantly brings it to mind. Stirring in some pesto adds a lovely pop of colour.

CAULIFLOWER CARBONARA

w/ leftover pesto

First steam your cauliflower until tender, stalks included, for about 10–12 minutes. Or you can boil the cauliflower in a pan of water for around the same time, but make sure to drain it well if you opt for this method. Set aside.

Cook your pasta according to type, then drain well and put back into the pan with 1 tablespoon of olive oil. (Feel free to omit this, but I find it prevents the pasta from sticking together.)

While the pasta is cooking, you can make the sauce. Place the cooked cauliflower in a blender with the plant milk, garlic, nutritional yeast, lemon juice and zest, turmeric, nutmeg and mustard. Blend until smooth. Season with salt and pepper and add water/olive oil if you want to loosen.

Add the cauliflower sauce to the pot of pasta and stir well. Slowly heat through again on a low heat, stirring carefully to combine. Add the fresh basil and stir.

To serve, you can stir the pesto into the pan, or serve up and add some to each bowl. Season with more salt and pepper if you like, and chilli flakes if you want a kick.

1 large cauliflower, leaves included, roughly chopped

approx. 350–400g fettuccine/ linguine/rotini/ tagliatelle (see tip)

1 tbsp olive oil (optional)

250ml unsweetened plant milk (I like cashew for thickness, but oat, almond, soy, coconut all work)

4 cloves of garlic, crushed

4 heaped tbsp nutritional yeast

1 lemon, juiced, plus a dash of zest

a pinch of ground turmeric

¼ tsp grated nutmeg

1 heaped tbsp mustard (Dijon or wholegrain)

salt and pepper

2–4 tbsp water, to loosen (olive oil can also be used)

a medium handful of fresh basil, roughly chopped, being careful not to bruise

3–4 tbsp pesto of choice (see page 359 for basil, page 360 for broccoli, or page 359 for kale)

a pinch of chilli flakes

Waste tips:

Typically 80–100g pasta is enough for one person, but feel free to vary depending on who you are feeding and how hungry they are. The pesto adds a nice texture, but omitting it is not the end of the world, so if you don't have any, you could instead stir through a larger handful of roughly chopped basil and some additional lemon zest.

Most vegetarian pâtés rely on mushrooms to help create a meaty texture or flavour, but using cauliflower, especially when roasted, produces a deep umami flavour. It's a pâté that's better for the environment and uses just a few simple ingredients. Rich, creamy, garlicky, zesty, what more could you want from a pâté? It's perfect as part of the bruschetta recipe overleaf.

Makes approx.
350–400g

CAULIFLOWER PÂTÉ

Preheat your oven to 180°C fan. Put your cauliflower, whole onions and garlic into a large roasting tray and mix with your hands. You can drizzle on a little olive oil, but I prefer them left without. Roast for about 30 minutes, until the onions have cooked through and the cauliflower is tender. Remove from the oven and set aside.

Once the cauliflower, onions and garlic have cooled slightly, remove the skins from the onions and garlic. You can save for your stock box or compost as you wish.

Put the cauliflower, onions and garlic into a blender with the lemon juice, tahini, thyme leaves, coriander seeds and chilli flakes/cayenne, and season with salt and pepper. Blend to a relatively smooth paste. I like to keep some texture, but you can add water depending on your desired consistency. Adjust the seasoning if you need to.

Put your pâté into an airtight container and place in the fridge. This will allow it to thicken as it cools completely. It will keep in the fridge for about 4–5 days. Use as a side for salads, a topping for toast or bruschetta (see overleaf), or just as a snack with crudités of choice.

1 small cauliflower, roughly chopped, stalks and leaves included

2 small onions or shallots, skin on, whole

3 cloves of garlic, skin on, whole

1–2 tbsp olive oil (optional, for roasting)

1 lemon, juiced

3 heaped tbsp tahini

3–4 sprigs of thyme, leaves only (pop the stalks into your stock box)

1 tsp coriander seeds

a pinch of dried chilli flakes or cayenne pepper

salt and pepper

A definite 'don't knock it until you try it' dish. The pear perfectly complements the cauliflower pâté, adding a bit of sweetness to the umami flavours and using salt to balance it all out. Bruschetta is great for entertaining, whether it's a casual barbecue or a dinner party; either way this dish is undeniably a great surprise.

Serves 2

SALTED PEAR AND CAULIFLOWER PÂTÉ BRUSCHETTA

Put the slices of pear into a pan with the soy sauce or tamari, a dash of water, the oregano and smoked paprika, and place on a very low heat. Season with salt and pepper, and simmer until the pear is tender and slightly browned. This should take around 8–10 minutes.

To assemble, toast your bread either in the oven or in a toaster (I like mine super-crispy). Top with the cauliflower pâté, spreading it to cover the toast. Add the pear and some extra salt and pepper to taste.

Drizzle a little olive oil on top, and serve.

1 small pear, thinly sliced, core removed (add it to your stockpot)

1 tbsp soy sauce or tamari

1 heaped tsp dried oregano

½ tsp smoked paprika

salt and pepper

2–4 pieces of your preferred bread, depending on size (I usually use sourdough, fresh or frozen)

2–4 tbsp cauliflower pâté per slice (see page 37)

a drizzle of olive oil, to serve

Waste tips:

I tend to make this recipe if I have bread I need to use up, and have yet to freeze it, or if I have some 'on the turn' pears . . . or apples, which work nicely too. The good fats in the olive oil bring this dish to life. If you have any garlic or chilli oil to hand, that's also great. This makes a tasty alternative to your morning toast, or is ideal for when you want something a little fancier to serve as a starter or snack.

I'm a huge fan of baking vegetables whole, especially cauliflower. This dish is deceptively simple but will have others believing you've gone to real effort, because of the intensity of the flavours. Baking the cauliflower whole preserves all its moisture, so the result is a beautifully tender showstopper. I love this dish simply paired with a cooked grain and greens. It looks pretty wow served with all the garnishes and is great for guests in need of a hearty dinner.

Serves 4

WHOLE BAKED HARISSA CAULIFLOWER

Preheat your oven to 200°C fan. Remove the leaves from the cauliflower and put to one side. Using a sharp knife, cut into the core of the cauliflower at various angles to slightly separate the florets/branches. You want to keep it intact, so don't cut too deep.

Using a steamer or steamer basket, steam the cauliflower, stalk side closest to the water, for 8–10 minutes. You don't want it to be cooked, just enough that a knife will remove with ease when poked in. If you don't have a steamer, you can boil it for around the same time.

Remove the cauliflower from the steamer and place it upside down to allow any excess water to drain – you can pat it dry too. Prepare a baking tray with a dash of oil or line with a Silpat baking mat if you have one, or parchment paper (remember to re-use if possible).

In a small bowl, mix the water, harissa paste, lemon juice and any extra salt and pepper. With the cauliflower stalk side up, spoon some of the mix into the cuts you made in it. This will allow the mix to drip through the entire cauliflower. Tap and shake it a little to help it on its way. Make sure you keep some of this mix for the top surface.

Flip the cauliflower so that the core is facing down and brush a little olive oil, salt and pepper over the surface. Put into the oven and roast for about 10 minutes. Remove from the oven, add the rest of your harissa mix to the top

1 large head of cauliflower (whole – leaves separated and either left whole or chopped)

4 tbsp water (or use half olive oil, half water, depending on how much oil is in your harissa)

2–4 tbsp harissa paste (see page 361)

1 lemon, juiced

salt and pepper

1–2 tbsp olive oil/coconut oil

a handful of fresh herbs, to garnish

of the cauliflower, then roast for a further 30–40 minutes. You want the cauliflower to be brown on top and to look relatively dry. A knife will easily score through.

I like to dry-fry the leaves (whole or chopped), letting them get nice and crispy, or you could put them into the oven about 10 minutes before removing the rest of the cauliflower. If you're dry-frying, heat a pan until hot, add the leaves, season with salt and pepper and fry until tender but crispy – approximately 8 minutes.

Remove your cauliflower from the oven and serve whole, adding the crispy leaves on top and a handful of chopped fresh herbs. Cut into thick slices for 'steak' style pieces, or as you wish.

Waste tips:

The cauliflower leftovers work well as a pâté (see page 37) or even mashed for another dinner. I've also tried this recipe successfully with broccoli. The harissa can be jazzed up with seasonal herbs or made milder with less chilli. If you are out of harissa, or want to skip that part entirely, you can make up a quick sauce using oil, a little maple syrup, a variety of spices, salt and pepper. You could also use any other sauce or pesto, should you want to.

Inspired by a trip to California, where I discovered a deconstructed take on Caesar salad, I've created my own version for the spring months. It's a hearty salad with a subtle hint of paprika that lifts it out of the ordinary.

Serves 4

CAULIFLOWER CAESAR SALAD

w/ crispy broad beans, tahini dressing

Preheat your oven to 190°C fan. Put the cauliflower, paprika, soy sauce or tamari, oregano and nutritional yeast into a bowl and mix well to coat the florets. Roast for about 20 minutes, until tender and slightly crispy.

To make croutons, toss the torn bread with the olive oil, garlic, salt and pepper. They only need about 10 minutes in the oven, so you can put them in while the cauliflower is cooking.

To make the rest of the salad, put the drained chickpeas, lettuce, onion, celery and capers into a bowl. Set aside while you make the dressing and crispy broad beans.

For the broad beans, heat the coconut oil on a low heat. Add the broad beans, garlic and some salt and pepper. Stir to prevent them from burning and fry until the beans become a more vibrant colour with some slight browning. The outer part may start to shrivel slightly – this is normal.

For the dressing, whisk or blend together the tahini, garlic, nutritional yeast, soy or tamari, lemon juice and zest, mustard, paprika and oregano. Season with salt and pepper. Add a little water if you want the dressing runnier.

To assemble the salad, add the roasted cauliflower to the bowl of chickpeas. Add half the croutons and half the broad beans. Pour in half the dressing and mix slowly, coating the salad. To serve, sprinkle over the rest of the broad beans and croutons and drizzle with the dressing. You can plate separately or serve in one big bowl.

For the salad

1 small/medium cauliflower, in florets, stalks included

1–2 tsp smoked paprika

3–4 tbsp soy sauce or tamari

4 tsp dried oregano

3 heaped tbsp nutritional yeast

3–4 slices of stale bread, torn into small chunks

2 tbsp olive oil

2 cloves of garlic, crushed

salt and pepper

about 200g cooked chickpeas, rinsed

1 medium lettuce (butter, romaine, cos, iceberg)

1 small red onion, thinly sliced

2 stalks of celery, leaves included, thinly sliced

2 tbsp capers, drained

For the crispy broad beans

1 tbsp coconut oil

180g podded broad beans (inner skins removed)

1 clove of garlic, crushed

salt and pepper

For the tahini dressing

2 heaped tbsp tahini

2 cloves of garlic, crushed

3 tbsp nutritional yeast

2 tbsp soy sauce or tamari

1 lemon, juice and zest

2 tbsp Dijon mustard

½ tsp paprika

2 tsp dried oregano

salt and pepper

These croutons are a great way to use up stale bread. They are ideal for salads, with roasted veggies, or even ground to garlicky breadcrumbs that'll keep in the fridge for a few days. Broad beans do require a bit of effort if they are in their skins. The outer shells can be placed in your stock box, but have a slightly bitter taste, so be sure to have enough other 'scraps' in there before making a stock (see page 352.) As an alternative, you can use dried split broad beans. Parboil them first and then roast using the same method.

This almost raw salad combines some of the best spring produce. Paired with a zingy orange dressing and crumbled almond feta, it's the perfect salad for a warmer day, as a main or a side with some crusty bread. Spreading some extra almond feta on the bread will also never go amiss.

Serves 4–6
depending on
main or sides

SHREDDED CAULIFLOWER, ASPARAGUS AND BROCCOLI SALAD

w/ crumbled almond feta

Preheat your oven to 180°C fan. Grease a baking tray with a dash of oil or line with parchment paper.

To make the almond feta, drain and rinse the almonds. Ideally use a high-speed blender for the next process. Put the almonds into a blender along with the lemon juice and zest, salt, miso paste, oregano, garlic, apple cider vinegar, pepper, plant-based milk and nutritional yeast. Blitz in the blender until the mixture starts to reach a smoother consistency. You can add water here if the mix is a little chunky or needs a bit of extra liquid to get it going. The more liquid you add the smoother the texture. I like to keep some texture/'bittiness' to it, helping to replicate a feta-like cheese.

Transfer the mixture to the baking tray. You'll want it to be relatively thick and even; the shape doesn't matter. Sprinkle on some extra salt, then put into the oven and bake for around 30–40 minutes. It will start to brown and crisp on top and be slightly firmer to touch. Remove and allow to cool completely.

For the salad, put your shredded cauliflower and broccoli into a bowl. Lightly steam the asparagus, approx. 5–6 minutes, then run it under cold water to stop the cooking process. Halve the spears lengthways and widthways, and add to the cauliflower and broccoli. Go ahead and add the

For the almond feta

110g almonds, soaked for at least 2 hours, and best overnight

1 small lemon, juiced, plus a dash of zest

1 heaped tsp salt

1 tsp miso (preferably yellow or light-coloured)

2 tsp dried oregano

2 cloves of garlic, crushed or finely chopped

1 tsp apple cider vinegar

a pinch of pepper

80ml plant-based milk

3 heaped tbsp nutritional yeast

For the salad

1 small cauliflower, shredded, grated or very finely chopped, either with a knife or a mandolin

1 broccoli (I like to use a variety of Tenderstem/broccolini if I can find them), shredded, grated or very finely chopped, with a knife or a mandolin

1 bunch of asparagus, approx 10/15 spears

6 spring onions, finely sliced

1 apple, thinly sliced, core removed

2 stalks of celery, thinly sliced

salt and pepper

olive oil, to finish

»

spring onions, apple and celery. Mix well and season with salt and pepper.

For the dressing, either in a blender or using a whisk/fork, mix together the orange juice and zest, garlic, ginger, tahini, mustard, maple syrup, vinegar, cayenne and some extra salt and pepper. Add water if you want a thinner consistency.

Pour your dressing over the salad and begin to mix slowly with your hands, coating everything and massaging slightly as you go to help soften the vegetables.

Either plate up individually or serve in a large bowl. Using your hands, start to grab pieces of the almond feta and crumble them over the salad. Drizzle over a little olive oil – you could also do this directly on to the feta before crumbling it over. Season with salt and pepper if necessary.

For the dressing

2 oranges, juiced, plus zest from half

1 clove of garlic, crushed or finely chopped

a couple of cm of fresh ginger, finely chopped or grated

2 heaped tbsp tahini

2 tsp wholegrain mustard

1 tsp pure maple syrup, or any other sweetener of choice

1 tsp apple cider or white wine vinegar

a pinch of cayenne pepper

salt and pepper

broad beans

Sweet little 'buttery' tasting beans: a real springtime favourite. Half the joy for me is removing them from their pods – it's not a huge task but feels like an achievement, especially when enjoying them afterwards. To be honest, despite encouraging creativity, my favourite way to enjoy broad beans is when tossed into a salad, simply seasoned with salt and pepper and a good squeeze of lemon. They taste like spring to me, sweet, tender, succulent. They are often referred to as fava beans in the culinary world, so sometimes in restaurants you'll see that name on a menu, but fear not, they are ultimately the same thing although not to be confused with dried fava beans, as these are fresh. They often last until late summer in the UK, still just as delicious, and towards the end of their season you'll occasionally find them in a larger form, with thicker, fluffier pods.

Waste tips:

Here's the catch. For all the mouth-watering, flavourful taste of the beans after a simple steaming or boiling, the pods are a little different. Despite the common thought that you should toss them into the compost, there are a few things you can do to ensure you use the whole vegetable. The pods make a great fried dish, whole or chopped with some salt and pepper, plain flour and herbs/spices of choice, such as ground cumin or coriander, then fried on a low heat in a shallow amount of oil. Maybe not the healthiest thing in the world, but delicious all the same, and lovely as a side dish to a spring spread. The pods are very bitter and fibrous if they are not cooked, but can easily be chopped and added to stews, towards the end of cooking, just as you would with a thicker green.

So often overlooked, broad beans are such a bold and versatile vegetable. With their subtle sweetness, creamy texture, earthy and nutty tones, this recipe really shows them off. I like this as a snack or as part of a spring spread, a thick slice of warm toast piled high with the broad bean mix. Toast never looked so good!

BROAD BEAN BRUSCHETTA

Cook your broad beans in boiling salted water, about 5 minutes. Drain, rinse and transfer to a dish. Using a fork, begin to mash them.

Add the lemon juice and three-quarters of the zest, the grated courgette, olive oil, mint, garlic, chilli and nutritional yeast. Season with salt and pepper and continue to mash and mix with the fork. The texture will be quite rough, but smooth enough to form a nice clumped mix.

Toast your bread and cut it into smaller pieces. You could also grill the bread or toast it on a hot pan over the stove. Spoon your broad bean mixture on to your bread slices, piling it as high as you desire. Serve drizzled with a little extra olive oil, sprinkled with the rest of the lemon zest and garnished with mint leaves.

240g podded broad beans

1 lemon, juice and zest

1 small courgette, grated

2 tbsp olive oil, plus extra for serving

a small handful of mint, finely chopped (2 tsp if using dried), plus extra leaves to garnish

2 cloves of garlic, crushed or finely chopped

a pinch of dried chilli flakes

1–2 heaped tbsp nutritional yeast

salt and pepper

bread of choice (depending on size, 4–8 slices, toasted, will suffice)

Waste tip:

You could add a vegan baked cheese to this dish, crumbling it on top, or a drizzle of another sauce or extra olive oil. If you can't get hold of courgettes due to seasonality, simply omit them. You could try other green vegetables such as peas, or even cucumber. The taste will be different but just as good, and it helps to make use of what you have in. The broad bean mix is a great dip should you want to make extra, adding a dash more olive oil. The looser consistency is also a great sauce for pasta – hot or cold. You could chuck in a handful of fresh basil and steam some other greens and you've got a simple pasta. This recipe is another great way to use up stale bread, or bread stored in the freezer.

One of my favourite pastas, fregola feels a lot more like a grain, similar to giant couscous – the main difference being their country of origin. A Sardinian pasta made from wheat flour, rolled and sun-dried, fregola is perfectly chewy and acts as a great base to many dishes. This recipe is ideal as a hearty brunch, a rustic lunch or a warming dinner. The pop of colour from the broad beans and lemon zest really makes it feel like spring has sprung.

SLOW-COOKED BROAD BEAN FREGOLA

w/ lemon zest, nut Parmesan

First cook your fregola. Simmer it in lightly salted water for around 10–12 minutes, stirring occasionally. The fregola once cooked will be softer on the outside but will still hold some texture when bitten – similar to giant couscous. Once cooked, drain and put back into the pot with a dash of olive oil to prevent it from sticking. Put to one side.

In a separate pan, begin to cook your onion in some water until soft and fragrant, then add a pinch of salt followed by the garlic, and continue to cook for another minute or so. Add the broad beans and lightly fry, then add the olive oil. Slowly pour in the stock until the beans are covered. Bring to the boil, then reduce to a simmer. You may not use all of your stock initially, so just place the rest to one side.

Add the lemon juice and zest, nutritional yeast, tahini, parsley, mint and oregano. Season with a good amount of salt and pepper and mix well. Cover and continue to simmer until the liquid starts to thicken, usually around 15 minutes or so. If it dries up a little too much, you can add a dash more stock or water.

While your broad beans are simmering, make your nut Parmesan. Place the cashews in a blender and blitz until they break up slightly. Add the sunflower seeds, salt,

200g fregola

1 large onion, white or brown, finely chopped

salt and pepper

4 cloves of garlic, crushed or finely chopped

450g broad beans, podded and skinned

2 tbsp olive oil

500ml stock

2 lemons, both juiced, 1 zested

2 tbsp nutritional yeast

1 tbsp tahini

a handful of fresh parsley, finely chopped (2 heaped tsp if dried)

a handful of fresh mint, finely chopped (2 heaped tsp if dried)

2 tsp dried oregano

a pinch of chilli flakes or cayenne pepper

For the nut Parmesan

70g raw cashews

45g raw sunflower seeds

1 tsp salt

3 heaped tbsp nutritional yeast

¼ tsp garlic powder

¼ tsp ground turmeric

nutritional yeast, garlic powder and turmeric. Blitz again until a nice crumb-like texture forms. Be careful not to over-blend, as you don't want to make a paste. Transfer to a jar and place in the fridge.

Add the chilli to the broad beans and stir, seasoning if necessary. The beans by this point should be very soft, and may start to break down slightly. Add the fregola to the pot and stir well to combine. Again, season if necessary. You want the mixture to be like a stew – there will be some liquid, but not a whole load.

To serve, transfer to bowls, topping with a good sprinkle of your nut Parmesan and any additional herbs of choice.

I'm a big fan of hummus, so using one of my favourite vegetables to make it naturally always leaves me wanting more. Light and fresh, this is ideal for pairing with salads, vegetables, grains, or even just as part of a snack. The chopped mint really brings that spring feeling!

Makes approx. 8–10 servings

BROAD BEAN AND MINT HUMMUS

Cook your broad beans in boiling salted water, about 5 minutes. Drain, rinse and transfer to a blender.

Add the lemon juice, zest, olive oil, tahini, mint, garlic and chilli. Season with salt and pepper and blend until you reach your desired consistency. If you like it a little chunkier, you can blend a little less. For a super-smooth consistency, add a dash of water as you go.

Scoop into an airtight container and drizzle over a little olive oil to prevent it from drying out. Serve with salads, as a snack with crudités, or as another way to top your toast.

450g podded broad beans

1 lemon, juice and zest

2 tbsp olive oil, plus extra for serving

2 heaped tbsp tahini

a small handful of mint, finely chopped (2 tsp if dried)

2 cloves of garlic, crushed or finely chopped

a pinch of dried chilli flakes

salt and pepper

Once I got my head around the idea of couscous in vegetable form, I was quick to learn that cooking the cauliflower really makes all the difference. This is a meal on the lighter side, or a great topping for a baked potato, with hummus or a dip.

HERBY GARLIC CAULIFLOWER COUSCOUS

w/ pea shoots and broad beans

To make the 'couscous', put the cauliflower florets into a blender or processor and blitz to coarse crumbs. You can do this in batches, scraping down the sides as you go.

Place the 'couscous' in a pan with a thin layer of water, just to cover. Add a dash of salt, then cook/steam over a low heat for about 5 minutes, with the lid on. Transfer the cauliflower to a large tray or pan to dry and cool.

Heat a teaspoon of oil in a separate pan and briefly fry the garlic, spring onions, coriander seeds and celery, just until they are fragrant and starting to brown.

Cook your broad beans in boiling salted water for a few minutes, then drain and rinse under cold water.

Combine the 'couscous', celery mixture and broad beans in a large bowl. Add the dried and fresh herbs, pea shoots, raisins/sultanas, lemon juice and zest, vinegar and mustard. Carefully mix with your hands, making sure it is all coated, with no clumps of mustard left. Season with salt and pepper and a drizzle of olive oil, and serve.

1 cauliflower, cut into florets

salt

1 tsp olive oil

4 cloves of garlic, crushed or finely chopped

4 spring onions, chopped finely

½ tsp coriander seeds

2 stalks of celery, chopped finely

120g podded broad beans

1 tsp each of dried oregano, mint and thyme

a large handful each of fresh parsley and mint

70/80g fresh pea shoots (or any kind of micro sprout will work, and chives are also a good option)

80g raisins or sultanas

1 lemon, juice and zest

1 tsp white wine or apple cider vinegar

1 tbsp wholegrain mustard

salt and pepper

a drizzle of olive oil

Waste tips:

I love adding fruit to this, for extra texture and sweetness. Use apples, pears, pomegranate seeds, or any fruit you want to use up. Toasted nuts or seeds are another great addition. You can make the cauliflower couscous in a bigger batch and keep it in the fridge with a dash of lemon, salt and olive oil to help it stay moist, for adding to salads, or even stews. This salad also keeps in the fridge for a few days, as it's quite moist. Cooking the cauliflower helps preserve it, as does the addition of vinegar when mixing. Leftovers make a great sandwich filler, along with some fresh lettuce and tomatoes.

rhubarb

A beautiful plump and juicy fruit . . . well, botanically
speaking, it's a vegetable, but with its distinctive taste – a
combination of sweet and sour – it's treated as a fruit. It's
fleshy and shows off with its attractive pink appearance.
Rhubarb is a great ingredient to experiment with, as it
works well with a lot of savoury dishes. It's quite common
to see and eat it stewed or in crumbles, but it also makes
great dressings, paired with healthy fats such as nuts or
avocados. It's also good with citrus, so if I make a dressing
with it I'll often use a lot of lime, honouring its tart flavour
with an added hit of zest. When rhubarb season hits, I am
truly filled with glee, again perhaps something to do with
the sense of nostalgia that it triggers for me, but as it's
quite a short-lived season I think it's only natural to
get excited.

Waste tips:

In my opinion, we want to savour
this fibrous ruby fruit and, as I said,
its season is short, so batch cooking
is great. It'll keep in the fridge for a
good 5 days or so and the flavour
gets better each day. You can also
store it in the freezer once cooked,
keeping it for up to a month. Leaving
the leaves on until you're ready to
eat and cook it helps to keep it fresh
– often they get trimmed down
because of their size, but if you can
manage it, leaving them on is a good
idea. Leftovers make great crumbles,
on top of a breakfast or, as you'll
have discovered above, in dressings.
One of my favourite salads, on page
60, features rhubarb as a dressing,
keeping things interesting and new,
in honour of spring of course.

When rhubarb comes into season, I get overly excited and end up buying too much of it, so I'm always thinking of new things I can use it for. This recipe is perfect for that. A fridge or freezer cake that will not let you down, the rhubarb is stirred through carefully, helping to balance out the rich creaminess from the cashew-baked cake. It's one to please a crowd.

RHUBARB CASHEW CHEESECAKE

First, cook the rhubarb. Place the rhubarb, maple syrup, lemon juice and zest, ginger and salt in a small saucepan. Slowly add about 60ml of water bit by bit. You want there to be enough to almost cover the rhubarb, making sure to not swamp it – you can always add more if need be. Over a low heat, slowly simmer until the rhubarb softens and starts to form a 'compote' or sauce-type consistency. You want it to be quite thick and well mixed rather than loose and liquidy.

For the base, put the nuts into a blender or processor and blitz to a rough crumb consistency. Add the pitted dates, coconut oil and maple syrup and blitz again until the mixture starts to form a nice rough dough.

Grease your cake tin with coconut oil, making sure to not skip the sides. Press the base evenly into the tin and put into the freezer to set while you make the topping.

Put the soaked cashews into a clean blender with the maple syrup, coconut oil, plant-based milk, lemon juice and zest, plus salt. Blend on high until you start to get a smooth creamy consistency. If the mixture is a little thick, you can add some more plant-based milk.

Once the mix is smooth, pour it into a bowl, followed by your rhubarb. Very gently and slowly, using a spatula or large spoon, swirl the two together. You don't want them to combine.

For the rhubarb

approx. 4–5 stalks raw rhubarb, roughly chopped

60ml pure maple syrup

½ lemon, juice and zest

1 tsp fresh ginger, finely chopped or grated

a pinch of salt

For the base

240g almonds or walnuts, or a combination of the two

140g dates, pitted

1–2 tbsp coconut oil, melted, plus extra for greasing

1 tbsp pure maple syrup

For the topping

300g cashews, soaked overnight

2–3 tbsp pure maple syrup (use more or less for sweetness preference)

2 heaped tbsp coconut oil – approx 30–50g

approx. 150ml plant-based milk (you may need extra)

2 lemons, juice and zest (save some zest for garnish)

a pinch of salt

Remove your cake tin from the freezer and pour your swirled mixture on top of the base. Add the remaining lemon zest and put back into the freezer to set. This can take anything from 2 hours onwards, depending on your freezer. If you want to serve it as a dessert later in the evening, I'd go ahead and prepare it earlier in the day.

To serve, remove from the freezer. Allow to sit for a few minutes, then pop the base to remove. It should be easy to remove so long as you greased your tin enough. Slice, serve and enjoy!

I remember the day I discovered Bircher muesli – and I've never looked back. It seemed to have everything I wanted and more, and over the years I've played around with different ingredients to create different textures, realizing that flaked grains and seeds work just as well as regular oats. This recipe has a subtle burst of cardamom, making it feel somewhat fancy.

Serves 2–3

THREE-GRAIN BIRCHER MUESLI

w/ stewed rhubarb and cardamom

Ideally, prepare your muesli and let it sit over-night in the fridge. This helps with digestion and also allows the mix to really thicken and the grains to soak. Put the oats, spelt flakes, rye flakes, pumpkin seeds, sesame seeds, coconut, salt and cinnamon into a bowl. Mix to combine. Slowly start to add your liquid, mixing as you go. The measurement is approximate, so you may need more or less. You want the mixture to be quite thick but with liquid still apparent. Cover, then place in the fridge and leave overnight. The longer you leave it the better, but if you only have a few hours, make it a bit ahead of time.

Put the rhubarb into a pan and add enough water to almost cover it. Add the sugar, lemon juice and zest, crushed cardamom, ginger and salt, and stir to combine. Bring to the boil, then lower to a simmer until the rhubarb is cooked. This could take between 10 and 15 minutes. If the pan becomes dry, add a little more water, stirring occasionally. Once cooked, place to one side to cool.

Remove your Bircher from the fridge and give it a good stir. If the mixture is quite thick and you want it looser, simply add a few tablespoons of milk until you reach your desired consistency.

To serve, spoon the Bircher into bowls and add a hefty serving of the stewed rhubarb. You'll have extra rhubarb, which you can simply place in an airtight container in the fridge. Sprinkle over any extra toppings and dig in.

For the muesli

100g rolled jumbo oats

50g spelt flakes

50g rye flakes

1 tbsp pumpkin seeds

1 tbsp sesame seeds

1 tbsp desiccated/ shredded coconut

a small pinch of salt

approx. 1 tsp ground cinnamon (if you like a subtle cinnamon flavour, start with less)

approx. 350ml plant-based milk (you could also use half water, half milk, any of choice), plus a few tbsp extra after soaking

For the stewed rhubarb

approx. 400g fresh rhubarb, roughly chopped

2 heaped tbsp coconut sugar/ palm sugar/any other natural raw sugar

1 lemon, juiced, ½ zested

4–5 cardamom pods, shells removed, seeds crushed, or 1–2 tsp dried

approx. 2.5cm ginger, finely chopped or grated

a pinch of salt

Waste tips:

This has been one of my go-to breakfast recipes for a long time. I like to change up the
grains every so often, depending on what I have in. Occasionally if I have batch-cooked a
grain I will use that in place of one of the other flakes. You can also make a larger quantity
of the Bircher base and keep it in the fridge for a few days to have each morning, changing
up what you add on top – berry compote from page 371 is a favourite and a classic, or
even the pumpkin seed granola on page 220 should you be in a more autumnal month.
It's a great breakfast or brunch recipe that keeps you full and has a variety of taste and
texture. If you fancy eating this hot, you can also add a little more liquid, spoon some
into a saucepan and simmer over a low heat until warm.

Optional toppings

---

granola (see page
  366 for
  inspiration)

extra seeds

crushed nuts

plant-based
  yoghurt

fresh fruit

A pretty rustic recipe for a see-what-you-have-in-the-fridge, end-of-the-week kind of meal. The dressing keeps it interesting, rhubarb being one of those fruits you would never typically think to use in a dressing. It creates a deep, tart flavour, bringing to life the vegetables in the salad, not to mention also being very pleasing to the eye.

Serves 4 as a
side, 2 as a main
—

FRIDGE DINNER SALAD
—
w/ rhubarb dressing

First make the dressing. Heat 1–2 teaspoons of olive oil in a pan and sauté the chopped rhubarb until tender and starting to break down and brown. Add the garlic and sauté for another minute or so.

Put the rhubarb and garlic into a blender along with the remaining olive oil, lemon juice, lime juice and zest, maple syrup, tahini, dried oregano and dried chilli flakes. Season with salt and pepper, and blend until you have a smooth, thick consistency. If you want it a little looser, add some water and blend again. Put to one side while you make your salad.

For the salad, put the dark greens, fresh mint, parsley, radishes and your chosen leftover vegetables into a bowl. Squeeze over the lemon juice and add the vinegar and 1 teaspoon of salt. Using your hands, begin to mix the salad, massaging slightly to allow the vegetables and greens to soften slightly. Once they begin to soften, add half the dressing and mix the salad, again using your hands.

Add the apple and the toasted nuts, season with salt and pepper, and mix again. To serve, you can either add the rest of the dressing straight to the main bowl, or portion the salad out with a drizzle of dressing on top.

For the dressing
—

2 tbsp olive oil

125g rhubarb, chopped

2 cloves of garlic, crushed or finely chopped

1 lemon, juiced

1 lime, juice and zest

1–2 tsp pure maple syrup (this will help to remove any bitterness from the rhubarb)

1 tbsp tahini

2 tsp dried oregano

a pinch of dried chilli flakes, for some spice

salt and pepper

For the salad
—

a large handful of dark leafy greens (this will depend on where you are and what you can get – kale, collard greens, chard), roughly chopped

a handful of fresh mint, roughly chopped

a handful of fresh parsley, roughly chopped

4 small radishes, thinly sliced, leaves included

approx. 800–950g finely chopped raw veggies (use what you have in the fridge – cauliflower, broccoli, roots, etc.)

1 lemon, juiced

1–2 tsp apple cider or white wine vinegar

1 tsp salt

1 apple, finely sliced

70g nuts of choice, lightly toasted (almonds, cashews, hazelnuts, or a combination)

salt and pepper

Waste tip:

The dressing recipe can easily be doubled and keeps in the fridge for up to a week. It's a great way to mix up your dressings and be a little adventurous. As for the veggies that go into the salad, that's entirely up to you. If you have lots of roots left over, you could grate these and add anything else you have lying around in the fridge.

asparagus

Until a few years ago, I didn't realize how great roasted asparagus is. I don't know why it hadn't occurred to me to roast it, but my go-to was to always lightly steam it until it reached its peak vibrant green, cooking it quickly to avoid any browning. It really is a sublime vegetable and when in season is everywhere at the markets. I often see it in the supermarkets throughout the year, which somewhat annoys me because I feel its unique woody flavour is somewhat watered down when it's past its heyday. Throughout the spring and leading into the summer, it matures in flavour, making it a great ingredient to combine with less pungent ones. To be honest, in a good old classic way, adding it to a risotto has got to be at the top, whether that's simply steamed or griddled to get a slight char. It's perfect when paired with just a simple vinaigrette of olive oil, vinegar, mustard, lemon juice and a pinch of salt, and if you're feeling a little bit more adventurous, a very finely chopped shallot. Of course asparagus spears are commonly known to be of a green variety, but we occasionally see them slightly paler or even a white shade – although those ones are often imported/grown in hotter climates across Europe. The white asparagus spears tend to also be a little thicker in width, with a slight tinge of pale green to them, almost anaemic in colour, which intrigues me even more, especially when finding they are actually more bitter, when I think you'd suppose the opposite. They tend to be more common in other European countries and I've seen them many times in France when catering, bundles of them sold at markets for an absolute steal.

Waste tips:

One of the greatest ways to use asparagus ends is to pop them into soups or sauces. They are completely edible, but because they are quite a lot tougher than the rest of the spear, they need a tad more time cooking, otherwise it's common to think we should chuck them when they are still more on the chewy al dente side. They add a great depth to a dish when cooked, even if they are a little stringy, so blend them in to remove that texture.

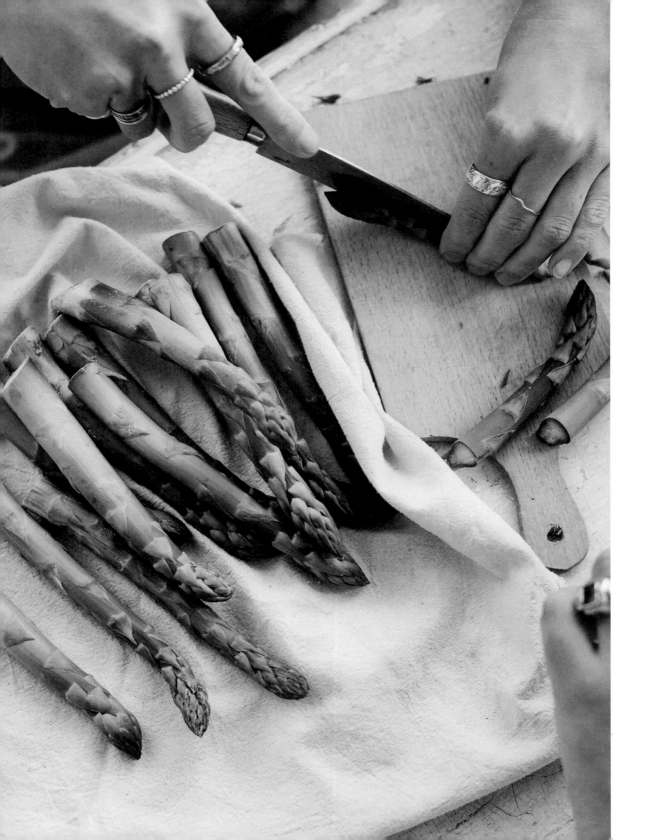

On a solo trip to Bali, I stumbled across a beautiful, off-the-beaten-track café, owned by two sisters with a passion for cooking and sharing. I found myself in there almost every day, trying most of their menu. I was a total sucker for their delicious garden soup, packed to the brim with Balinese vegetables and herbs, served with rice and toasted shallots. So this is my tribute to those sisters and their recipe: veg heavy, easy on the stomach but perfectly filling.

Serves 4–6

SPRING BALINESE SOUP

With this recipe, prep work is everything. Once you have all your ingredients ready to go, the rest is pretty quick.

Put the coconut oil into a pan on a low heat and sauté the shallots until they become soft and fragrant. Add the garlic, coriander seeds, ginger, lemongrass and chopped coriander stalks and continue to cook until browned. You can add a dash of water if it starts to dry out too much.

Add the soy sauce or tamari, stock and cayenne pepper. Bring to the boil, then add the carrots. Reduce the heat and simmer for a few minutes. The carrots take slightly longer than the other veggies to cook through, so allow them to soften slightly before the next step.

Add the tomatoes, asparagus, broad beans and chopped chosen greens. Continue to simmer gently to cook the vegetables.

Add half the coriander leaves and season with salt and pepper. You can decide here if you'd like a little extra heat, adding cayenne to taste or green chilli if you wish.

As your soup simmers, it will thicken slightly and the tomatoes will become very soft. Once your vegetables are tender, add a little more coriander, saving the rest of the leaves to garnish.

To serve, ladle into bowls and top with the toasted cashews and the rest of the fresh coriander leaves.

2 tsp coconut oil

2 shallots, finely chopped

4 cloves of garlic, crushed or finely chopped

1 tsp coriander seeds

a large knob of fresh ginger, finely chopped or grated

1 large stick of lemongrass, finely chopped

a large handful of fresh coriander, stalks finely chopped, leaves left whole

4 tbsp soy sauce or tamari

approx 1.5 litres stock

1 tsp cayenne pepper

2 carrots, any variety, thinly sliced

2 medium (or 4 small) tomatoes, quartered

approx. 10–15 spears of asparagus, sliced lengthways and then in half

200g podded broad beans

200g chopped greens (spinach, chard, kale – you could also use Asian greens if available)

salt and pepper

70g cashews, toasted

*If you like spice, a finely chopped fresh green chilli is great in this soup. Add with the rest of the vegetables when simmering.

Waste tips:

You can serve this dish with a grain or legume if you fancy, piling the soup on top of some rice or millet, for example, or chucking in some cooked chickpeas. The soup also works well blended if you have some of it left over. Simply blend half or all the leftovers, reheat on the stove and enjoy. You can also use the base of this and adapt it by adding whatever vegetables you may have in the fridge or happen to have bought that week.

A savoury-meets-sweet kind of dish, in which the earthy, nutty tones from the rice are met with sweetness from the coconut and paired with a spring-time favourite, asparagus. It's a vegetable that's not around for long and really should be eaten in its prime for optimal taste.

COCONUT BLACK RICE SALAD

w/ balsamic roasted asparagus

Preheat your oven to 180°C fan. Before cooking your rice, make sure to rinse it well, letting the liquid run clear, then put it into a saucepan with about 1 litre of water and a pinch of salt. Bring to the boil, then cover the pan and lower to a simmer.

After about 20 minutes, add the coconut oil, desiccated coconut, garlic and ginger to the pan. Continue to cook until the rice is tender with a tad of bite left, about 30–40 minutes in total. Once cooked, leave to cool slightly. You can add a little more water at this stage if need be. You don't want the rice to burn on the bottom of the pan. Black rice will have more bite than regular rice once cooked.

While your rice is cooking, lay your asparagus and red onions on a baking tray and drizzle over the balsamic vinegar and 1 tablespoon of olive oil. Season with salt and pepper and roast for about 15 minutes.

Once your vegetables have roasted, transfer them to a bowl and add the fresh herbs, celery, raisins or sultanas, pomegranate seeds or other fruit, lime juice and half the zest. Season with salt and pepper and mix well.

To serve, spoon a helping of black rice on to a plate, and top with the salad mix and a dash of the remaining zest for garnish. Drizzle over some extra olive oil.

250g uncooked black rice

1–2 tbsp coconut oil

1–2 tbsp desiccated coconut

2 cloves of garlic, crushed or finely chopped

1cm ginger, finely chopped or grated

10–15 spears of asparagus, halved

3 small red onions, skins removed, quartered, layers separated

2–4 tbsp balsamic vinegar

1 tbsp olive oil, plus extra for drizzling

salt and pepper

a handful of fresh herbs of choice (coriander, parsley, mint, or a mix)

2 stalks of celery, finely chopped

35g raisins or sultanas

1 pomegranate, deseeded (this may not be in season or available, but for a fruity citrus kick, add a fruit of choice, sliced and chopped small)

2 limes, both juiced, 1 zested

Waste tips:

The recipe for the rice on its own is great for jazzing up other salads or eating as is, no extras. With its coconutty taste it's good for Asian-inspired dishes, even Indian. You could also add some fresh chopped greens and herbs to it and serve it along with other bits for a picnic or buffet-style spread. It keeps well in the fridge for around a week, as the oil helps to preserve the additional ingredients as well as the rice.

This is one for those somewhat colder spring nights when it can feel like we've suddenly fallen back into winter. Mash to me is the ultimate comfort food, and mustard in mash, a little trick I learnt from my dad, is a winner. This recipe calls for Dijon but I've been known to use English mustard for a slightly more fiery take. Paired with some spring vegetables, the wintery slump won't feel like such a thing.

Serves approx. 6

POTATO, WHITE BEAN AND MUSTARD MASH

w/ sautéd asparagus, tenderstem broccoli

Bring a large pan of water to the boil, and add a pinch of salt and the cubed potatoes. Bring back to the boil and cook the potatoes until soft and fluffy. Drain and put back into the pan.

While the potatoes are still hot, add the garlic, mustard, beans, plant-based milk, olive oil and salt and pepper to taste. Use a potato masher (if you don't have one you can use a fork, it'll just take slightly longer) to mash the potatoes. Test for seasoning and add more if need be, along with the smoked paprika. Continue to mash until you reach your desired consistency. Cover the pan while you sauté your vegetables.

Put the olive and coconut oil into another pan, over a low heat. Add the asparagus and Tenderstem broccoli and sauté for about 5 minutes. Once they start to brown slightly, add the vinegar, lemon juice, oregano, peppercorns and salt and continue to sauté until the vegetables are cooked, about another 5 minutes or so.

Put the pan with the mash back on the stove and heat up over a low heat, stirring with a wooden spoon.

To serve, spoon out the desired amount of mash followed by some of the sautéd veggies. Sprinkle over a handful of crushed and toasted nuts (whatever you have in, or a mixture) and season again if necessary.

For the mash

4 large baking potatoes, washed well, cubed, skins on

salt and pepper

6 cloves of garlic, crushed or finely chopped

2 heaped tbsp Dijon mustard

approx. 200g cooked white beans (tinned beans are fine)

250ml plant-based milk, plus extra if you like a slightly smoother mash

2 tbsp olive oil

½ tsp smoked paprika

For the sautéd vegetables

1 tbsp olive oil

1 tbsp coconut oil

12 spears of asparagus, whole

12 Tenderstem broccoli stalks, whole

1 tsp white wine vinegar (you could also use white wine if you have some in the fridge)

1 lemon, juiced

2 tsp dried oregano

1 tsp peppercorns, crushed

salt

early summer

I don't know about you, but there's something about the smell of summer that sends me into a whirl of happiness. The smell in the air is one of my favourite things about the season, especially when we're at that in-between stage where spring turns into summer. A light and fresh smell in the morning that lingers for a good part of the day, the occasional whiff of freshly mown grass and the subtle scent of floral blooms . . . and don't get me started about the smell of the air by the ocean, I'm an absolute sucker for it; it's my happy place. Once summer commences, I love dining alfresco. It really is the best part of my day: a long drawn-out picnic, watching the sunset, chilled drink in hand, friends and a great spread. Even when I'm away it always feels like a great idea – laid-back suppers on the lawn, or sandy sundowners on the beach. Given that daylight saving has only just commenced at this time, I'll admit I love pulling on a cosy jumper during the evenings. As a fantasizer, naturally I find myself daydreaming about upcoming summer events, planning all the details – decor, colour theme, dishes and ingredients, totally in my element, delving into the realm of summer party hosting.

To me, summer screams salads, barbecues, whole roasted corn, condiments of every kind – dips, salsas, pestos, and in my case, mustards! There is a misconception around salads which I want to debunk from the get-go. Whoever said a salad was boring was clearly on another planet. I mean, sure, leaves are simple, but even they can be turned into what I like to call a sexy salad with some grated lemon zest, lemon juice, salt and pepper, a wee bit of olive oil, vinegar and a spoon of mustard, and that's 'fussy'. We have such a handsome variety of produce that sticking to your cucumber, lettuce, tomato situation just isn't always justified (although, don't get me wrong, that can be a great combination, especially when in season). Salads are great for bringing together a whole bunch of food groups, balanced out with salt, acidity, healthy fats, and occasionally some heat (cooking-wise and chilli-wise). Use different methods to chop your veggies, and don't be afraid to add fruit . . . dried fruit even!

star produce:

Apricots

—

Aubergines

—

Courgettes

—

Fennel

—

Jersey Royal potatoes

—

Other seasonal produce: Artichokes, chicory, lettuce (a variety), cherries, runner beans, samphire, Swiss chard, summer squash, chillies, cucumbers, gooseberries, marrows, blackcurrants, beetroot varieties, peas, chives, nectarines, strawberries, rocket, corn.

———

You will of course notice some of these fruits/vegetables in other seasons as well. There is a big overlap these days, due to the climate and average temperatures we experience, regardless of where you are.

———

Grains harvested at this time of the year: Corn, millet/pearl millet, rye, amaranth, freekeh, kamut, bulgur, spelt, sorghum.

———

apricots

I'll be honest, apricots haven't always been a star fruit for me. I wasn't a fussy kid, but apricots would ever so slightly wig me out. I wouldn't say I hated them, it was more a subtle dislike, and the idea of a few scoops of vanilla ice cream was a lot more attractive than an apricot for dessert. Now, however, the combination of their delicate fuzzy skin and grainy but smooth texture is something I find quite special. Their usually firm flesh is not as juicy as other stone fruit, yet is just as delightful. When I see a punnet of fresh apricots, I can't help but purchase a whole load, eager to get home, of course enjoying one or two en route and then stewing a batch to keep for the week, sometimes served hot, sometimes cold. Weirdly, given my dislike for them when I was younger, I still find them nostalgic. Apricots are the perfect combination of tart and sweet, making them a great ingredient to add to salads, served with a grain; I can guarantee you'll be hooked. If I can recommend one thing with apricots it's that you will not regret buying them organic, and of course local if possible. They should be a delicate orange tone, fragrant to smell and elegant to touch, especially when they're at peak ripeness.

Waste tips:

Two words: apricot jam. A real jazzy number in my opinion, easily whipped up, full of flavour, subtle sourness but ever so sweet. You can stew a batch with any desired sugar, a dash of water, some lemon juice and a pinch of salt. Simmer until they have completely softened and gradually become thicker and thicker. A little trick I picked up from a childhood friend's mum is adding jams to dressings . . . yep, you heard right. It makes perfect sense if you'd add the fruit to a salad anyway, and using apricot jam or any jam for that matter creates a beautiful texture, as well as helping to level out the components of the dressing, i.e. adding some sweetness to balance a sharp or citrus taste, or even something that's too salty or vinegary. Compotes are another great way to use up on-the-turn or super-ripe apricots, using them as you desire or creating a crumble, bars, cakes . . . even mixed with olive oil, fennel seeds and a bit more salt and using as a glaze for tofu.

Pancake day should be every day if you ask me, especially when they're as fluffy and textured as these. I'm really into using blends of flours with an addition of whole oats; it makes it more interesting, and texture for me has always been a big thing. Served with juicy spiced apricots, this recipe feels super special, especially if you're having it on, say, a Tuesday!

Makes approx. 4 small pancakes, or 2 large (mixture easily scales up for more)

MULTIGRAIN PANCAKES

w/ maple and cardamom apricots

First cook your apricots. In a small pan, on low, heat the maple syrup and coconut oil. Add the salt, followed by the cardamom, then wait a few seconds before adding the apricots. Slowly stir to coat the fruit. Keeping the pan on a low heat, allow the apricots to simmer, soaking up the flavours and becoming tender. Remove from the heat once cooked.

For the pancakes, put the buckwheat flour, oat flour, oats, baking powder, salt, cinnamon and chia seeds into a bowl and stir to combine.

Slowly add the maple syrup and plant-based milk, starting with the smaller amount of liquid. Whisk as you go to ensure there are no lumps in the batter and that you have a smooth, loose mix. You don't want it to be too runny, but it should be pourable. Add more liquid if necessary.

Get your pan very hot. Add coconut oil if using, but keep on a low heat and allow it to heat up slowly. Ladle either a quarter or half the batter into the hot pan. If you have a large enough pan, you can do all the pancakes at once. Cook them for about 2–4 minutes on each side. You want bubbles to form on top and the edges to brown before flipping. Flip and cook for a further 2–4 minutes.

Top the pancakes with the apricots. Serve with a drizzle more maple syrup and any other toppings you like.

For the maple and cardamom apricots

2 tbsp maple syrup

1 tbsp coconut oil

a pinch of salt

either ½ tsp dried ground cardamom or approx. 3 cardamom pods, shells removed, seeds crushed

4 small apricots, stones removed, quartered

For the pancakes

approx. 70g buckwheat flour

approx. 70g oat flour, plus 1 tbsp normal oats

½ tsp baking powder

a pinch of salt

¼ tsp ground cinnamon

1 tsp chia seeds

1 tsp maple syrup

125–250ml unsweetened plant-based milk

coconut oil (optional, for frying, but dry fry if you have a good non-stick pan)

Spelt, in my opinion, and especially in its whole form, is a mighty grain. It's perfectly chewy, beautifully nutty and quite similar to barley. This recipe is really brought to life by the spelt, a perfect dish when you want simplicity and freshness, particularly at the start of summer when we typically think more about salads and less about stews.

APRICOT AND GRAIN SALAD

w/ toasted walnuts, greens

Bring about ½ litre of water to the boil in a pan. Add the rinsed soaked spelt and a pinch of salt, and adjust the heat to a medium or gentle rolling boil. Cook the spelt until tender, about 25 minutes. Once cooked, drain any remaining liquid and rinse under cold water for a few moments, to remove any extra starch.

Place the sliced onion in a bowl and cover with enough vinegar to submerge it. Using a fork, stir it around, pressing fairly firmly, allowing the onion to soften. This helps with the digestion of raw onion, as it removes a lot of the fructose from the vegetable. Leave to one side.

Heat the olive oil in a medium frying pan. Go ahead and add your chopped kale. After a few minutes or so, once it starts to wilt, add the chopped garlic and continue to sauté until the kale is nice and soft. Allow to cool slightly, then put into a large mixing bowl.

Add the apricots, rocket, cherry tomatoes and walnuts. Squeeze over the lemon juice, add the zest and mix well. Add the softened onion (plus any leftover vinegar) and season with salt and pepper.

If you like, you can add the spelt to the bowl and mix together. If you prefer to serve it separately, spoon it on to plates, followed by a hefty serving of the salad. Season with extra salt and pepper and some olive oil if you wish.

approx. 180g spelt, soaked for at least 1 hour, drained and rinsed well

salt and pepper

1 large red onion, finely chopped

2–4 tbsp apple cider or white wine vinegar

1–2 tbsp olive oil

5 stalks of kale, any variety, finely chopped, stalks included

2 cloves of garlic, chopped finely and small

4 apricots, stones removed, quartered

80g fresh rocket, washed well

a small handful of cherry tomatoes, quartered

80–100g walnuts, toasted then roughly chopped

2 lemons, both juiced, 1 zested

Waste tips:

You are not restricted to spelt here. If you don't have any or simply aren't a fan, use any grain you like or have in. The quantities are about the same. You could also do a mixture of grains, or use any that you may have already batch-cooked. This salad is also great with pesto, either mixed through or spooned on top as a condiment.

A summer delight, inspired by a trip to Morocco, where griddling apricot halves was a daily ritual. They're paired in this recipe with a subtle burst of Persian flavour from the caraway seeds, to cut through the sweetness. A real flavour-matching dish, it works served on a platter or in a glass ramekin or tumbler.

ROASTED APRICOTS

w/ caraway and toasted quinoa

Preheat your oven to 180°C fan. If you have an oven with more than one shelf, you can do this all at the same time. Prep your apricots and place them, cut side up, on a baking tray. Evenly sprinkle over the caraway seeds, cinnamon and lemon zest. Squeeze over the lemon juice and drizzle over 2 tablespoons of maple syrup. Put into the oven and roast for about 15 minutes in total, checking halfway through and giving a little mix/shake to make sure everything is still coated and cooking relatively evenly.

Put the well-rinsed quinoa into a bowl with the coconut oil, 1 tablespoon of maple syrup and a pinch of salt. Spread evenly on a baking tray and roast for about 12–15 minutes, again checking a few times and stirring/shaking the quinoa. You want it to be nice and crunchy.

You can serve this as a sharing dessert, laying the apricots on a large serving plate, followed by the crunchy quinoa, or serve it individually or as a snack.

- 10–12 apricots, halved and destoned
- 2 tsp caraway seeds
- 1–2 tsp ground cinnamon
- 1 lemon, juice and zest
- 2 tbsp pure maple syrup or other sweetener of choice, plus 1 tbsp for the quinoa
- 200g quinoa, rinsed thoroughly
- 2 tbsp coconut oil
- salt

Waste tips:

This recipe is also great with any other stone fruit or a combination. If you have leftovers from the recipe, you can use a compote-type mix on porridge, with yoghurt, or just eat as is. Occasionally, I'll add it to summer salads, as the roasted fruit brings a nice variety to a meal, and you'll also find these apricots in the panzanella salad on page 104 – sweet fruits can work very well in savoury dishes. The crunchy quinoa will keep in an airtight container or jar for up to 2 weeks, ready for sprinkling on sweet or savoury dishes, such as simply roasted vegetables.

aubergines

One of the many things my best friend and I have in common is our love for aubergines. As soon as the season hits, we pretty much don't go without one for the entire summer . . . and really a zone in the fridge dedicated to aubergines is a must. Whether we're cooking together or just grocery shopping, we always go to our favourite local grocer's in Nunhead, south London. Because of the frequency with which we go there, even if sometimes it's simply to have a nosey at what fresh produce they have in, or to pick up an apple en route to somewhere else, naturally the owners know us well, and know only too well our summer aubergine addiction.

An absolute staple at this time of the year, aubergines are one of those vegetables that I could definitely eat every day, whether roasted, grilled, stuffed, or turned into that real showstopper, babaganoush. I know aubergine isn't everyone's cup of tea given its often slimy texture, but this dip is always a winner. Its smoky flavour and creamy texture overcome any aubergine dislikes. The trick to babaganoush really is getting that smoky flavour, and you'll see in the recipe on page 85 that holding the aubergines over a flame, whether that's just your stovetop or a barbecue, is where it's at. You don't even have to do much with the vegetable – something as simple as grilling it with a little olive oil, salt, pepper and dried oregano is incredibly delicious. My mouth is watering just thinking about it. We're very lucky now to be able to get hold of aubergines for a larger portion of the year, more so than ever before, and it's definitely in its prime all summer long . . . babaganoush for all, I say!

Waste tips:

Just in case you thought I hadn't written about babaganoush enough, a great little tip for leftovers of the luscious dip is to stir them through a risotto. Sounds a little wacky, but trust me when I say it's a real game-changer. It adds a lovely texture and of course flavour, complementing the rice perfectly. Another great thing to do, especially if you have an 'on-the-turn' aubergine, is to roast it whole. You can then scrape out the middle and stuff it with your favourite grain, of course not wasting the delicious inside and adding it to the stuffing mix. It's a great vegetable for replicating a kind of 'meaty' texture, so it's ideal to add to most pasta dishes, bakes, curries . . . you name it.

Pasta salad takes me straight back to my childhood, with vivid memories of my parents using whatever we had in the fridge to make it 'exciting' and piling it into Tupperware on sunny weekend mornings, before we headed out for the day. The dressing in this recipe brings out all the flavours, and having enough veg is key. If you're still dubious about pasta salad, trust me when I say this one will change your mind.

Serves 4–6

SUMMER PASTA SALAD

w/ grilled aubergine, stone fruit, shaved fennel

Bring a large pan of salted water to the boil and cook the pasta until al dente, usually around 7–8 minutes depending on variety. Drain and rinse under cold water to stop the cooking process. Put back into the pan with a drizzle of olive oil to avoid any sticking and cover.

If you have a grill setting on your oven, switch it to high. Or you can roast the aubergines, but the result will be slightly different. Place your aubergine slices on a large tray, add a sprinkle of salt, and grill for 10–12 minutes. Once cooked, remove from the grill and place to one side.

Put the stone fruit, shaved fennel, cabbage, fresh herbs, and half the toasted nuts into a serving bowl. Add the paprika, lemon juice and zest, nutritional yeast, olive oil and garlic. Season with salt and pepper and mix well, massaging to slightly soften the cabbage and fennel.

Add the aubergine slices to the bowl. While cooling, they may have seeped a little liquid – pour this in too, then add the cooked pasta. Mix carefully to coat everything.

Serve with the rest of the toasted nuts on top and season again if necessary.

approx. 200g dried pasta of choice (I love rotini or fusilli for this)

2 medium aubergines, sliced 1cm thick

salt and pepper

6 small stone fruit of choice (apricots, plums, etc.), halved, stone removed, then cut into 1cm thick slices

½ fennel bulb, halved, then shaved, with a mandolin or sharp knife

¼–½ a small cabbage (any variety), thinly sliced

a large handful of fresh herbs (basil, mint, parsley), roughly chopped

50g pine nuts (or pistachios, hazelnuts or almonds as substitutes), lightly toasted

1 tsp smoked paprika

2 lemons, both juiced, 1 zested

2 tbsp nutritional yeast

2 tbsp olive oil

2 cloves of garlic, finely chopped

Waste tip:

This keeps well in the fridge and is great for balmy evenings or picnics. You can use any variety of pasta you like here, even a smaller pasta type such as orzo.

A little recipe I'd describe as a vegetarian go-to; so simple but incredibly tasty, working mainly with what you have in your store cupboard. The marinade really helps to bring the aubergine to life, cooking it until soft and gooey with an ever-so-slightly caramelized situation on top. Garnished with fresh herbs, spring onions and a little crunch from the sesame seeds, it's perfect as a main or a side.

Serves 4
as a side

GINGER, PARSLEY AND MISO AUBERGINE

Preheat your oven to 180°C fan. Place your aubergines on a baking tray. Lightly score them using a sharp knife in a criss-cross pattern on one side. Brush them lightly with the sesame oil and sprinkle with a pinch of salt. Put them into the oven for around 15 minutes, until they start to brown on top and slightly shrivel.

Make the rest of the marinade while the aubergines are in the oven. Whisk together the miso paste, mirin, rice vinegar, soy sauce or tamari, sugar, garlic, ginger and chopped parsley stalks.

Remove the aubergines from the oven and pour over the marinade, making sure they're entirely covered. Roast again for another 5–10 minutes, depending on your oven and the desired consistency of the aubergines.

Remove from the oven and serve with the chopped parsley leaves, spring onions, sesame seeds, lime juice, zest and salt.

Waste tips:

These are great for making a dip if you have leftovers – similar to a babaganoush but without the smokiness. They are also great added to pasta sauces, salads or eaten cold just as they are, maybe with some hummus and toasted bread.

6 small aubergines, Japanese or baby, or 2 average size aubergines, sliced diagonally, approx. 1–2cm thick (if you have the small Japanese type, you can slice them in half)

1 tbsp sesame oil, plus a pinch of salt for pre-seasoning

3 heaped tbsp miso paste (yellow, brown or red)

2 tbsp mirin

2 tbsp rice vinegar

2–3 tbsp soy sauce or tamari

1 tbsp coconut/palm sugar (natural cane or brown sugar is also fine)

2 cloves of garlic, crushed or finely chopped

2 tbsp ginger, finely chopped or grated

a small handful of fresh parsley, stalks and leaves separated and roughly chopped

2 spring onions, roughly chopped

2 tbsp sesame seeds

1 lime, juice and zest

salt, if needed (there is already a lot of salt/sodium in the miso and soy, so don't over-salt)

Babaganoush has always been one of my favourite dips, hands down. The smokiness, garlic, creaminess . . . it really gets my taste buds tingling. Perfect to complement any summer spread, over the years I've tested this on clients, friends and family members, so safe to say it's one to please a crowd!

Makes approx.
8–10 servings

BABAGANOUSH

The key to the smokiness is to cook the aubergines on a gas flame/hob. You can also use a barbecue, should you feel inclined. One by one, or at the same time if you have enough burners, place the aubergines over the flame. As they char and become soft, slowly move them around to cook on all sides. They will start to juice or ooze slightly.

(If you don't have a gas hob, you can cook the aubergines in the oven. Pierce all over to prevent exploding and place in the oven on 180°C fan for 25–30 minutes until softened and cooked through. Once cooked, remove from the oven and allow to sit before continuing.)

Once the aubergine has cooked through and charred on the outside (don't worry if some parts look blacker than others), place in a dish to cool entirely. While cooling, the aubergine will ooze more liquid; save this for the dip.

Once cool, carefully peel off as much of the skin/charred layer as you can. These can go into your food scraps. Any charred bits left behind will just add to the flavour.

Put the aubergines back into the bowl with the aubergine juice and add the garlic, tahini, lemon juice and zest, chilli flakes, salt and pepper. Using your hands, mix this together, breaking down the aubergine as you go. If it's a little dry, add more tahini or olive oil, seasoning again if necessary. (You can also do this in a blender, but the consistency will be a lot smoother.)

To serve, drizzle over a tad of olive oil and any other seasonings or garnishes you desire. Great for a summer evening dinner dip.

- 3 medium aubergines
- 4 cloves of garlic, crushed or finely grated
- 4–5 heaped tbsp tahini
- 1½ lemons, juiced, plus a dash of zest
- a pinch of dried chilli flakes
- salt and pepper
- olive oil (optional, for garnish)

Waste tips:

I never usually have leftovers of this, but should you have some left or want to pre-make a batch, it'll keep in an airtight container in the fridge. Jazz this recipe up to make a Greek-style favourite by adding some finely diced tomatoes and red onion, plus a dash of oregano, and you have a more traditional 'eggplant salad'. If you have no tahini, you can also sub this with olive oil. I would start with 3–4 tablespoons and see how you go. Another great way to use babaganoush is to swirl it into a risotto. It adds an amazing smoky flavour as well as a nice texture.

A roasted aubergine, especially whole, is a beautiful thing. The skin chars and the flesh becomes soft and juicy, with a subtle caramel taste. When using whole vegetables, it's key to bring them to life with seasoning or sauces, and this aïoli really complements the succulent star of the show.

Serves 2
as a side

ROASTED AND SMOKED WHOLE AUBERGINE

w/ greens and vegan aïoli

Preheat your oven to 200°C fan. To make the aïoli, put the cashews in a blender with 100ml of water, the garlic, mustard, vinegar, lemon juice and zest plus a good pinch of salt and blend to a smooth creamy texture. Taste and adjust the seasonings and liquid if necessary. It should be thick but pourable. Place in a jar or airtight container and pop into the fridge while you make the rest of the dish.

Pierce your aubergine/s all over (to prevent exploding while cooking), place on a baking tray and roast on a middle shelf for about 10 minutes, then remove.

In a small bowl, whisk the garlic, paprika, cumin, chilli flakes, olive oil and a pinch of salt. Where you pierced the aubergine/s, very slightly and carefully pull the incisions apart. Pour some marinade into each hole, then roast the aubergine/s for a further 20 minutes. You will notice them start to shrivel slightly and ooze some juice – this is good.

To cook the greens, either steam or lightly boil in salted water. Once they're a vibrant green, remove and blanch under cold water to stop the cooking process. If you want your greens hot, don't run them under water for too long. Place them in a bowl with the lemon juice and zest and a good grind of salt and pepper, and cover to keep warm.

Remove the aubergine/s from the oven. You can serve it whole or sliced lengthways down the middle. Serve with the greens, a dollop of aïoli, a sprinkle of crushed nuts and a drizzle of olive oil to bring it even more to life.

For the aïoli (makes extra)

120g cashews, soaked overnight in cold water (or for 4 hours in boiling water)

approx. 100ml water (or more to loosen)

3 cloves of garlic

2 tsp Dijon mustard

½ tsp apple cider vinegar

½–1 lemon, juiced, plus a dash of zest

a pinch of salt

For the aubergine and greens

1 large aubergine, or 2 small ones,

4 cloves of garlic, crushed or finely chopped

2 tsp smoked paprika

1 tsp ground cumin

a pinch of chilli flakes

1–2 tbsp olive oil

salt and pepper

5–6 stems of your chosen greens (kale, chard, spring greens)

1 lemon, juice and zest

a handful of crushed nuts (I love pistachios)

Aubergine cooked in this way acquires a slightly smoky flavour, which means leftovers are ideal for babaganoush (see page 85). The aïoli will keep for about a week in your fridge; it's great as a condiment, for adding to dressings or mixing with pesto or harissa for a creamy version. It's also delicious as a marinade.

Every time I smell ras el hanout, it takes me right back to a
Moroccan-style market, buzzing with locals, spices, fresh
produce, a shop dedicated to all things wicker . . . it's a really
magical spice. Inspired by my trips there, this recipe is a
little dedication to some of the amazing people who taught
me the tricks of their trade – well, when it comes to putting a
spice like this together, that is. Heady and aromatic, it's most
certainly their signature blend.

**Serves 2 as a
main, 4 as a side**

RAS EL HANOUT BAKED AUBERGINE

w/ tahini tapenade

Preheat your oven to 200°C fan. Slice your aubergines
and place them on a baking tray. Sprinkle over the ras el
hanout, and add the cherry tomatoes, olive oil and garlic.
Season with salt and pepper and mix well, making sure
the aubergines and tomatoes are coated. Put into the
oven and roast for about 20–25 minutes. You can add
a little water about halfway or further on towards the
end if you want or need a little more juice in the tray.

If you are serving this dish with a grain, put this on to
boil now, cooking until the desired texture is reached
and covering to keep warm.

For the tapenade, put the olives, pine nuts, capers, garlic,
olive oil, parsley and lemon juice into a blender or small
processor. You could also use a mortar and pestle for
a chunkier tapenade. Blitz or smash until you reach a
paste-type mix. Transfer to a bowl and season with salt
and pepper, stirring in the tahini as you go. If you want
the mixture a little wetter, you could add a little more
lemon juice.

Once the aubergines are cooked, remove them from the
oven. Serve hot, with a dollop of tapenade on top and
your chosen grain alongside. Season with salt and pepper
if necessary, and add any extra parsley or some chilli
flakes if you fancy.

For the aubergine

- 2 medium
  aubergines,
  sliced diagonally,
  approx. 2cm
  thick
- 3 tbsp ras el
  hanout (see
  notes opposite)
- approx. 150g
  cherry tomatoes
- 3–4 tbsp olive oil
- 2 cloves of garlic,
  crushed or finely
  chopped
- salt and pepper
- 90–180g grain
  of choice,
  for serving,
  i.e. spelt, pearl
  barley (omit
  for a light dish
  or side)

For the tahini tapenade (makes approx. 150ml)

- 160g pitted black
  olives (any
  liquid drained)
- 35g pine nuts
- 1 heaped tbsp
  capers
- 2 cloves of garlic,
  crushed or finely
  chopped
- 2 tbsp olive oil
- a small handful of
  parsley, roughly
  chopped (dried
  is also fine,
  approx. 1 tbsp)
- ½ a lemon, juiced
- salt and pepper
- 2 tbsp tahini
- dried chilli flakes
  (optional), for
  serving

»

Notes:

Ras el hanout is one of those spice blends that you can make very easily yourself at home if you don't want to buy it. It's pretty much a blend of all the aromatic spices – what could be better? To make your own blend, simply place the following ingredients together in a jar, mix with a dry spoon and voila! This recipe is for about 35g worth, so a small spice jar will suffice.

2 tsp ground ginger

2 tsp ground cinnamon

2 tsp ground allspice

2 tsp ground cardamom

2 tsp ground coriander

1 tsp ground nutmeg

1 tsp ground turmeric

½–1 tsp cayenne pepper (or more for a kick)

½ tsp ground fennel seeds

½ tsp ground cloves

½ tsp ground pepper (white or black)

courgettes

Part of the summer squash family that grows in a variety of shapes, sizes and colours, you'll often see beautiful striped courgettes around this time, as well as the yellow variety. Later in summer we start to see the more familiar darker green ones. I often still call them zucchini, just as I sometimes call an aubergine an eggplant, thanks to my time spent living in Australia. I think the name zucchini makes them sound sexier, which they so rightly deserve.

Courgettes are very versatile. I always find them exciting: grilling them, grating and adding them to salads, and I have many go-to recipes for when the season hits. I remember my dad being very fond of courgettes too – they usually made their way into his infamous pasta dish, which you'll discover on page 160. I've experimented a lot with them, appreciating their ease and accessibility, and most of my recipes have come from playing around with other things I have in the fridge or re-creating a dish I used to love.

Let's not forget about the gorgeous, short-lived flowers. They're quite hard to come by, as once picked from their fruits (the courgettes) they start to close and wilt. If you do happen to see some, especially if they are still attached to their courgettes, snap them up! I feel like I've totally lucked out when I stumble across them. I like to whip up a batch of nut-based ricotta and carefully stuff them. You have to be patient with the flowers, as they are very delicate, but it's so worth it. Once stuffed, you can lightly fry them or pop them into the oven for about 5–6 minutes, heating them through and cooking them ever so slightly. They're not as fragrant as you might think, given their appearance, but they are well and truly delicious.

Waste tips:

Lots of salads call for 'ribboned' courgette. It's all too easy to then discard the middle once you can ribbon no more. It may not look as pretty as the ribbons, but the middle part of the vegetable is where most of the flavour usually is, given that's where the seeds are. You can thinly slice it and use it just as you would anything else. Grating is also an excellent way to use up either a half-used or a slightly limp-looking courgette – they're lovely in salads and also great for adding a bit of colour to a grain. They hold quite a lot of liquid, so if you are grating, once left for a few minutes they will start to release that, adding a natural liquid to a salad dressing. Occasionally, you will want to squeeze out the liquid, for example if you are using them for patties, when you may need the courgette to be drier. Don't chuck the liquid though, as I really am serious about using it in a salad dressing.

An alternative to the traditional dish but just as good. Using a vegetable – courgette in this instance – in place of the pasta layers is a revolution. Layered with rich tomato sauce, creamy vegan ricotta and a thick pesto, my mouth waters just at the thought. A great one to prepare a little earlier in the day when you have more time, to be served later with a fresh salad.

Makes one serving dish, approx. 9 squares in a 20 x 25cm dish
——

COURGETTE 'LASAGNE'
——

Preheat your oven to 180°C fan.

First make the ricotta. Drain and rinse the almonds well, then roughly chop and put them into a high-speed blender. Add the lemon juice and zest, salt, miso paste, oregano, garlic, vinegar, nutritional yeast and pepper. Slowly add the milk, starting with the lower quantity, and blend until the mixture starts to have a smoother texture, adding any remaining milk if necessary. The mixture should be thick and textured. Place in the fridge and allow to harden slightly.

For the tomato sauce, sauté the onion in a dash of water until it starts to become translucent. Add the garlic and continue to fry for another minute or so. Add the tomatoes, tomato paste, water, basil and dried oregano. Season with salt and pepper and allow to simmer on a low heat for about 12 minutes. You want the sauce to become thick and rich, but if it starts to dry up, add a dash more water. Leave to simmer for about 10 minutes. Meanwhile, do the next steps. Once the sauce is cooked, turn off the heat and allow it to sit.

For the pesto, place all the ingredients in a clean blender and blitz until they form a paste or pesto-type mix, adding any extra olive oil if necessary to loosen.

Next make the béchamel. Put the cooked beans into a blender or food processor along with the lemon, olive oil, water, nutritional yeast, mustard, nutmeg and oregano.

For the ricotta topping (makes extra)
——
120g almonds, soaked for at least 2 hours, and best overnight, roughly chopped

1 small lemon, juiced, plus a dash of zest

1 heaped tsp salt

1 tsp miso (preferably yellow or light-coloured)

2 tsp dried oregano

2 cloves of garlic, crushed or finely chopped

1 tsp apple cider vinegar

4 heaped tbsp nutritional yeast

a pinch of pepper

60–125ml plant-based milk

For the tomato sauce
——
1 small white or brown onion, finely chopped

2 cloves of garlic, crushed or finely chopped

12 cherry tomatoes or 6 larger ones, quartered

2–4 heaped tbsp tomato purée/ paste

125–250ml water

a handful of fresh basil, roughly chopped (be careful not to bruise it)

2 tsp dried oregano

salt and pepper

»

Season with salt and pepper and blend until it is as smooth as possible, like a flour-based béchamel.

To assemble, place a layer of courgettes at the bottom of your dish. Spread over a layer of the tomato sauce, followed by a layer of the pesto, then a layer of béchamel. Repeat, starting with another layer of courgettes, followed by the sauces until you have used them all up. Don't worry if they start to merge slightly when layering. The top layer will, however, be a layer of ricotta rather than béchamel. If you're feeling fancy, you could use a fork to make a light marking on top, scoring from one end to the other.

Put into the oven for around 15 minutes, or until the lasagne is browned on top and the courgettes have cooked through. You can test this by poking a sharp knife through the centre.

Once cooked, allow to sit for a few moments before slicing into squares.

Waste tips:

This is one of my favourite dishes to have as a leftover, whether that's reheated or cold with a side salad. It will keep in the fridge for about 5 days, and in the freezer for a lot longer, approx. 3–4 weeks . . . so it's a great one to make in advance for the freezer for times when you're feeling a bit lazier. You can also experiment with using different vegetables for the layers: squash, pumpkin, potatoes, etc. would be great. I have also made this same recipe using regular lasagne sheets for a more traditional outcome. You may need a slightly deeper or bigger dish to do so, though.

For the pesto

150g walnuts

4 cloves of garlic, crushed or finely chopped

a large handful of fresh basil (approx. 60g)

2 small lemons, both juiced, 1 zested

approx. 125–250ml olive oil

6–8 heaped tbsp nutritional yeast

a pinch of dried chilli

salt and pepper

a pinch of grated nutmeg

a pinch of cayenne pepper

For the béchamel

1 x 400g tin of white beans, drained (approx. 240g)

½ a lemon, juiced

1 tbsp olive oil

60–125ml water

2 tbsp nutritional yeast

½ tbsp mustard

a pinch of grated nutmeg

a pinch of dried oregano

salt and pepper

For the courgettes

6 large courgettes, cut into slices approx. 1cm thick

A favourite at my retreats, this is packed with summer flavours, simmered in a light white wine, cooked until tender – heaven in a dish! It's great served with crusty bread to mop up the juices. You can use fresh globe artichokes when in season. Boil in salted water for 25–30 minutes, until the leaves puff and can be removed (compost them along with the stalk). The hearts are at the centre. If using fresh, you may want to use less than the recipe calls for.

CREAMY GARLIC WHITE BEANS

w/ courgette, artichokes, white wine

In a large frying pan, cook your onion in a dash of water. When it starts to soften and become translucent, add the garlic, parsley stalks and a small pinch of the leaves. Continue to cook until fragrant. Turn the heat low and add the courgettes, stirring as you go. You'll notice the pan is a little drier now, which is what you want.

Add the cooked beans, nutritional yeast, tahini, 125ml of plant-based milk, the lemon juice and zest, and the mustard to the pan. Season with salt and pepper, stirring to combine.

If your mixture is quite thick, go ahead and add the other 125ml of plant-based milk, then add the paprika, oregano, soy sauce/tamari and chilli flakes. Allow to simmer for around 8–10 minutes, letting the beans soak up the liquid and the flavours deepen.

Add the artichoke hearts and white wine, stirring slowly to mix. You want the white wine to slightly burn off but still have a strong taste in the dish. Continue to simmer for a further 10 minutes or so.

You'll have quite a thick mix and the beans will be lovely and soft, as well as the vegetables. Add the rest of the parsley leaves and season with salt and pepper if necessary. Serve hot, with a drizzle of olive oil.

1 medium brown or white onion, thinly sliced

4 cloves of garlic, crushed or finely chopped

a large handful of parsley, approx. 100g, stalks included, finely chopped

2 courgettes, quartered, then cubed

250g cooked/canned cannellini beans, drained and rinsed well (if using dried beans, approx. 125g, soak overnight, then boil until tender)

2 tbsp nutritional yeast

2 tbsp tahini

125–250ml plant-based milk

½ a lemon, juice and zest

1 tbsp Dijon mustard

salt and pepper

1 tsp smoked paprika

1 tsp dried oregano

1 tbsp soy sauce/tamari

a pinch of dried chilli flakes

200g artichoke hearts, tinned, preferably in water (see note)

60–125ml white wine

olive oil (for serving/garnish)

Waste tips:

You can use any type of bean if you don't have white beans; chickpeas are also great, or kidney beans for a Mexican feel. You can vary the spice levels too. Another great addition is a handful or two of greens, i.e. spring greens, spinach, finely chopped broccoli, etc., thrown in to wilt at the end.

Summer screams freshness and simplicity and this salad ticks both of those boxes. Who'd have thought a salad made up of just one vegetable could have such an impact? It's one to tickle the taste buds with a tangy citrus hit, cut with some good quality olive oil and a hefty seasoning of salt and pepper.

COURGETTE RIBBON SALAD

w/ lemon zest, crushed garlic

Using an ordinary peeler, ribbon the courgettes until you can't go any further and reach the core. Thinly slice this and put it all into a serving bowl.

Squeeze in the lemon juice, add the zest, olive oil, garlic, vinegar, mint and oregano. Season with salt and pepper.

Using your hands, begin to mix the courgettes with the dressing, making sure everything is coated nicely. You'll start to notice that a bit more liquid comes out of the courgettes and they become nice and soft.

Serve as a side to a main, or as part of a picnic/buffet-style spread.

- 3 medium courgettes, top chopped off, peeled until you get to the core, core thinly sliced
- 2 small lemons, both juiced, 1 zested
- 2–4 tbsp olive oil
- 2 cloves of garlic, crushed or finely chopped
- 1 tsp apple cider or white wine vinegar
- a small handful of fresh mint (or 1 tsp dried)
- 1 tsp dried oregano
- salt and pepper

Waste tips:

This is one of my favourite salads in the summer; it's super refreshing and has so much flavour. You can play about with different-coloured courgettes and even add a cucumber or some spring onions for a bit of texture. If you have other fresh herbs left over they'll also work well here. This salad is also perfect for using up older courgettes, making a light, zesty and fresh salad.

A total whim of a recipe, inspired by some leftover pesto and vegan ricotta in my fridge. I'd always stuffed marrows, part of the same family, so it made sense to try with courgettes. I use the entire courgette, mixing the scraped-out flesh into the stuffing, so it really highlights how to use a whole vegetable.

STUFFED COURGETTES

w/ walnut pesto, vegan ricotta

First make your ricotta. Drain and rinse your almonds well, then roughly chop and place in a high-speed blender. Add the lemon juice and zest, salt, miso paste, oregano, garlic, vinegar, nutritional yeast and pepper. Slowly add the milk, starting with the minimum quantity and blending until the mixture begins to have a smoother texture, only adding the remaining milk if necessary. The mixture should be thick and textured but all the nuts broken down. Place in the fridge and allow to firm up slightly.

Place all the pesto ingredients in a clean blender. Blitz to form a paste or pesto-type mix, adding any extra olive oil if necessary to loosen.

Preheat your oven to 180°C fan. Slice the courgettes in half lengthways and carefully, using a teaspoon, remove the centre. Place this to one side. Put the courgettes, flesh side up, in the oven with a pinch of salt for about 5 minutes, just to help them cook through.

Finely chop the middle part of the courgette. Add about 6–8 tablespoons of the pesto, the breadcrumbs and 2 tablespoons of the ricotta. Mix well, seasoning if necessary.

Take the courgettes out of the oven and fill with the pesto ricotta mix, as full or shallow as you wish. Put back in the oven for 10–12 minutes, or until golden brown on top.

To serve, add any additional pesto and ricotta, salt and pepper and a drizzle of olive oil. This will stop them being too dry and add some extra flavour.

For the ricotta (makes extra)

120g almonds, soaked for at least 2 hours, or overnight ideally, roughly chopped

1 small lemon, juiced, plus a dash of zest

1 heaped tsp salt

1 tsp yellow or light-coloured miso

2 tsp dried oregano

2 cloves of garlic, crushed or finely chopped

1 tsp apple cider vinegar

4 heaped tbsp nutritional yeast

a pinch of pepper

60–125ml plant-based milk

4 medium courgettes

60–120g bread-crumbs (depends on size of courgettes)

olive oil, to serve

For the pesto

150g walnuts

4 cloves of garlic, crushed or finely chopped

1 large handful fresh basil, approx. 60g

2 lemons, both juiced, 1 zested

125–250ml olive oil

6–8 heaped tbsp nutritional yeast

a pinch of dried chilli

salt and pepper

a pinch of grated nutmeg

a pinch of cayenne pepper

Waste tips:

You can also use this pesto and ricotta for the courgette lasagne on page 92.

fennel

There's something about fennel and its leaves/fronds that very much looks like dill, and which almost seems to wave at me when it comes into season. I think its anise-like flavour is one of its top qualities, though it might not be everyone's cup of tea. Fennel is one of those vegetables that can offer a totally different experience depending on how it's cooked. I went through a stage of roasting it, stalks and leaves on, with just a good pinch of salt, oregano and olive oil, and enjoying it as a side with a meal. It becomes a little sweeter when cooked and offers a softer taste to the palate, very delicate in texture, and a great vegetable when you're wanting to add something a little different. Eating it raw is especially nice when paired with a citrus and another crunchy vegetable, helping to balance out its frequent liquorice taste. I remember on a trip to Copenhagen when dining at a restaurant I'd been following for years, it was served in what I'd called 'fennel steaks' with a thick, creamy vegan yoghurt, toasted almonds and orange rind. It was a tastebud explosion.

Waste tips:

The leaves, or fronds as they are commonly known, make for a great fresh fennel tea. You can just chop these off before cooking, keeping some of the stalk and brewing with hot water. It's a great digestive-type tea, so having it after a larger meal is ideal. Fennel is also a great base for a stock, so whether you have some left over that needs using or you just want to pop a bit into the pot when making your homemade stock, you'll soon see how much it lifts it. I love chopping it into almost anything when I have a bunch a home (salads, soups, bakes, pasta dishes) and adding it to a pesto or salsa presents a new dimension to what could otherwise be pretty ordinary. You can also preserve or pickle fennel, it's really something special. If you have some in the fridge that's looking a bit sad, slice it up nice and thin, and add it to a mix of salt, vinegar and a dash of lemon juice – you won't regret it. See page 372 for some other homemade pickles. You can easily adapt any of those and sub in fennel, or even a combination.

A salad with a real punch, and a great side to a summer spread! The orange in the dressing really holds this together, adding a great citrus hit to balance out what can sometimes feel like a bitterness from the fennel. This salad really goes a long way, and if I'm eating it as leftovers or have made it a little in advance, I find the fresh vegetables have had time to soak up that ever-so-luxurious dressing.

FENNEL AND KOHLRABI SALAD

Put the kohlrabi, fennel, grated courgette, parsley, greens of choice, caraway seeds and spring onions into a large bowl. Season with salt and pepper and roughly mix.

Add the orange juice and zest and begin to massage the vegetables to help them to slightly soften. Add half the toasted walnuts, the mustard, vinegar, olive oil and maple syrup, seasoning again and mixing to coat well.

To serve, sprinkle with the remaining toasted walnuts and some extra parsley, plus any extra salt and pepper if need be.

2 medium kohlrabi, skin peeled (put in compost), shaved with a mandolin or a sharp knife

1 fennel bulb, stems removed, shaved with a mandolin or a sharp knife

1 courgette, grated

a large handful of fresh parsley, finely chopped (save some to garnish)

approx. 150–200g greens of choice (spinach, chard, watercress, rocket, or a combination)

1 tsp caraway seeds

2 spring onions, finely sliced

salt and pepper

1 orange, juiced, plus a dash of zest

55g walnuts, lightly toasted

1 tbsp wholegrain mustard

2 tsp white wine vinegar

1 tbsp olive oil

1 tbsp pure maple syrup, or any other sweetener of choice

I'm a huge advocate of fruit in salad and this recipe is my tribute to that. Roasted apricots add a lovely tanginess but aren't too sweet, so this is a gentle introduction to the idea. It's a real crowd-pleaser and great for a picnic.

Serves 4 as a main, 6 as a side

SOURDOUGH PANZANELLA SALAD

w/ roasted apricots and fennel

Preheat your oven to 180°C fan. Place the apricots on a baking tray, cut side up. Evenly sprinkle over the caraway seeds, cinnamon and lemon zest. Squeeze over the lemon and maple syrup, plus a pinch of salt. Roast for about 15 minutes, giving them a little mix/shake halfway through to make sure they are coated and cooking evenly.

Toss the torn bread with 2 tablespoons of olive oil and a pinch of salt. Spread evenly on a baking tray and roast for about 5 minutes. The bread will crisp up quite quickly, so keep an eye on it. Give it a little shake halfway through. You want it brown and crisp but still slightly spongy to touch. Once cooked, remove from the oven and allow to cool.

For the rest of the salad, put the onion, tomatoes, capers and fennel in a bowl. Drizzle over the other 2 tablespoons of olive oil, the vinegar and lemon juice. Mix until well coated. Add the roast apricots, toasted bread, basil, oregano and season with salt and pepper. Carefully mix until combined, taking care not to smash up the apricots. Dish up with extra fresh basil if you have some left.

For the apricots

10–12 apricots, halved, destoned

2 tsp caraway seeds

1–2 tsp cinnamon

1 lemon, juice and zest

2 tbsp pure maple syrup, or other sweetener of choice

salt

For the salad

approx. 4 slices of stale sourdough bread, torn into bite-size pieces

4 tbsp olive oil

salt and pepper

1 red onion, thinly sliced

12 cherry tomatoes or approx. 7 larger ones, in a variety of shapes (sliced, quartered, halved, etc.)

60g capers (drained weight)

1 fennel bulb, finely shaved/ sliced

1 tbsp balsamic vinegar

1 lemon, juiced

a handful of fresh basil (or 2 tsp dried)

2–4 tsp dried oregano

Waste tips:

Panzanella is a great way to use up leftover or stale bread. Any type is fine, but I particularly love the bubbly texture of sourdough when it's toasted. I usually have a fresh loaf of sourdough weekly, from whichever local bakery or market I've been to. I often slice half when fresh and put it in the freezer if I know I won't get through it all, or just for when I want a quick salad like this. The use of fennel here is a lovely seasonal twist, but feel free to omit and/or add another vegetable you may have in your fridge (sliced courgettes, cucumber, etc.). You can also bulk this out with a grain, or perhaps try adding fresh lettuce for a different take on the traditional version.

Spelt is such a versatile little grain, one that I've always loved and used, whether in its whole form or as a flour. I became a little obsessed with this recipe a few summers back; I'm certain I made it more often than seems normal. It's so simple and you really can't go wrong. Served with a thick layer of rustic homemade sauce and seasonal veggies, even if the sun isn't quite shining, this pizza certainly makes it feel like it is, cliché?

Makes 4–6 mini pizzas

SPELT PIZZA

w/ charred fennel, green cabbage and tofu cream

Preheat your oven to 200°C fan. To make the base, put the dry ingredients into a large bowl and mix well. Slowly add the water until the mixture starts to stick together.

Using your hands, knead the mixture into a dough, adding more water if necessary or flour if it is sticking too much. Place to one side (leaving in the bowl) while you make your sauce and prepare toppings.

For the tomato sauce, sauté the onion in a dash of water until it starts to become translucent. Add the garlic and continue to fry for another minute or so. Add the tomatoes, tomato purée/paste, sun-dried tomatoes, water, basil and dried oregano. Season with salt and pepper and allow to simmer on a low heat for about 12 minutes. You want the sauce to become thick and rich, but if it starts to dry up slightly, add a dash more water. Leave to simmer very low for about 10–12 minutes while you do the next steps. Once cooked, turn off the heat and allow the sauce to sit. You can either leave it chunky, or blitz it slightly using a blender/processor to make a smoother tomato sauce.

To make the tofu cream, put the silken tofu into a blender along with the apple cider vinegar, mustard, garlic, lemon juice, zest and oregano, plus some salt and pepper. Blend until you have a smooth creamy texture. Set aside or

For the base

300g spelt flour

4 tsp baking powder

a pinch of salt

5 tsp dried oregano/mixed herbs

250ml water (you may need less, you'll be adding it bit by bit)

For the tomato sauce

(This sauce has the same base as the lasagne on page 92, so you could double it up and store it to use for both at some point)

1 small white or brown onion, finely chopped

2 cloves of garlic, crushed or finely chopped

12 cherry tomatoes, or 6 larger ones, quartered

2–4 tbsp tomato purée/paste

6 sun-dried tomatoes, roughly chopped

250–375ml water

a handful of fresh basil, roughly chopped (be careful not to bruise it)

2 tsp dried oregano

salt and pepper

»

place in the fridge. If you are opting to use truffle oil, you can stir it in after removing from the blender.

To char the fennel, take your slices and hold them over a flame for a few seconds, turning them over to brown each side. Use a pair of tongs to do this. The fennel will continue to cook in the oven.

Sprinkle some flour on a clean worktop and split your dough in half or quarters depending on how many pizzas you are making. Using a rolling pin, covered with flour to avoid any sticking, roll each piece into a base. Make sure to flip halfway through. You'll want it to be around ½–1cm (depending on the thickness you like).

Transfer the bases to a baking sheet/parchment paper that will fit on an oven tray or wire oven racks.

Using a ladle or a large serving spoon, cover your bases with sauce. You don't want them to go soggy, but don't hold back.

Add the onions, charred fennel, greens, cabbage and half your basil. Depending on how many pizzas you are making, you can mix this up and get creative with arranging. Place your baking sheet on the middle shelf of the oven and bake for around 8 minutes. Again, either on the wire racks or a tray.

Add the dried oregano and nutritional yeast and season with salt and pepper. You want the base to be cooked through, making sure the dough is not soggy. Cook for another 4–5 minutes or so, until the vegetables are tender and cooked through. A few minutes before the end, drizzle over the tofu cream, letting it cook ever so slightly – it will start to turn a yellow-brown colour.

Once cooked, serve hot with any other garnishes.

For the tofu cream (makes 1 small jar, approx. 580ml)

300g silken tofu, drained

1½ tsp apple cider vinegar

2 tsp Dijon mustard

1 clove of garlic, crushed or finely chopped

1 small lemon, juiced, plus a dash of zest

2 tsp dried oregano

salt and pepper

truffle oil (optional)

For the toppings

1 medium sized fennel, cut into thin slices, top to bottom

1 small red onion, thinly sliced

a couple of large handfuls of greens of choice (spinach, kale, cavolo nero)

¼ a small head of cabbage (any green variety), thinly sliced, including any core

fresh basil, roughly chopped

dried oregano, to sprinkle

nutritional yeast (optional)

salt and pepper

Waste tips:

If you are feeling a little more adventurous, adding thinly sliced potatoes to pizza makes a really nice change, and given that many potato types are in their prime during the early summer months, you'll have plenty to choose from. The dough will keep for a few days in the fridge if you don't happen to use it all up: roll it into a ball and leave it covered in a bowl in the fridge. The same goes for the sauce. Of course, you are not tied to the vegetables above, and using whatever you have left over is a great way to make a pizza a little different and creative.

I was first introduced to gnocchi on a trip to Tuscany, where I had it freshly made, served with a whipped olive oil pesto and a couple of sides, one of which was a whole slow-roasted fennel – needless to say, this really stood out for me, not only in taste, but also in texture and presentation. I then tried my hand at making gnocchi on my own, and was surprised to find how easy it is. This recipe is like a trip down memory lane to that meal; what could be better than imagining basking in the Tuscan sun munching on some fresh homemade gnocchi!

Serves 2–3
as a main

ROASTED FENNEL, PESTO GNOCCHI

w/ crispy potato skins

Preheat your oven to 180°C fan. Peel and chop the potatoes, putting the skins to one side. Bring a large pan of salted water to a boil and cook the potatoes for about 12–15 minutes, until they can be easily pierced with a fork. Drain in a colander, shaking off any excess water, then set them aside and let them cool entirely.

While your potatoes are cooling, you can crisp up the skins. Heat the oil in a pan, add the skins and season with salt and pepper. Add the cinnamon, if using it. You should keep the skins on a relatively low heat, as they will crisp up quickly and you don't want them to burn. Once crispy, set aside on kitchen paper to let any excess oil dry off. They will continue to crisp up as they cool.

Spread the fennel evenly on a baking tray. I like to roast it dry with a bit of salt and pepper, but feel free to use an oil of your choice. Roast until browned and tender, about 15 minutes. Once cooked, remove from the oven and cover to keep warm.

For the pesto, put all the ingredients into a clean blender and blitz until they form a paste or pesto-type mix, adding any extra olive oil if necessary to loosen. Place to one side while you make the gnocchi.

For the gnocchi

approx. 500g russet/King Edward/jacket potatoes, peeled and cut into cubes (keep the skins, see below)

approx. 120g plain flour, plus extra as needed and for dusting

½ tsp salt

1 tbsp olive oil

For the crispy potato skins

skins from the potatoes (see above), chopped/torn as desired

1–2 tbsp olive oil

salt and pepper

1–2 tsp ground cinnamon (optional)

For the fennel

1 fennel bulb, roughly chopped, any direction

a handful of fresh basil, roughly chopped

2 tbsp walnuts, lightly toasted, then crushed

1 lemon, juiced, plus a dash of zest

olive oil, to dress/garnish

»

Mash the cooled potatoes with a masher – if you have a potato ricer, you can also use that. To the mashed potatoes add the flour, salt and olive oil, gently kneading with your hands. Make sure you have floured your hands first, to avoid the mixture sticking. If it is a little sticky, go ahead and add a bit more flour, or add a tad more oil if it is too dry. You want the dough to be soft but not sticky.

Flour a work surface and divide the dough into 4 equal pieces. Roll each one out into a rope-type shape, about 2cm in diameter. Using a sharp knife, cut the dough into approximately 2.5cm pieces. Using a fork, make small dents on the top and bottom of each gnocchi piece. This is optional, for effect. Continue until you've used all your dough.

To cook, bring a large pan of water to the boil. In batches, place the gnocchi in the boiling water and let them cook for a couple of minutes. The timings will vary, but the gnocchi are cooked once they float to the top of the water. It's important to do this in batches, to avoid the gnocchi overcooking.

To finish off the gnocchi, heat a dash of olive oil in a pan and add the gnocchi carefully (you may need to do this in batches depending on the size of your pan). Fry for a couple of minutes each side, to allow them to brown and crisp. This also helps the mix to stay together a little better if you are stirring them through a sauce.

To serve, put your gnocchi into a bowl and add the roasted fennel, fresh basil, crushed walnuts and a few heaped scoops of your pesto, as well as the lemon juice and zest. Top with the crispy potato skins and an extra drizzle of oil if you like. Season with salt and pepper.

For the pesto

150g walnuts

2 cloves of garlic, crushed or finely chopped

a large handful of fresh basil (approx. 60g)

2 small lemons, both juiced, 1 zested

approx. 125–250ml olive oil

6–8 heaped tbsp nutritional yeast

a pinch of dried chilli flakes

salt and pepper

a pinch of grated nutmeg

Notes:

If you have the time, you can bake the potatoes instead. That way the skins will already be crispy and you keep more moisture in the flesh, giving a slightly different texture to the gnocchi dough. Bake the potatoes whole for roughly an hour, then follow the same instructions as above. You may need less flour, so start with just under 120g and see how you go.

Waste tips:

You can also freeze the gnocchi and save them for another time. Chop the dough into pieces and sprinkle them with a little extra flour to prevent them sticking. They freeze for around a month like this. To re-cook, simply thaw the gnocchi until they are soft all the way through and cook in water as above, then lightly fry to crisp each side. This dough also doubles up as a great potato-based roti. Follow the same process to make the dough, then take small chunks, forming each one into a ball with your hands before rolling out into a flat pancake/roti shape. You can make them as big or as small as you like, serving them similar to above, making pesto garlic breads, salad, etc.

Jersey Royal potatoes

The most sought-after potato, as soon as the season arrives I am always on the lookout for them. Although they are relatively normal-looking, with occasional ridges or dips, and usually quite small, I can confidently say that they are by far the king of potatoes (despite a couple of other potato varieties being actually called 'king', which we'll get to shortly). Quintessentially British, they are distinctive, nutty and somewhat sweet, and to me they really taste of summer. Potatoes are often considered quite boring. I don't agree, and the day you try a Jersey Royal, perfectly roasted with just a bit of salt, olive oil and a sprig of rosemary, is the day I hope you will reconsider. Jersey Royals are part of the new potato family, which is why they work so well in salads. They add an oomph that really finishes things off. They need just a few small and simple details when cooking and they are delicious every time.

Over the years I've learnt that the key to cooking potatoes, and this goes for all types, is not to overcrowd them. They need space to show their true flavours, and because they can often be floury, pairing with other vegetables helps cut through that, so be sure not to pile a load in a pan when cooking, but work with other seasonal vegetables to help balance out the flavours and textures. Jersey Royals have a lovely crispy skin when roasted, and when boiled they retain a less floury texture than other varieties (such as King Edward potatoes, another favourite of mine, which are better for the gnocchi recipes in this book as they are less waxy and usually all-year-rounders). Potatoes love salt, so don't be shy, be consistent – flake it accordingly, with just the right amount of oil. Smothering potatoes in oil doesn't actually bring out their flavour and doesn't always make the best crispy skin, variety dependent.

Waste tips:

Leftover potatoes always make great mash, whether that's if they have been cooked or are still a little sad sitting in the basket. Leftover roasted potatoes are always great for a savoury brunch. Most of my friends know that I'm not usually a savoury lover in the morning, but using leftover spuds in a bubble-and-squeak-type dish, or stir-fried with other leftover veggies, tomatoes and onions, paired with a sexy slice of sourdough, really gets me. Lots of recipes call for the removal of potato skins, but rather than putting them in the bin or compost, keep them and lightly sauté them with some oil, herbs, salt, pepper and a dash of cinnamon for something a little different.

We all love roast potatoes, right? This recipe is a tribute to my favourite potatoes, Jersey Royals, served as they are, with a few extra flavours, crushed ever so slightly. Crispy and golden on the outside, soft and fluffy on the inside. The prep comes together in less than 5 minutes, and once they're in the oven, they work their own magic.

Serves 6
as a side

JERSEY ROYALS – STRAIGHT UP, PARSLEY, GARLIC, TARRAGON

Preheat the oven to 200°C fan. The key to crispy potatoes is parboiling them first. Immerse the potatoes in a pot of water, add a pinch of salt and bring to the boil. Reduce to a simmer and cook for about 10 minutes, or until cooked through but before they turn fluffy. Be careful not to over-boil.

Once the potatoes have cooked, drain and shake them to remove any excess water. Put them on a baking tray with the garlic, three-quarters of the fresh tarragon, three-quarters of the fresh parsley and the dried oregano. Add the olive oil (I'd recommend starting with 2 tablespoons first), and season with salt and pepper. Mix together until the potatoes are coated nicely, adding any extra olive oil if needed.

Roast in the oven for around 30 minutes, until the skins are crispy and golden. They should be soft and fluffy inside. Serve hot.

approx. 700g Jersey Royal potatoes, cut into large chunks, smaller ones left whole

1 whole bulb of garlic (approx. 10 cloves), halved, thinly sliced

a few sprigs of fresh tarragon, roughly chopped

a small handful of fresh parsley, roughly chopped

1 tsp dried oregano

2–4 tbsp olive oil

salt and pepper

Waste tips:

These make great mash! If you have any leftovers or have cooked a double batch, you can mix it up a little. Try adding a dollop of pesto and coconut yoghurt before mashing. Cold or leftover potatoes are always great for frying (similar to previous recipes). Chop up small and they become the base for a hash-brown-type dish. Roasting potatoes is also a good way to use potatoes that may be slightly old or on the turn. Boiling them before roasting removes any bad bacteria and they will still have the usual texture when roasting. They're quick and easy to do and make a great side to summer salads or in a picnic/barbecue situation.

For the love of hosting summer spreads, celebrating the season's produce and generally cooking for others, this is always my go-to potato salad dish. It doesn't involve much prep work and I'm always salivating when adding the warm potatoes to the creamy dressing. You get a little kick from the chilli and a salty one from the capers, and paired with the world's quickest pickles, it's definitely a summer veg-spread must!

CRUSHED POTATO SALAD

w/ quick cucumber dill pickles

First make your quick cucumber pickles. Peel your cucumbers into ribbons until you reach the core and place in a bowl. Finely chop the core and add to the bowl with the ribbons.

Add the vinegar, sugar, coriander seeds, cumin seeds and salt and mix, coating everything and submerging the cucumbers in the liquid. You want to use enough vinegar to cover the cucumber, hence why there is not a specific quantity. Put into the fridge while you prepare the rest of the salad.

Bring a large pan of salted water to the boil and add the potatoes. Cook until a knife goes through and can be removed easily, about 12 minutes. Be careful not to over-cook the potatoes, as you don't want them too fluffy. Drain and shake off any excess water, then allow to cool.

Put the cooled potatoes into a bowl along with the celery, spring onions, 2 teaspoons of capers, the mustard, tahini, 2 tablespoons of olive oil, the fresh dill, chilli flakes, salt and pepper. Using a fork, begin to mix, carefully crushing the potatoes as you go. You could do this with a masher, but I find you end up with a much nicer texture when crushing with a fork. It also allows the mustard and tahini to fully coat the potatoes.

For the cucumber pickles (enough for 2–3 as a side/nibble)

- 2 small cucumbers or 1 large
- apple cider or white wine vinegar (or a combination)
- approx. 1 tsp sugar of choice (coconut, palm, raw, etc.)
- 1 tsp coriander seeds
- 1 tsp cumin seeds
- a hefty pinch of salt

For the potato salad

- approx. 700g Jersey Royal potatoes (or other small 'salad' potatoes), skins on, cut into rough cubes of a similar size
- 2 stalks of celery, finely sliced
- 4 spring onions, finely sliced
- 2–4 tsp capers
- 2 tbsp mustard
- 2 tbsp tahini
- 2–4 tbsp olive oil
- a few sprigs of fresh dill, finely chopped
- a pinch of dried chilli flakes
- salt and pepper

Take your pickles out of the fridge, spoon out the cucumbers and add them to the mix. You can use as much or as little of the remaining liquid as you like. Saving it for another batch tends to be what I'd do. Mix again with a fork and adjust with salt and pepper if necessary.

To serve, add any extra olive oil and capers, should you wish, and enjoy.

Waste tip:

You could very easily have this as a mash, served hot rather than cold. Boil the potatoes a little longer and mash as you normally would, then add the rest of the ingredients. Skip adding the pickles to the dish and serve as is, or pile the pickles on top of the potatoes if you don't want to mix it. Leftovers of this salad also work great when fried, similar to a bubble and squeak. You could add some leftover vegetables, chopped small or grated, or use the mix as it is, heating up a little oil in a pan and frying, seasoning with any spices you might fancy.

I'm all for combining sweet and savoury things, yet I have always been a sweet kinda gal when it comes to breakfast or brunch. This recipe was inspired by that, creating something that still had a subtle sweetness to it, but satisfied the savoury craving. Better still, it doesn't have to be for the morning – it's also perfect for a hearty but light lunch or supper. Umami meets earthy.

Serves 4

SAVOURY MILLET PORRIDGE

w/ Jersey Royal potatoes and miso

Heat the coconut oil in a small saucepan, then add the onion and fry until it starts to brown and becomes fragrant. Add the garlic, ginger and coriander stalks and continue to fry for another minute or so. Turn the heat down low and add the millet, stirring it around initially before adding the stock.

Bring the stock to a boil, then lower to a simmer and cook the millet for approx. 12 minutes. Midway through, once the millet starts to soak up the liquid, stir in the miso paste, cayenne pepper and tahini and season with salt and pepper. Continue to simmer until the millet is cooked.

In a separate pan, cook the potatoes in boiling salted water until cooked through, around 10–12 minutes. Drain well, then add to the millet and stir. Add the fresh greens and let them wilt in the dish. If the liquid has disappeared and the mixture is a little thick, loosen with extra water accordingly. Season with salt and pepper.

To serve, dish up, drizzling some olive oil on top, and scatter over the spring onions, coriander leaves and sesame seeds.

1 tbsp coconut oil

1 medium brown or white onion, finely chopped

2 cloves of garlic, crushed or finely chopped

2.5cm piece of ginger, finely chopped or grated

a small handful of fresh coriander, finely chopped, stalks included

100g millet

approx. 375ml stock

2 heaped tbsp miso paste (yellow, brown or red)

½ tsp cayenne pepper

2 tbsp tahini

approx. 5–6 Jersey Royal potatoes, quartered, skins on

salt and pepper

a large handful of fresh greens of choice (spinach, kale, chard)

olive oil, for drizzling

2 spring onions, thinly sliced

1–2 tbsp sesame seeds

Notes:

This recipe is great with fresh sweetcorn. Although it can sometimes be hard to get hold of and often isn't in season until a little later in the year (depending on where you are), you might count yourself lucky for an early appearance. You can cook the corn in the oven with the husks on for about 30–40 minutes depending on the size, or boil it in water. Once cooked, take off the husks if still on and remove the kernels using a sharp knife close to the core. Once you've removed the kernels, pop them into the mix and stir through.

Waste tips:

This is a great dish to add to a weekend brunch. As it is a little more involved and hearty, it's a great one for a slow morning. Of course you could also have it for lunch or dinner. You can play about with grating potatoes in here too, cooking them at the same time as the millet. The potato offers a different texture and makes it a little less like a thick stew. Fresh chives are great with this dish, and if you do add corn to it, the combination works extremely well.

One for a cooler summer's day when it's a little cloudy outside or for when you don't have as much time, this nourishing number fixes any baked potato cravings. They can often be looked down on, but a hearty baked potato with all the trimmings is where it's at for me. The filling for this recipe can be whipped up and made ahead of time, or prepped just as you take the potatoes out for the first round. Baking them twice helps the flavours from the filling to seep into the potato flesh, but keeps the skin crispy, just the way it should be!

Serves 4

TWICE-BAKED POTATOES

w/ courgette filling

Preheat your oven to 200°C fan. Scrub your potatoes, removing all dirt/soil from the skins. Prick the potatoes a few times over the whole surface. Lightly brush each one with some oil – this will help them crisp up. Sprinkle with salt, rotating as you go to cover the entire potato. Place on a baking tray and put into the oven for around 45 minutes. You want the skins to be crispy and golden brown. To test the inside, poke with a sharp knife.

While your potatoes are in the oven, make the courgette filling. In a bowl, mash your cooked chickpeas with a fork. You'll start to notice the skins coming away – this is normal. Add the grated courgette, celery, red onion and garlic, and mix with a fork until well combined.

Add the tahini and mustard, starting with the smaller amount first. Add the lemon juice and zest, nutritional yeast, parsley, smoked paprika, chilli flakes and season with salt and pepper. Mix well. Add more tahini and mustard accordingly. If your mixture is a little drier than you'd like, you could also add some olive oil.

Remove your potatoes from the oven. Carefully, slice them in half lengthways to expose the inside, and put back on the baking tray, cut side up. Put a large dollop

4 medium baking-style potatoes (any variety, large enough to have one each, or, if using smaller potatoes, try 3–4 depending on variety)

approx. 1 tbsp olive oil (or another high-quality oil such as avocado)

salt, flaky if possible

For the courgette filling

approx. 240g cooked chickpeas or 1 × 400g tin of chickpeas, drained

1 large courgette or 2 small, grated

1 stalk of celery, very thinly sliced

1 small red onion, finely chopped

2 cloves of garlic, crushed or finely chopped

2–3 tbsp tahini

1–2 tbsp Dijon mustard (wholegrain will also work)

1 lemon, juiced, plus a dash of zest

2 tbsp nutritional yeast

a small handful of fresh parsley, finely chopped

½ tsp smoked paprika

a pinch of dried chilli flakes

salt and pepper

118   the whole vegetable

of the courgette mix on each potato half. Put back into the oven for a further 10 minutes, to allow the courgette filling to heat through and turn slightly golden on top.

Remove from the oven and serve with any additional sides or toppings. Season with salt and pepper.

Waste tips:

On-the-turn or older potatoes are ideal for baking like this. The texture is always great and they will still go crispy in the oven even if they are a little softer beforehand. You can also make this ahead of time, baking the potatoes and keeping them in foil to preserve the moisture. Cut them open when you wish and fill as above. The courgette filling also works great raw as a side salad, or even as a sandwich filler. You can fry the filling if you have leftovers or simply want to make extra, similar to a patty. Form balls with the mixture, then flatten them and lightly fry them in oil. You can add a variety of grated vegetables to the mix, adjusting the wet ingredients accordingly. If you don't have courgettes in season, try carrots, parsnips or even cabbage. You'll notice that the courgette part of this recipe also features later on in another seasonal chapter – I won't give the game away, but it's just as great a topper as it is a filler.

Optional serving suggestions

fresh herbs, finely chopped (chives, parsley, dill)

plant-based yoghurt

any other dressings/creams you desire (see the basics section, page 353, for inspiration)

the
height of
summer

I'm a true sun baby. A lover of the coast, sandy feet, idyllic evening light, and the frequent relaxed social situations the summer brings, with a 'carefree' attitude floating around. As much as I also love autumn (as you'll discover later), summer is definitely the time of year I savour most, clinging on to every last moment that I can, hoping for a balmy 'Indian summer' September – and I'm sure I speak for many when I say that.

Less is more in the summer and produce is always stunning, so I can only encourage a carefree attitude in the kitchen too, treating cooking as a leisurely affair. There is something so special to me about easygoing suppers after a successful market trip, letting those ingredients shine through, at their very best. Tomatoes are juicer, tastier and more vibrant, simply sliced and perfectly paired with grilled vegetables and some crispy homemade garlic bread. It's easier to be a bit more impulsive in the summer, a little more spontaneous, because no one expects too much from you, other than perhaps some sort of spread and a cold beverage. 'Potluck' dining situations are, in recent years, something I've become very fond of. I find it incredibly therapeutic putting ingredients together for a little impromptu get-together (though actually, let's face it, among me and my friends these are usually planned). I love every moment, from the preparation to the sharing to watching people dine.

I remember spending summers in Cornwall, close to where I grew up, basking in the evening sun and finding glee in every part of the day. It was always over far too quickly, and the appreciation I have now for the summer wind-down was definitely not the same back then. We'd come back salty from the beach, impatiently waiting for Dad to present us with a dinner concoction that he had no problem rustling up. I now admire my dad's bravery with the flavours he'd sometimes make us try, and usually it wound up with us asking for more, especially in my case if green beans were involved, of which I still can't get enough!

star produce:

Cherries

—

Carrots

—

Green beans

—

Lettuce

—

Tomatoes

—

Other seasonal produce: Apricots, aubergines, courgettes, fennel, damsons, French beans, runner beans, peppers, potatoes (a variety), mangetout, samphire, sweetcorn, strawberries, raspberries, spring onions, cucumber, celery, plums, parsnips (summer variety), loganberries, greengages, watercress, summer squash.

—

You will of course notice some of these fruits/vegetables in other seasons as well. There is a big overlap these days due to the climate and average temperatures we experience, regardless of where we are.

—

Grains harvested at this time of the year: Oats, buckwheat, pearled millet, farro, couscous (a variety, giant, Israeli, made from wheat), kamut, quinoa (red in particular), orzo.

—

cherries

Kinda like the queen of the fruits, right? Luscious in so many ways, with their heart-shaped appearance and ever so slightly sour but juicy bite. You may have guessed it, I adore cherries . . . how could you not? I could compliment them forever. They are one of those fruits that people get excited over when they spot them in a local shop, but there is nothing worse than a bad batch. You want them rich in colour, plump, voluptuous and without any sourness. Cherries can be pretty tricky to grow, which is even more of a reason to appreciate them. Often they are covered in pesticides, so naturally they are one of the most important fruits to eat in their seasonal prime, when this is less likely. We should wash all our produce, but cherries in particular should be washed well under cold water. I tend to empty a punnet straight into a sieve, wash them and store them in the fridge.

Cherries are most often just eaten as a snack, or used in crumbles, tarts, pies . . . all quite obvious choices when it comes to cooking cherries. But a little something I learnt at a young age is that cherries are amazing paired with a strong herb such as basil or lemon thyme, or even lemongrass. The combination brings them to life, particularly in a salsa or a salad, and the overall look is incredibly pretty too. One of my favourite recipes in this book was inspired by a trip to Marrakech, where I discovered smoked cherries, a flavour I was so intrigued by and would never otherwise have thought of. Thus, the recipe on page 164 was born: slow-cooked, home-smoked cherries, cooked into a chutney-type mixture, with fresh basil, and served with butterbeans and tomatoes, my other love at this time of the year.

Waste tips:

There really isn't anything quite like a homemade cherry compote. If you can get your hands on a cherry 'de-pipper' this will of course make your life a little easier, but if you are using some miserable-looking cherries you can actually bung them into a pot with a little water, a squeeze of lemon and a dash of zest, and as they start to wilt, the flesh will come away from the pip, so you can easily remove them with a spoon as you go. You can of course do this with fresher cherries and the removal will be a similar process, but getting the pip out will require a little more effort.

Picture this: a sunny summer's morning, the sun beaming down on you, a cosy spot outside; breakfast crumble, tart cherries in their prime. I found myself on a job with a whole bunch of cherries left in the fridge, breakfast on my mind and some creativity bubbling inside. I like to add nuts to my crumble mix to give a bit of oomph and keep it on the healthier side. It's served here with homemade coconut milk, which believe me when I say is a real game-changer and probably one of the most delicious plant-based milks going.

Makes approx. 10–12 servings

CHERRY BREAKFAST CRUMBLE

w/ toasted coconut milk

Preheat your oven to 180°C fan. In a bowl prepare your crumble topping. Place the flour, oats and chopped nuts in a bowl and gently mix. Add the maple syrup, coconut oil, cinnamon, cardamom and a pinch of salt. Using your fingertips, begin to mix, rubbing the ingredients to help them stick together, forming crumbs with larger pieces. If the mixture is quite dry, add more coconut oil, a tablespoon at a time. Pop into the fridge to firm up slightly while you prepare the cherries.

Pit and halve the cherries. The best technique I have found for this is scoring around the whole cherry in the middle, twisting it to open, then carefully removing the pip. Place the pitted cherries in the bottom of your baking dish. Add the coconut sugar, lemon juice and zest, vanilla, cinnamon and salt. Mix using your hands or a spoon until the cherries are well coated.

Remove the crumble mixture from the fridge and evenly top the cherries with the mix, patting it down slightly as you go. Bake in the oven for around 25–30 minutes. The topping will go a dark golden brown and the cherries will be tender and slightly bubbling.

While your crumble is cooking, make the coconut milk. Lightly toast the coconut flakes either in the oven or in

For the crumble

You will need a 20–23cm baking dish

120g flour of your choice (spelt, rye, buckwheat, plain, almond)

30g oats (I like to use jumbo, but any you have are fine)

45g nuts of your choice (walnuts, almonds, hazelnuts, cashews, etc., or a combination), chopped

3 tbsp pure maple syrup

125ml coconut oil, room temperature (not melted but soft), plus extra if needed

1 tsp ground cinnamon

1 tsp ground cardamom

a pinch of salt

For the cherries

approx. 600g cherries, pitted, halved

90g coconut sugar, palm sugar, or any other raw/natural sugar (if your cherries are quite soft and sweet, you can use less sugar)

½ a lemon, juiced, plus a dash of zest

1 tsp vanilla paste/extract

1 tsp ground cinnamon

a pinch of salt

a pan, dry. They won't take long to go slightly brown, so be careful they don't burn. Allow to cool slightly, then place in a blender with the water, salt and the optional date. Blend on high for a few minutes, until you have a smooth, creamy consistency.

Using a nut milk bag/fine strainer or cheesecloth, strain the liquid to remove any fine nut particles that haven't been blended. You can keep this dry mix for other recipes (see below). The milk will keep in an airtight bottle in the fridge for about 4–5 days.

Remove the crumble from the oven. I like to serve the coconut milk warm with the crumble, so I heat a little in a pan on the stove.

For the toasted coconut milk

approx. 105g coconut flakes, lightly toasted

1 litre water (use more for a thinner milk)

a pinch of salt

1 pitted date (optional, for sweetness)

Waste tips:

If you don't have cherries, this recipe works with pretty much any fruit. Stone fruits are great, apples or pears make a more traditional crumble, or perhaps there's a variety that you may have left over or just stocked up on. You'll also notice that this is a great cupboard recipe, as you're likely to have a lot of the ingredients in and can use nuts/flours of choice.

A pairing to tickle the taste buds, where sharp meets tart and you wouldn't have thought it would work, but it more than does, so it's a must. Roasting cherries allows them to lose some of their tartness and they become a whole lot sweeter, which is why the combination works so well. They're served with a biscuit that's crunchy on the outside, soft on the inside – a cliché of a biscuit, full of aromatic flavours, a pinch of orange and a pinch of salt, the perfect flavour and texture combinations.

Serves approx. 6

SUMAC ROASTED CHERRIES

w/ tahini orange biscuits

Preheat the oven to 180°C fan. Pit and halve your cherries if you haven't done so already, and put them into a mixing bowl. Add the sumac, maple syrup, lemon juice, zest and a pinch of salt and mix until the cherries are well coated. Transfer to a baking tray, then put into the oven on the bottom or middle shelf and cook for about 15–20 minutes. The time will vary depending on your oven, but they should be extremely soft by this point and starting to ooze and caramelize slightly. You can check them halfway through, stirring if necessary and making sure they haven't stuck to the tray. Once cooked, remove from the oven and place to one side to cool slightly.

While your cherries are in the oven, prepare the biscuits. Put the dry ingredients – ground almonds, cinnamon, cardamom, nutmeg, turmeric, salt and pepper – into a clean mixing bowl, and mix to combine.

Start adding the wet ingredients – date syrup, tahini, vanilla, orange/lemon juice and zest – and slowly mix until you start to form a dough. If the mixture is a little wet, add more ground almonds, or if a little dry, add a little more tahini. You want the mixture to be relatively soft and slightly sticky, but firm enough to be able to form little balls when rolling.

For the cherries

600g pitted cherries, halved

1½–2 tbsp sumac

1–2 tbsp pure maple syrup

½ a lemon, juice and zest

a pinch of salt

For the biscuits (makes approx. 10)

125g ground almonds/almond flour

1 tsp ground cinnamon

½ tsp ground cardamom

¼ tsp grated nutmeg

¼ tsp ground turmeric

a pinch of salt and pepper

60ml date syrup (or another sweetener of choice – maple syrup also works)

120g tahini

2 tsp vanilla extract

either 1 orange or 1 lemon, zested, plus a dash of juice

2 tbsp sesame seeds (or crushed nuts/seeds of choice)

Optional serving suggestions

plant-based yoghurt

tahini, to drizzle

dash of milk, to drizzle

Grease a baking tray with a little coconut oil to prevent the cookies from sticking, or use baking paper if you wish. Start to form little balls with the dough, flatten them ever so slightly between the palms of your hands, and place them on the baking tray with some space between them, about a finger width or so. They will spread out as they cook, so you don't need to make them too flat.

Sprinkle over the sesame seeds/nuts and pat gently. Bake in the oven for about 10–12 minutes, or until browned and slightly crispy on top. Once cooked, remove from the oven and allow to cool.

To serve, put the desired amount of cherries into a bowl or bowls, serving with a cookie on the side, or perhaps crumbling it over, as desired.

Waste tips:

Sumac is great paired with a lot of fruits, especially stone fruits, which are very easy to find in the summer, and berries of any variety, so use what you have and can get your hands on. The tahini biscuits can be served whole or crumbled, and can be stored in the fridge in an airtight container for over a week, although they are of course great served slightly warm from the oven. I also love serving this dish with a plant-based yoghurt or cream, which really brings it together. These cherries can double up as a compote for porridge and are great both hot and cold. They work well as a chutney too. Simply fry some red onions beforehand, adding the cherries afterwards. Add a dash of balsamic vinegar and some garlic too, if you like.

Discovering the beauty of vegan cheese was a great day for me; who knew that soaking nuts would be the key to that? This recipe is a summer love story in my eyes: cashew-based cheese served just as you would a regular one (on a fancy wooden board, of course) with a refreshing cherry salsa to break through the richness of the cheese. A real show-off dish to serve to friends, or great as a snack board for eating at home.

Makes 1 big batch, enough for approx. 20 servings

BAKED CASHEW CHEESE, BALSAMIC CHERRY SALSA

Preheat your oven to 160°C fan and line a flat baking tray with baking paper.

First make the cheese. Drain your cashews and put them into a high-speed blender/processor. Add the lemon juice and zest, apple cider vinegar, nutritional yeast, dried herbs, mustard, garlic, milk and 125ml of the water. Season with salt and pepper and blend. You want this to be a smooth consistency, so it will take a few minutes or so. Depending on your blender/processor, you may have to scrape down the sides every so often. If your mixture is a little thick, add more water. You want it to be smooth, but thick enough so it doesn't fall or run off a spoon.

Start to scoop the cashew mix into the middle of the prepared baking tray. I like to pour it all out first into a pile so that it forms a rough circular shape. Even out the top using a spatula or the back of a spoon, then sprinkle a good pinch of salt on top and add a light dusting of extra dried herbs.

Put into the oven on the middle shelf and bake for around 30–40 minutes. The time will vary depending on your oven. The top should start to crack and turn a lovely golden brown. The top will be crispy but the inside a little softer. Once cooked, remove from the oven and allow to cool and firm up slightly.

For the salsa, place the cherries, chilli, red onion, basil and coriander seeds into a bowl, and mix to combine.

For the baked cashew cheese

240g cashews, soaked overnight in cold water (or pour over boiling water and soak for 4 hours)

1 lemon, juiced, plus a dash of zest

1 tsp apple cider vinegar

50–70g nutritional yeast

2–4 heaped tsp dried oregano, thyme, rosemary or a combination

1–2 tbsp Dijon mustard

2 cloves of garlic, crushed or finely chopped

125ml plant-based milk

125–250ml water, plus more if needed

salt and pepper

For the cherry salsa

approx. 280g cherries, pitted, roughly chopped

1 small green chilli, deseeded and finely chopped

1 small red onion, finely chopped

a large handful of fresh basil, finely chopped

1 tsp coriander seeds

2 tsp balsamic vinegar

1 lime, juiced, plus a dash of zest

salt and pepper

Optional serving suggestions

bread of choice

crackers of choice

vegetable crudités

Drizzle over the balsamic, lime juice and zest and season with a good pinch of salt and pepper.

Serve with toasted bread, crackers, vegetable crudités, etc. Slice off some cheese, add a dollop of salsa and enjoy.

Waste tips:

If you can't find cherries, you can replace them with any fruit of your choice. As my good friend Jaime always says, 'Strawberries are great in salsa, who knew?' . . . and it's true, but apricots or other stone fruit, etc. are also good. A soft or stone fruit will be better suited to this recipe, but go ahead and be creative. This cheese has become an absolute staple for me. I like to make a big batch every so often and keep it in the fridge, as it will last for over a week in a container. It's great to crumble on salads, to have on bread or with crackers, and as a snack, like this recipe. It's a great crowd-pleaser, so rustle this up for guests to serve on a vegan cheeseboard, and you'll be praised forever. You can try using macadamias or Brazil nuts if you don't have cashews, or even a combination. You'll find a similar recipe for an almond-based cheese on page 365, which is better for nuts with tougher skins.

carrots

Feeding people is a hobby of mine – I enjoy the whole process, combining flavours and textures and watching the expressions when I present a particular dish. I am definitely a people-pleaser and would much rather serve up something I'm proud of to others than enjoy it myself. That feeling of knowing I've filled hungry bellies always puts a smile on my face. Although simple, the carrot-top pesto in this section is most certainly one of those dishes, delicious served thick or made thinner with a little more lemon juice and olive oil and paired with the carrots themselves, roasted on a low heat until almost cake-like inside. I've quite often made this dish for supper clubs or catering jobs over the summer, and it's a great way to make use of those rather stringy, peppery carrot tops in order to encourage using up the whole vegetable. It's also a great dish for a picnic. You can vary the type of nuts in the pesto, as well as trying different ratios of basil to carrot tops and some fresh chilli for a little kick. I've always been extremely partial to a carrot, especially when kept simple and just steamed. We're pretty lucky with a long carrot season – to be honest, they are almost an 'all-year-rounder' – but they are particularly almighty in the summer.

Waste tips:

Aside from the carrot-top pesto, the tops are great as a fresh herb. They'll need to be chopped quite finely, as they can be on the tough side, but they have a lovely peppery, almost rocket-like taste. Faced with a glut of carrots? They make a delicious hummus, roasted or steamed, then added just as you would with any other hummus. Better yet, a roasted carrot muhammara-type dish will blow your mind, a non-traditional take on a classic Mediterranean dip. You could omit the peppers if you're feeling very untraditional, or add them with the rest of the mouth-watering spices.

Carrots have always been one of my favourite vegetables, which may be a surprise to some. These days they are pretty much an all-year-rounder, making them a versatile little veg, but they are in their prime in the warmer summer months. Roasting carrots brings out their sweetness: they're juicy and full of flavour, and what better than using another part of their growth to serve with? This little trio gets me thinking of summer barbecues or antipastos, creating a spread that takes no time to rustle up but will have you coming back for more.

Serves 4–6
as a side

WHOLE ROASTED CARROTS, TWO WAYS

w/ cherry salsa, carrot top pesto

Preheat your oven to 200°C fan. Chop off the leafy part of your carrots, putting it to one side for the pesto. Wash your carrots well, then place them whole on a baking tray. Drizzle over the olive oil, making sure they are coated all over. Season with salt and pepper, then put into the oven and roast for about 30–40 minutes. The timing will depend on your oven – you want them to be browned on their surface with a slight crisp, but soft all the way through. Test with a sharp knife.

While the carrots are roasting, make your salsa. Put your pitted and chopped cherries into a bowl with the green chilli, red onion, basil, coriander seeds, vinegar, lime juice and zest, plus a good pinch of salt and pepper. Mix to combine and put into the fridge to cool.

For the pesto, wash and chop the carrot tops. They can be quite tough, so chopping them smaller will help them to blend and not get stuck around the blade.

Place in a blender along with the basil, walnuts, nutritional yeast, garlic, olive oil, lemon juice and zest, chilli, salt and pepper. Blend until a relatively smooth paste forms, adjusting with extra olive oil if needed. Remove from the blender and put to one side.

1kg carrots (any variety, preferably with leaves for the pesto)

1–2 tbsp olive oil

salt and pepper

For the salsa

approx. 280g cherries, pitted, roughly chopped

1 small green chilli, seeded and finely chopped

1 small red onion, finely chopped

a large handful of fresh basil, finely chopped

1 tsp coriander seeds

2 tsp balsamic vinegar

1 lime, juiced, plus a dash of zest

salt and pepper

For the pesto

the tops from a 1kg bunch of carrots

a large handful of fresh basil (or try parsley if you can't get basil, or a combination)

50g walnuts (or try almonds, cashews or hazelnuts, or a combination)

4 heaped tbsp nutritional yeast

4 small cloves of garlic, crushed or finely chopped

approx. 125–250ml olive oil

1 lemon, juice and zest

a pinch of chilli flakes

salt and pepper

»

This next step is optional: add a couple of tablespoons of the pesto to the cooked carrots, making sure they are coated all over, and put back into the oven for 4–5 minutes. This crisps the pesto a little as well as the carrot skins themselves.

To serve, pile on some more pesto and a good spoonful of salsa. The acidity and citrus from the salsa pairs really well with the carrots, making them also ideal to serve with or without the pesto. Roasted carrots two ways – you decide.

Waste tips:

It doesn't just stop at carrot tops: beetroot leaves, celeriac and celery leaves, and kohlrabi leaves are also great bases for pesto. Often we find our vegetables being sold without the tops, but check local shops or markets and you'll usually have better luck. You can use a combination of leaves and herbs, playing about with the taste; the possibilities are endless. The roasted carrots themselves will also double up for the roasted carrot, ginger and chickpea dip on page 140. Haven't got any carrots? Parsnips are also great for this kind of recipe, and when roasted whole have a lovely crispy outside and a cake-like centre. You could also use this recipe to jazz up a larger salad if you fancied having it as a main. Follow the directions above, then chop the carrots with either/both the pesto and salsa, adding some crunchy lettuce, a grain/legume and some olive oil and an extra squeeze of lemon to dress. The pesto will keep for a while in the fridge, usually over a week. Make sure it has a layer of oil on top to help to preserve it and keep it moist. Use as you desire . . . on vegetables, pasta, rice, as a snack, stirred into your favourite sauces, soup, bread – the possibilities are endless. You can also use a mixture of greens/tops for this recipe, getting creative with celery tops, beet tops . . . whatever you can find in season. Or you can use a variety of herbs for a slight twist on a classic basil pesto.

My dad was always fond of making mash with different vegetables. If it was ever straight up potatoes, I'd be surprised. Sweet potatoes, swede, celeriac, you name it, he probably did it. My favourite combination was a buttery swede and carrot mash, usually served with some of his infamous Polish red cabbage and an onion sauce. There was something so buttery about the mash, yet to my surprise, no butter in there. The mix of oils and stock creates the perfect liquid to add to the mash, helping to avoid any dryness, or 'ungyness' as I used to say.

'BUTTERY' SPICED CARROT MASH

Bring a large pan of salted water to the boil. Add the carrots and garlic, and boil for about 15–20 minutes. You want them to be nice and tender, so a knife can easily slide in and be removed.

Once cooked, drain the carrots and garlic, give them a quick chop (to help the mashing process), and then put them back into the pan. Add the coconut oil, olive oil, stock, mustard, cayenne pepper, nutmeg, cinnamon, cumin and dried chilli flakes, and season with salt and pepper. Using a masher, begin to mash everything in the pan until it reaches your desired consistency. You can use a blender if you like your mash super-smooth, but I prefer a slightly more rustic consistency.

To serve, place in a large bowl, season again and add a sprinkling of chopped herbs.

roughly 10–12 large carrots, sliced in half widthways

4 cloves of garlic, left whole, skins removed

2 tbsp coconut oil, melted

1 tbsp olive oil

125ml vegetable stock

1 tbsp Dijon mustard (add a dash more for a big mustardy hit)

1 tsp cayenne pepper

½ tsp grated nutmeg

½ tsp ground cinnamon

½ tsp ground cumin

a pinch of dried chilli flakes

salt and pepper

fresh herbs of choice, roughly chopped, for garnish (parsley, coriander, chives)

Waste tips:

You could try this mash using parsnips in place of carrots, or even try adding 1–2 sweet potatoes or large baking potatoes for a more dense and traditional mash. This mash also doubles up as a great dip: add it to cooked beans and blend. It's great when you want something a little warm with a salad, or even as a side for a barbecue. The combination of olive and coconut oil creates the dip's buttery taste, but you could try any other oils you have to hand such as a nut-based oil or even avocado oil if you have that in.

At the end of a week I often tend to have a glut of carrots left – I'm always shocked at how far they go. I've already mentioned my love for roasting carrots, and if, like me, you're a bit of a hummus fiend, this dip is definitely for you. Perfectly creamy with a subtle fiery kick, balanced out with the earthy but sweet roasted carrots, it's great to serve with breads, crudités, or, let's face it, on its own, spoon at the ready.

Makes 12–16 servings

ROASTED CARROT, GINGER AND CHICKPEA DIP

Preheat your oven to 200°C fan. Wash/scrub your carrots, removing all dirt. Place on a baking tray, whole, and drizzle over the olive oil, using the full amount if needed to coat. Season with salt and pepper and roast for 30–45 minutes. You will need to flip and move the carrots about halfway through. They will be browned on the outside, soft and tender in the middle. Once cooked, remove and set aside.

Meanwhile, put the garlic, lemon juice and zest, chickpeas, tahini, cumin, ginger and 2 tablespoons of water into a blender and blitz until they form a rough paste.

Once your carrots have cooled slightly, roughly chop and add them to the blender. Add another 2 tablespoons of water and the chilli flakes and season with salt and pepper, blending again until the mix has a hummus-type texture. You can add a little more water to make it smoother.

I like to eat this dip slightly warm, or you can refrigerate it before serving if you prefer. To serve, place in a bowl, drizzle over some olive oil to make it nice and moist, and scatter with fresh coriander and some salt and pepper.

approx. 4–5 medium carrots

2 tbsp olive oil, plus extra to finish

salt and pepper

2 cloves of garlic, crushed or finely chopped

1 large lemon or 2 small, juiced, plus a dash of zest

250g cooked chickpeas (or 1 × 400g tin, drained)

3 tbsp tahini

1 tsp ground cumin

approx. 2 heaped tsp finely chopped or grated ginger

a pinch of dried chilli flakes

a small handful of fresh coriander, roughly chopped, to garnish

Waste tips:

Carrots are in season for a fair amount of the year, so this dip doesn't just have to be for summer. You could also make it with parsnips, pumpkin or even sweet potato. The ginger adds a nice kick but you could try adding extra herbs and spices, getting creative with what you have. A spoonful of pesto swirled through it, or even harissa or a creamy sauce, really brings it to life. The dip will keep in an airtight container for about 5–7 days in the fridge. Adding olive oil on top keeps it moist and helps to preserve it.

green beans

As the weather warms up, some of the finest ingredients start to show their faces. While green beans aren't commonly known for being the most versatile vegetables, it seems a shame not to let them show off their little lanky selves. Traditionally, we would smother them in salted butter and have them as a side to some kind of veggie-heavy spread, but these days I omit the butter and use them in one of my favourite Sri Lankan inspired dishes, almost buttery tasting and pan-fried – it makes me drool just thinking about it. One of the greatest things I have learnt about cooking green beans is that when boiling them you want to heavily salt the water. It should be as salty as the sea once at a rolling boil. Add the beans and cook until tender, drain and serve. This little trick helps add that 'buttery' taste but still 'au naturel'! As I've said, I believe in summer we should be a little more relaxed in the kitchen, so don't be afraid to serve the beans straight up, steamed, with a hefty pinch of salt, a squeeze of lemon and a drizzle of olive oil. Or jazz them up with crushed toasted nuts, pair them with a creamy white wine sauce . . . their amazing flavour always shines through and because of their quick cook time and simple presentation, those relaxed recipes are easy to achieve.

Waste tips:

Just like that old-school classic 'sour cream and chive', green beans make a perfect dip. Lightly steam them, then blend with a plant-based yoghurt, some chopped spring onions, lemon juice, garlic, fresh chives and a dash of vinegar. You've pretty much replicated a very luscious dip. You could also blend them with a nutty herbed cheese recipe (see pages 364 and 365 for examples) and create a similar dipping situation.

Without a doubt, this is one of my most loved recipes, inspired by many trips to Sri Lanka and cooking lessons with the locals. Think 'everything fresh' in terms of the herbs and spices, cooked down slowly in coconut oil and simmered until a vibrant green. This one always has me reminiscing over my trips, remembering eating local food the way it should be.

Serves 4
as a side

PAN-FRIED SRI LANKAN GREEN BEANS AND SHALLOTS

Heat ½ tablespoon of coconut oil in a large frying pan. Once hot, go ahead and add your mustard seeds, gently frying them on a low heat until they begin to pop. Once the majority of them have started popping, transfer them to a small bowl and put to one side. Put the pan back on the heat and add the other ½ tablespoon of coconut oil, followed by the shallots. Fry these for a few minutes until they begin to soften and are fragrant.

Add the garlic, ginger, ground turmeric, pepper and green chilli, frying for another minute or so. Add the curry leaves, green beans, lime juice and curry powder, and sauté until the green beans turn more vibrant in colour. By this stage you'll notice the mixture starting to dry up a little, so make sure to keep stirring while you fry.

Put the mustard seeds back into the pan, as well as the grated coconut (if you used dried, you can use this soaking water instead of adding extra) and season with salt and pepper. Add enough water to remove any sticky bits from the pan, and stir frequently to combine.

Once your green beans are tender and everything smells nice and fragrant, you're good to go. Season with salt and pepper and serve. I like to give it another squeeze of lime on top to add a little zest.

1 tbsp coconut oil

1 tsp black mustard seeds

2 shallots, finely chopped

4 cloves of garlic, crushed or finely chopped

2 tsp ginger, finely chopped or grated

1 tsp ground turmeric

a grind of black pepper

½ a small green chilli, finely chopped

5–6 fresh curry leaves

500g green beans, washed

½ a lime, juiced, plus a dash of extra juice for serving

2 heaped tbsp unroasted curry powder

3 tbsp fresh grated coconut (or if dried, rehydrate by soaking in a little water beforehand)

salt and pepper

2–4 tbsp water

Waste tips:

These will keep in the fridge in an airtight container for at least 5 days. They're great for adding to salads, or you can heat them up again with a dash of coconut milk to make more of a curry-style version. Add any legumes you fancy or pair with rice. Any type of green will work in this recipe – okra is also great, as are courgettes. You could try a combination and be creative with what you have in your fridge. For some extra colour, grate in a carrot when adding the coconut or even add a couple of chopped tomatoes. If you happen to get your hands on some fresh pandan leaf, a Sri Lankan herb, it's well worth adding it to this recipe – about 5cm will suffice.

Black rice is great for salads. It doesn't cook as much as white rice so always keeps a bit more bite. Adding a variety of textures and flavours into salads is what makes them so great, not to mention a lot more nutrient dense. Pairing this with a stone fruit, you get a little reset for the taste buds, a bit of freshness and zing, making it feel light but filling. Great on its own or served as a side for a summer spread.

GREEN BEAN SALAD

w/ stone fruit, pistachios, nut Parmesan, crispy black rice

Cook your black rice as follows, or according to the packet instructions (these may vary depending on the brand/variety). Place the rice in a large pan of cold water with a pinch of salt. Bring to the boil and allow to simmer for about 35 minutes. Once cooked, drain and set aside to cool. Black rice tends to have a little more bite when cooked and has a lovely nutty aroma.

Either steam or boil your green beans until vibrant and tender, usually about 8 minutes. Once cooked, blanch under cold water to stop the cooking process and to hold the nutrients (and colour). Leave to drain thoroughly.

Put the onion, stone fruit (see notes about charring), radishes, fresh parsley, fresh chives, capers and three-quarters of the pistachios into a bowl. Once your green beans have drained, go ahead and add these to the bowl.

Once the rice has cooked and drained, we're going to crisp it up slightly. Heat the coconut oil in a pan and slowly add the rice to the pan, stirring it to soak up some of the oil. Leave it for about 2 minutes before stirring again. Repeat this process until your rice starts to crisp up. Depending on the size of your pan, the time this takes may vary, with some grains of rice not as crispy as the others, but this is totally normal. Once you've reached your desired crispness, set to one side to cool while you make your nut Parmesan.

150g black rice, uncooked

salt and pepper

300g green beans, sliced in half widthways

1 brown onion, thinly sliced

2 large or 4 small stone fruit of choice (peaches, nectarines, plums, or a combination), stones removed, thinly sliced

4 small radishes (any variety, lots in season), thinly sliced

a handful of fresh parsley, roughly chopped

a handful of fresh chives, roughly chopped

1 tbsp capers, drained

70g shelled pistachios, roughly chopped

1 tbsp coconut oil (you can also use olive oil, avocado oil, etc.)

2–4 tbsp red wine vinegar

1 tbsp wholegrain mustard

1 lemon, juiced, plus a dash of zest

a pinch of dried chilli flakes

For the nut Parmesan

60g raw cashews

35g raw sunflower seeds

1 tsp salt

3 heaped tbsp nutritional yeast

¼ tsp garlic powder

¼ tsp ground turmeric

For the nut Parmesan, simply place the cashews, sunflower seeds, salt, nutritional yeast, garlic powder and turmeric in a blender or processor, and blitz until you have a fine crumb-like mix. Be careful not to over-blend. Transfer to a bowl or jar, ready to top the salad.

Add the crisped rice to the rest of the salad and stir carefully. Add the vinegar, mustard, lemon juice and zest and chilli flakes. Season with salt and pepper and stir carefully to dress the salad.

Serve on to plates and sprinkle over the rest of the pistachios and a good helping of the nut Parmesan.

Notes:

Often when I'm making this dish, I like to slightly char or grill the fruit. It's not essential, but it adds a lovely summery feel to the salad. You can place the slices under a grill for about 5 minutes, or even put them on a barbecue. If you have a ridged or griddle pan, you can also do it on that, griddling each side until a slightly browned colour. Add to the salad as above.

Waste tips:

Feel free to use any other fresh herbs you like or can find. Basil, dill and coriander are widely available and are great for this salad. If you don't have black rice, you can substitute any other rice you like. Quinoa is a great alternative, and has the same earthy and nutty aroma. The nut Parmesan will keep in the fridge for about 2 weeks, so if you do make extra or have leftovers, just store in the fridge and use as desired.

This is one of the dishes most loved by guests on my retreats. Upon arriving home from a trip, I often crave the flavours from the places I've just visited, and this little noodle number is a great way to hold on to the feeling of being in Thailand a bit longer. It's a great one-pot recipe (bar the noodles) and it involves minimal clean-up and just a little bit of chopping. You can vary the vegetables easily, making it a great dish for a number of seasons. I often add a dollop or two of pesto if I have a batch in the fridge – sometimes I just can't get enough of basil, especially when it's in season.

Serves 2–3

TAHINI THAI NOODLES

Put your noodles on to cook. Submerge them in salted boiling water, then simmer for about 7 minutes. (This will vary depending on the noodles you use, as some just require soaking rather than boiling.) Once cooked, drain and rinse under cold water to remove any excess starch.

In a large frying pan or wok, cook your spring onions with a dash of water until vibrant and fragrant – this should only take a few minutes. Add the garlic and ginger and cook for another minute or so.

Bash the lemongrass halves with the back of a spoon or a rolling pin and add to the pan along with the soy sauce, kaffir lime leaves, 2 tablespoons of water and half the basil and coriander. Make sure the heat is now down low. Mix well to combine.

Add the lime juice and zest, plus the green beans, carrot, pepper and green chilli. Stir to combine, add another 2 tablespoons of water, and cook for about 5 minutes, or longer if you want them softer (though I prefer mine with a bit of bite). Once your vegetables are vibrant and tender, add the tahini and the cooked and drained noodles, stirring to combine. Season with salt and pepper and simmer for a further few minutes, to reheat the noodles and allow them to soak up some of the sauce.

For the salad

180g brown rice noodles (any variety, flat, thin, etc.)

4 spring onions, finely chopped

4 cloves of garlic, crushed or finely chopped

approx. 5cm ginger, grated

2 stalks of lemongrass, chopped in half widthways

2 tbsp soy sauce

4–6 kaffir lime leaves, lightly scrunched in your hand to release the flavours

a large handful of fresh basil, roughly chopped (if you have access to Thai basil, you can use it here)

a large handful of fresh coriander, roughly chopped

1 lime, juiced, plus a dash of zest

150g green beans, roughly chopped

1 medium carrot, julienne peeled or finely sliced

1 small pepper, any colour or variety, finely sliced

1 small green chilli, finely chopped

4 tbsp tahini

salt and pepper

approx. 1 small head of lettuce of choice, finely chopped

6 plum tomatoes, sliced in half lengthways, then each half in quarters

a handful of seeds, to garnish (any you prefer/have in: sesame, sunflower, pumpkin, etc.)

»

Remove from the heat and transfer to a bowl. Add the chopped lettuce, the tomatoes and the rest of the basil and coriander. Season with salt and pepper again and carefully stir to combine. You'll notice the fresh herbs and lettuce will slightly wilt. This is normal.

Garnish with your seeds of choice and enjoy.

Waste tips:

As mentioned, don't feel restricted to the vegetables listed, just use what you have to hand. If you can't get lemongrass or kaffir lime leaves, just add extra ginger and lemon zest and you'll still have a great-tasting dish. You can also use rice in place of noodles. Adding an extra sauce (e.g. pesto) along with the tahini can be really nice, or even in place of tahini if you've run out.

lettuce

There is something so elegant about the leaves of a lettuce. Butterhead, romaine, red leaf, cos, iceberg . . . the list is long. I love the variety: some more bitter than others, some peppery, some fresh and ever so slightly watery, and some soft and buttery. I'm a big fan of salad in general, whether it's simple, with a refreshing vinaigrette, or doused in a richer creamy dressing. I adore tahini in dressings, often using it to recreate a particular one I used to order at Pizza Express. It was quite the ritual when we were younger to keep a stock of their House Dressing in our fridge and the taste has stuck with me. I very happily got experimenting a few years back, playing with the balance of salt, acid, citrus and herbs to recreate the real deal, with the addition of my much-loved tahini. I now have a few renditions of this dressing (see page 356), for jazzing up any kind of salad, straight-up lettuce or not.

When I was living in Australia there was a local taco spot I adored. The tacos were just how I imagined they must be in Mexico or California. They switched the ingredients frequently, making use of seasonal produce, and you could pick 'n' mix from more than one variety. One type really caught my attention: a taco in a lettuce cup, filled to the brim with grilled avocado (another revelation), pickled onions, a cashew-based chipotle sauce, charred cauliflower florets and lots of fresh coriander. It was simple but brilliant, the filling textures contrasting so well with the crunchy lettuce. Of course, normal tacos are great friends of mine too, but this lettuce cup version was special and has stuck with me ever since.

Waste tips:

We often think about lettuce as a fresh ingredient, serving it as part of a salad or side. Up until recently I had always struggled a little with wilting lettuce and would still try to bring it back to life in a salad by totally pimping it up. Much to my surprise, and probably yours, charred lettuce is a real game-changer. Depending on the size and variety of the lettuce, you can chop it lengthways, just in half, or into quarters. Heat a small amount of oil in a pan (a griddle pan if you're feeling fancy) and char the lettuce on each open side until you get a slightly crisped edge. It will start to wilt further, so if you're using an older lettuce, don't panic. Serve it the way you desire, with a crispy topping and smothered in your favourite dressing. A great tip for making lettuce last a little longer is washing it before you put it into the fridge. Keeping the stalk end on helps to preserve it, too. Make sure it's fully drained and dried, then either wrap it in a damp tea towel or store it in a flattish Tupperware with an airtight lid.

I'm a huge salad enthusiast. My aim when creating/making/ eating salads is to ensure they are far from 'boring'. Fresh crunchy lettuce, a flavoursome dressing and lots of herbs are always a good place to start. This recipe is a great way to use up leftover or stale bread, making the salad a little more filling too!

CHARRED LETTUCE AND TAHINI CAESAR
___
w/ capers, sourdough croutons

Start by making your croutons. Preheat your oven to 180°C fan. Tear the sourdough slices into bite-size pieces, as chunky as you like, and put them on a baking tray with about 2 tablespoons of olive oil and the oregano. Season with salt and pepper, mixing to make sure the bread is coated.

Put them into the oven for about 10 minutes, to crisp up. Be careful not to burn them – they will firm up as they cool. You want them to be a pale golden brown and crispy on the outside, but still slightly spongy to touch. Once cooked, remove from the oven and allow to cool.

Put your sliced red onion into a small bowl and cover it with the vinegar. You want it to sit in the vinegar to pickle slightly and remove the fructose, making it easier on the digestion as it is raw. Leave it in the vinegar while you prepare the rest of the dish.

Heat the remaining tablespoon of olive oil in a pan (if you have a ridged pan, you'll be able to create 'charred' lines) over a low heat. Once hot, carefully place your quartered lettuce in the pan for about 3–4 minutes each side. You want the two sides to brown and char slightly, so be careful not to burn or wilt the lettuce too much. Once done, remove to a plate to cool.

Put the tahini, lemon juice and zest, soy sauce or tamari, mustard, vinegar, oregano and capers into a blender.

For the charred lettuce
___

2 slices of sourdough (stale bread or frozen to use up leftovers, roughly torn)

2–3 tbsp olive oil

2 tsp dried oregano (or dried mixed herbs, thyme, rosemary, etc.)

salt and pepper

1 small red onion, thinly sliced

1–2 tbsp white wine vinegar

2 large heads of romaine or cos lettuce, quartered lengthways

2 tbsp capers

a handful of crushed nuts, lightly toasted (pistachios, almonds, cashews)

For the dressing
___

2 heaped tbsp tahini

1 lemon, juiced, plus a dash of zest

1 tbsp soy sauce or tamari

1 heaped tbsp Dijon mustard

1 tsp apple cider vinegar, or white wine vinegar

2 tsp dried oregano

1 tsp capers

salt and pepper

Season with salt and pepper and blitz until you have a smooth dressing. If you want to loosen it slightly, go ahead and add a dash of water until you reach your desired consistency.

To serve, put your lettuce on serving plates, charred side up. Carefully remove the onions from the vinegar and sprinkle them over the lettuce, along with the capers. Drizzle on as much dressing as you desire (you can save some for dipping, or serve on the side in a small bowl), followed by the crushed nuts and sourdough croutons. Season with extra salt and pepper if necessary.

Waste tip:

This is a great side at a barbecue or served with a dish that is a little heavier, as it's lovely and fresh, with simple flavours. It's a great way to use up leftover bread, and also any lettuce that may be a bit old. The recipe calls for cos or romaine, but it will work with a variety of lettuces – you'll just have a slightly different-looking outcome. If you don't have much else in the fridge and want to use this as a foundation to a dish, go ahead and follow the same instructions but chop the lettuce after charring. You could add any leftover vegetables you have in the fridge, or even some simple boiled potatoes to make it a bit more substantial.

As a kid, I remember my sandwiches being somewhat famous at school. On days when my parents felt creative, they'd pack me some weird but wonderful lunchtime surprises, from cream cheese and grapes to a concoction of vegetables mixed with mayonnaise and herbs. Inspired by my childhood sandwich memories, this one has definitely got it going on. A creamy dressing mixed with chickpeas creates a 'filling' filling, wedged between two slices of your favourite bread.

Serves 2–4, depending on bread choice/filling thickness

CHIVE AND CHICKPEA SANDWICHES

Put your cooked chickpeas into a bowl and mash with a fork. You'll start to notice the skins coming away – this is normal. Add the grated courgette or carrot, celery, red onion and garlic and mix with a fork until well combined.

Add the tahini and mustard, starting with less. Add the lemon juice and zest, nutritional yeast, chives, smoked paprika and chilli flakes. Season with salt and pepper and mix well. Add more tahini and mustard accordingly. If your mixture is a little more dry than you'd like, you could add some olive oil, but the tahini and mustard are usually enough.

To serve, take a lettuce leaf and place on one side of your sourdough, followed by a generous dollop of the chickpea mix. Top with another sourdough slice.

approx. 240g cooked chickpeas or 1 × 400g tin, drained

1 large courgette or carrot, grated (or 2 small ones)

1 celery stalk, very thinly sliced

1 small red onion, finely chopped

1 clove of garlic, crushed or finely chopped

2–3 tbsp tahini

1–2 tbsp Dijon mustard (or wholegrain)

1 lemon, juiced, plus a dash of zest

2 tbsp nutritional yeast

a small handful of fresh chives, finely chopped

½ tsp smoked paprika

a pinch of dried chilli flakes

salt and pepper

4 lettuce leaves (cos or romaine lettuce work well)

4 slices of sourdough, or more for additonal sandwiches (you could toast, for a variation)

Waste tips:

When I've cooked a batch of chickpeas I often like to use the leftovers in this recipe, sometimes also adding other things from my fridge. You can also use other kinds of beans, though the consistency will be a little looser, as chickpeas have a lot more texture than other white beans. If you like, you could make this feel Mexican by adding kidney beans and corn. If your bread isn't fresh, you could have this toasted, either putting the bread in the toaster beforehand or placing the whole sandwich under the grill for 5 minutes or so – or a hot pan will also do the trick. Drizzle over some olive oil to moisten it.

A very best very green salad. Tossed with a grain of choice and a trio of seasonal leaves, it may seem on the lighter side but it will leave you feeling fuelled and satisfied. I love to make a big batch of this salad, keeping the dressing separate until I'm ready for it, and having it during the week, just as it is. I have also been known to serve this alongside some very simple roasted potatoes, cooked simply with a little olive oil to help them crisp up, and salt and pepper.

LOADED LEAF SALAD, PEAS, GREEN BEANS, DILL DRESSING

Depending on your chosen grain, the cooking time will of course vary. Cook according to the packet instructions in salted boiling water, stirring occasionally. Once cooked, drain and set aside to cool to room temperature.

To make the dressing, put the tahini, garlic, lemon juice and zest, dill, mustard and maple syrup or sweetener of choice into a blender (you could also do this with a fork or hand whisk – the texture will be slightly different). Blitz/whisk until smooth, slowly adding water to reach the desired consistency. Season with salt and pepper and put into the fridge.

For the rest of the salad, bring a medium pan of salted water to a boil. Add the green beans and boil for about 5 minutes, then add the peas for a further 2–3 minutes. You want both to be tender and vibrant green. Once cooked, drain and briefly blanch under cold water to stop the cooking process. Place to one side while you make the rest of the salad.

Put the lettuce, spinach, celery, shallot, fresh dill and caraway seeds into a large bowl. Add your grain, green beans and peas and mix to combine.

Take the dressing out of the fridge and give it a quick whisk with a fork. Pour half of the dressing into the

For the dill dressing

120g tahini

2 cloves of garlic, crushed or finely chopped

1 lemon, juiced, plus a dash of zest

approx. 20–35g finely chopped fresh dill (I love dill, so I will use about 35g, but you can use less if you'd like the dill flavour to be a little less powerful)

1 heaped tbsp Dijon mustard

½–1 tbsp pure maple syrup (if you're using less dill, start with ½ tbsp – the sweetener helps to remove any bitterness)

salt and pepper

For the salad

approx. 180g grain of your choice (rice, millet, buckwheat, barley, etc.)

250g green beans, cut into thirds widthways

150g peas (you can use fresh and shell them beforehand, or use frozen and thaw)

1 small head of romaine lettuce, finely chopped (see notes opposite)

1 small head of butter lettuce/ red leaf lettuce, finely chopped

a large handful of spinach, finely chopped

2 stalks of celery, leaves included, finely chopped

»

bowl of salad ingredients. Season with salt and pepper and mix, making sure to coat everything.

To serve, drizzle on the rest of the dressing either now, or when portioned up into bowls. You could also drizzle on some olive oil for extra moisture, should you fancy. Using additional fats really brings a simple salad to life.

1 small shallot, finely chopped

a small handful of fresh dill, finely chopped

1–2 tsp caraway seeds, toasted

salt and pepper

olive oil, to drizzle

Notes:

This recipe came from having a variety of lettuces and green leaves in my fridge at one time, and I love how different they all are in their own way. Spinach adds a great darkness to the salad, as well as a nice variety of flavour. You could use cos, iceberg or butter lettuce in this recipe, depending on what you can get and what you like.

Waste tips:

This salad is great in various seasons, as you can use any lettuce you have as well as choosing an appropriate grain. You can switch dill for any other herb you might like, as it does have a short season, though it's great while you can get it. To bulk this up further, you could add some boiled or roasted potatoes, either in the salad or on the side. Try adding a squeeze more lemon when doing this, and a drizzle of olive oil, or feel free to add any oil of your choice. Occasionally I use avocado or sesame oil if I fancy something different, or simply if I have run out of olive oil.

tomatoes

I'm throwing it out there: a sliced tomato with a sprinkle of flaked sea salt, a grind of pepper and a drizzle of good quality olive oil . . . I mean, it's one of the greatest things. You can't beat a tomato in tomato season, juicy and plump, with a unique smell that cannot be replicated. A tomato is technically a fruit, part of the nightshade family, but we tend to know it as a vegetable and it's put into that category more often than not. To be honest, I'd say it's in a total league of its own. Tomatoes scream summer to me, and there are so many occasions when I'll serve them in a salad, using different varieties – heirloom, cherry, plum, green, yellow, beefsteak – and keeping it simple, as I described above. If I'm feeling more adventurous, a glug of balsamic vinegar and some finely chopped spring onion and basil is always a winner. What gets me is the different flavour profiles that each variety of tomato will give. I have strong memories of eating an abundance of them while holidaying in Europe, sometimes after a trip to the market where I picked up a bunch, or in a tomato salad enjoyed while out and about. One summer I became a little obsessed with experimenting with them, pairing them with a chewy grain or legume, a punchy zesty sauce, an occasional crunch from a nut or seed or a pop of salty goodness from a caper. It's often easier to experiment with ingredients you love, as you know you'll probably enjoy the end result and feel pretty smug with yourself. Tomatoes are versatile beauties, and despite often being dressed themselves, of course also make great sauces. Another all-time favourite of mine, again since I was young, is roasted vine tomatoes. Something about the vibrancy, taste, texture, and the utter glee when they burst upon eating . . . it's a real love affair.

Waste tips:

If you're someone who always has plenty of tinned tomatoes in the cupboard, for whenever you want to whip up a sauce, you might panic if you realize one day that you don't have any to hand. But using fresh tomatoes eliminates most packaging and creates a delightful rich flavour. Chop them up any which way, add a dash of water, some purée if you have some, a glug of balsamic and seasonings of choice, and you can create a much more delicious sauce, simmering until you reach your desired thickness and adding fresh herbs for a pop.

My dad claims not to remember my brother and me badgering him about a recipe very similar to this, but he's always been extremely good at throwing together a meal out of pretty much nothing. He also loved it, though he may not always agree. I'm keeping it simple, just the way my dad made it.

DAD'S ANY-VEGETABLE-GOES, CREAMY, ROASTED TOMATO PASTA BAKE

Preheat your oven to 200°C fan. Spread your tomatoes, whole or halved, on a large baking tray and add a good pinch of salt and pepper. Put them into the oven and roast for about 15–20 minutes. They'll start to juice and become lovely and soft, with a few starting to brown on top. Once cooked, remove from the oven and set aside.

Put your chopped vegetables on a separate baking tray. Toss them with a little salt and pepper and about 1 tablespoon of olive oil, and roast for about 15–20 minutes. The timing will vary depending on the size and type of vegetables you have chosen. Roast until cooked through and slightly browned. Once cooked, cover and set aside.

Bring a large pot of salted water to the boil and cook your pasta according to the packet directions. The time will vary slightly depending on what pasta you are cooking. Once cooked, drain, then put back into the pot with about 1 tablespoon of olive oil (to avoid sticking) and cover.

You'll most likely be making your sauce while all the above is cooking, making the cook time so much shorter. In a pan, sauté your shallots/onion in either roughly 1 tablespoon of olive oil or 2 tablespoons of water. Cook until slightly translucent and fragrant, then add the garlic and continue to cook for a further minute or so. Lower the heat and add the white wine, stirring to help

250g tomatoes, any variety, whole if small, halved if larger

salt and pepper

approx. 160–180g chopped seasonal vegetables of choice (aubergines, courgettes, fennel, green beans, mushrooms, etc.), chopped small

2–4 tbsp olive oil, or 2 tbsp olive oil + 2 tbsp water (see notes below)

approx. 270–340g pasta of choice (fusilli, orecchiette, penne)

2 shallots or 1 large white onion, finely chopped

6–8 cloves of garlic, crushed or finely chopped

2 tbsp white wine or 1 tbsp white vine vinegar

approx. 300–375ml plant-based milk, unsweetened if possible (oat, rice, soy are great)

250ml vegetable stock

3 tbsp plain flour, to thicken

2 tbsp nutritional yeast

2 tsp dried oregano

a large handful of fresh herbs (parsley, basil, or a combination), finely chopped

»

combine and 'burn off' the alcohol slightly, about 1 minute. Add your plant-based milk, stock, 2 tablespoons of flour, the nutritional yeast, oregano and three-quarters of the fresh herbs, and season well with salt and pepper. Mix well to combine and allow to simmer for about 8–10 minutes, stirring occasionally. Your sauce will start to thicken as it simmers, but you can always add the extra tablespoon of flour if it is still a little too runny after 10 minutes. Season again if necessary.

Add the sauce, tomatoes (including all of the residue in the baking tray) and roasted vegetables to the pot of pasta. Add the rest of the fresh herbs and stir carefully, making sure the pasta and vegetables are coated well.

Transfer it all to a baking dish, giving a little shake to let it settle. Place back in the oven for about 5 minutes, just to heat through and for the top to go a bit crispy.

To serve, dish up, adding a drizzle of olive oil should you wish.

Notes:

My dad would also make this sauce by sweating the vegetables in water, starting with the onion and garlic, then bit by bit adding seasoning, more water and the next round of vegetables. I definitely picked up this trick from him, as he would then serve it with a drizzle of olive oil instead, bringing the dish to life, using the oil as a garnish and flavour enhancer.

Waste tips:

This is a really great way to use up any vegetables in your fridge as well as using cupboard staples. You can also make it without the vegetables if you want something simpler, or just using one vegetable such as mushrooms to help complement the creamy sauce. Baking it isn't essential, although I do love the crispier topping that you get when doing so, and it gives me time to clear up a bit before sitting down and tucking in. This dish will keep in the fridge for about 4–5 days. It's lovely served cold, loosened with a little oil and with some chopped spinach thrown in to make it more of a pasta salad.

An almost 'one-pot' wonder, one to prep and pop on earlier in the day and not really have to think about. With a dash of liquid smoke this dish will have you thinking it has been cooked in a smoker. Liquid smoke is one of those ingredients that does so many amazing things to a dish, really bringing it to life, giving it some body and allowing you to taste all the smoked goodness just from a few drops. It can be pretty potent, so if you're new to using it as an ingredient, less is more, a bit like salt. You can always add but you can't take away. Here it's combined with fresh summer tomatoes, the noble butter bean and long-lasting flavoursome basil.

SLOW-COOKED, SMOKED TOMATOES

w/ cherries, butter beans and basil

Drain and thoroughly rinse your soaked beans. Put them into a large pot and cover them with water – you'll want the water to reach at least 10cm above the beans. Add a big pinch of salt and bring to the boil, then reduce the heat and simmer the beans for approx. 45–50 minutes. The time will vary depending on how long they have soaked for. Make sure there is always enough water in the pan. You want the beans to be al dente, as they will finish cooking in the tomato sauce. Once your beans have reached their al dente state, turn off the heat, cover and allow to sit.

While the beans are cooking, you can do the tomatoes. Heat up the olive oil in a large pan, then add the chopped onions and sauté until they start to brown and become fragrant. Add the garlic and fry for a couple of minutes, stirring continuously so that it doesn't burn. Add the tomato purée, fresh tomatoes, 500ml of water, the sun-dried tomatoes, 1 teaspoon of liquid smoke, 2 teaspoons of smoked paprika and the oregano. Season with salt and pepper, stirring to combine. Bring back to the boil, then lower to a simmer and cover the pan.

300g dried butter beans, soaked overnight

salt and pepper

1–2 tbsp olive oil

2 medium white onions, finely chopped

6 cloves of garlic, crushed or finely chopped

2 heaped tbsp tomato purée

approx. 600g tomatoes, roughly chopped

8 sun-dried tomatoes, roughly chopped

1–2 tsp liquid smoke (see page 185)

2–4 tsp smoked paprika

2–4 heaped tsp dried oregano

140g cherries, halved, then pitted

a large handful of fresh basil, roughly chopped

a pinch of grated nutmeg

1 tsp sugar (just to remove the acidity – any sugar you have in your cupboard will work)

olive oil, to serve

Allow your tomato mixture to simmer for about half an hour, making sure it's on a low heat, and stirring occasionally. Go ahead and add the cherries, half the fresh basil, the nutmeg, the other teaspoon of liquid smoke and 2 teaspoons of smoked paprika. Season with salt and pepper. Add the sugar and stir – you can add a dash more if your mix is quite sharp and acidy. If it's starting to dry up slightly, add some more water. Cover again and simmer for a further 10 minutes.

By now, your tomato mix will be nice and thick and the beans will be cooked to al dente. Drain the beans, reserving the liquid, and add them to your tomato pot. Stir to combine and slowly add some of the reserved liquid to loosen. If you don't have very much liquid left, you can simply add water to help loosen this. Leaving the lid off, simmer again for approx. 10–15 minutes, allowing the beans to cook fully and the mixture to become thick.

To serve, top with the rest of the basil and season with salt and pepper. You could drizzle on a little olive oil when dishing up – the fat from the oil will bring out the flavours.

Waste tips:

Using homemade stock in this recipe adds a little more flavour. You could use it for cooking the beans, or simply add it to the tomatoes instead of water. You could try baking the mixture for a little variety and a crispier top, adding some nutritional yeast for a little cheesy hit. If you have leftovers, you can blend them into a dip, creating a lovely rich and smoked tomato and butter bean-style hummus. I love to add this to roasted vegetables. If you don't have cherries, you can simply leave them out or try adding another soft stone fruit. The fruit adds a nice texture to the dish and also helps to balance the high fructose from the tomatoes, as occasionally they can be quite acidic in taste.

The perfect side dish to accompany the tomatoes. A twist on a little Greek classic, something that has worked its way into my week, and rightly so . . . and what's even better is that it can easily be turned into hummus, added to a salad (such as above) or thrown into soups/stews to make them a little heartier. Cooked with seasonal herbs and a touch of zest, I am yet to become bored with such a simple number.

Serves 2–3
as a side

MUM'S BEST BUTTER BEANS

Put your cooked beans into a pan with the lemon juice and zest, olive oil, water, garlic, oregano, 1 tablespoon of herbs, the chilli flakes and a hefty seasoning of salt and pepper.

Over a medium heat, allow the beans to heat up slowly. The liquid will reduce quickly, and once it does so and just as it starts bubbling, reduce the heat to its lowest. Let it simmer for about 10 minutes. If it starts to dry up, add a dash more water.

Add the other tablespoon of herbs and any extra seasoning that's needed.

Serve as a hearty little side, with salads, fresh bread, etc.

approx. 270g cooked butter beans (135g dried, soaked overnight and boiled)

2 lemons, both juiced, 1 zested

2 tbsp olive oil

4–6 tbsp water

2 cloves of garlic, crushed or finely chopped

1 tsp dried oregano

2 heaped tbsp chosen fresh herbs (parsley, basil, dill, or a combination), finely chopped

a pinch of dried chilli flakes (optional)

salt and pepper

TOMATO SALAD, THREE WAYS

Tomatoes to me scream summer. I love how many varieties there are, colours, sizes and so on! Tomato salads are a favourite, and in their prime are a regular occurrence at home. The following salads all feature the same base; with a few small additions it can be 'pimped' very easily, enabling you to tailor the salad to be either a side dish or a main.

—

TOMATO SALAD, STRAIGHT-UP

Serves 4–6 as a side. Use this as the base recipe for the two variations which follow

—

- 1 small red onion, finely chopped
- 1 small clove of garlic, crushed or finely chopped
- 1–2 tbsp white or red wine vinegar
- salt and pepper
- approx. 450g tomatoes (any variety/colour, combination), some halved or quartered, smaller ones whole

- a large bunch of fresh basil, roughly chopped (you can also use any other herb of choice, or a combination)
- 1–2 tbsp olive oil
- ½ a lemon, juiced, plus a dash of zest
- a pinch of dried chilli flakes

Put your onion and garlic into a small bowl, followed by 1 tablespoon of vinegar. Mix and add a pinch of salt. You want the onion and garlic to be submerged, so go ahead and add the other tablespoon of vinegar if there is not enough. Put to one side, for the acidity to be removed from the onion.

Put the tomatoes and basil into a large bowl. Season with salt and pepper, then add the olive oil, lemon juice, zest and chilli flakes. Mix to coat the tomatoes.

Add the onions and garlic to the bowl. I like lots of vinegar, and it helps to remove any bitterness from the tomatoes, but you can drain it off slightly if you wish – the amount of vinegar is definitely a matter of choice in this circumstance.

Serve as a side (see waste tips).

—

TOMATO SALAD WITH CELERY, FENNEL AND CAPERS

Serves 6 as a side

—

Base recipe, plus:

- 4 stalks of celery, finely chopped, leaves included
- 1–2 tbsp fennel seeds

- 2 tsp capers, drained, rinsed
- 2 tbsp tahini

Following the base recipe, once you have everything in the bowl, go ahead and add your celery, fennel seeds and capers. Mix well until combined. To balance it out, tahini is a great addition here, adding a creaminess to the salad, as well as bringing out the flavours in the fresh produce. Add the tahini and carefully mix to combine.

Serve as a side (see waste tips).

—

Waste tips:

My favourite thing about tomato salads is that they add such freshness and zest to any meal. They are great served over pasta, rice, noodles, on top of bread, bruschetta-style, with some pan-fried tofu – there really are so many options. These salads also make great salsas: chop the tomatoes slightly smaller, add an extra glug of olive oil, a dash of lemon or vinegar, and you're good to go. You can also add avocado to either of these salads. It isn't in season for a lot of the time and is often imported, but the height of summer is a great season to find it at its best!

TOMATO SALAD WITH ORZO AND CRISPY GREENS

Serves 4, as a main

—

Base recipe, plus:

approx. 210g dried orzo

2 tbsp olive oil

1 large bunch of dark leafy greens (kale, cavolo nero, etc.), roughly chopped

2 large cloves of garlic, sliced thin

1 small lemon, juice and zest

salt and pepper

a pinch of chilli flakes

Bring a large pan of salted water to the boil. Add the orzo and simmer for about 8–10 minutes, until al dente. Once cooked, drain the orzo, put it into a bowl with about 1 tablespoon of olive oil, and fluff it up to prevent sticking. Set aside while you prep the rest of the salad.

Following the 'straight-up' tomato salad recipe above, add this mixture to the orzo and mix well. This will help the orzo soak up any additional flavours.

Heat 1 tablespoon of olive oil in a pan over a low heat. Add your greens, garlic, lemon juice and zest, salt and pepper to taste and a pinch of chilli flakes. Cook until your greens become crispy. They will also reduce slightly in size. You'll notice them starting to dry up – this is normal and will help add some additional crunch.

To serve, you can either add the greens to the bowl of tomatoes and orzo, or, to keep them crispy, plate them up accordingly and scatter the greens on top. Season with extra salt and pepper if necessary.

—

GREEK-STYLE TOMATOES, TWO WAYS

One of the greatest things about cooking Greek dishes is that a lot of the ingredients tend to be the same: similar herbs and spices, flavours and fresh produce. A lot of their traditional dishes are of course not vegan, but many of their vegetarian classics are heavily tomato based and full of flavour, with plenty of oregano and good quality olive oil, and delicious served with fresh, warm bread. Growing up we spent a lot of time in Greece as we had relatives who lived there, and I have continued to travel to the beautiful islands for work with one of my best friends. To this day, I still express my love for Greek tomatoes, served simply with some salt and a drizzle of olive oil. You can't beat it.

—

RICE-STUFFED TOMATOES
(*yemista*)

Having a Greek best friend is great in so many ways, including her recipes, from her nanna herself. I remember the first time I made these after a phone call to Kat's nan, a frazzled me trying to note down what she was saying despite a questionable Greek phone signal, and I feared that they wouldn't live up to Kat's memories or expectations. But I'm happy to confirm that they did and have since become a regular, sometimes with peppers, sometimes with tomatoes, oozing herby goodness once removed from the oven and served with a traditional Greek salad.

»

10–15 large tomatoes (make sure these are ripe but not too soft and have a relatively flat base)

1 large white onion, finely chopped

1 tbsp olive oil

salt and pepper

8 cloves of garlic, crushed

a large handful of fresh parsley, roughly chopped, stalks included

a large handful of fresh mint, roughly chopped

1 × 400g tin of whole tomatoes

2–4 tbsp tomato purée

35g pine nuts

2 heaped tbsp dried oregano

300g long grain, jasmine or white basmati rice

approx. 560ml water (I like to use half water, half stock, optional)

2 tbsp raisins/sultanas (optional)

olive oil and balsamic, to serve

Preheat your oven to 180°C fan. Carefully cut the tops off your tomatoes and delicately remove some of the insides until they are slightly hollow. Make sure you don't break the bottom of the tomato. Place the tops back on as lids and roughly chop the tomato insides, then put to one side.

In a large pan, on a medium heat, sauté the onion in 1 tablespoon of olive oil with a pinch of salt and cook until the onion is fragrant and starting to turn translucent. Add the garlic and sauté for another minute or so, stirring frequently, then add half the parsley and half the mint, stirring again to combine.

Add the tinned tomatoes and 2 tablespoons of the purée. Stir in the pulp/insides from your hollowed tomatoes and add the pine nuts, oregano, rice and water/stock. Bring to the boil, then lower to a simmer. Season with salt and pepper.

You want to three-quarters cook the rice, so depending on the specific type you are using, simmer for about 20 minutes, until al dente. It will have some bite and there will not be much liquid left in the pan. If it dries up too quickly, go ahead and add some more water. Once you've tested your rice, season again if necessary and add the raisins/sultanas.

Carefully spoon some of your rice mixture into each tomato, spooning a little of the liquid from the pan over the top to help cook the rice a bit more. Fill them to just below the top and put the tomato lids on.

Place in the oven for about 20–30 minutes. Depending on the size of your tomatoes and how thick they are from the outside in, this will vary. You want the lids to turn a slightly golden brown and the rice to be cooked inside, plus of course the tomatoes should be lovely and soft.

Once cooked, remove from the oven. Dish up and drizzle with a little olive oil and balsamic, seasoning with more salt and pepper if necessary. I like to pour over some of the juice/residue in the pan, either over the whole thing, or lifting the lids of the tomatoes and pouring the tomato garlic goodness inside

Waste tips:

You'll notice that both these recipes contain almost identical ingredients for the tomatoes, showing how easy it is to use the same ingredients for an alternative dish, pairing them with different things – one option more filling because of the rice, the other more suited as a side dish to complement another grain, some grilled potatoes, salads, etc.

QUARTERED AND ROASTED TOMATOES

w/ crumbled vegan feta

A vegan rendition of a dish we used to make all summer long. I found out not so recently that I'd been calling it the wrong name for years; needless to say, it still tasted amazing. It's baked high, allowing all the juices from the tomatoes to cook with the garlic and herbs, and the vegan feta to soak it all up. I love to have mine with a hot crusty loaf, to help scoop up all of that juice!

Serves approx. 5

—

For the tomatoes

10 large tomatoes, quartered

4 tbsp olive oil

1 large white onion, sliced thin

8 cloves of garlic, crushed or finely chopped

a large handful of fresh parsley, roughly chopped, stalks included

a small handful of fresh dill, roughly chopped

a pinch of chilli flakes

35g pine nuts

2 heaped tbsp dried oregano

salt and pepper

For the almond feta (makes one large round, you will probably have extra)

120g almonds (soaked for at least 2 hours, and ideally overnight)

1 small lemon, juiced, plus a dash of zest

1 heaped tsp salt

1 tsp miso (preferably yellow or light-coloured)

2 tsp dried oregano

2 cloves of garlic, crushed or finely chopped

1 tsp apple cider vinegar

a pinch of pepper

125ml plant-based milk

4 heaped tbsp nutritional yeast

80–125ml water, plus more to loosen

Preheat your oven to 180°C fan. Put your quartered tomatoes into a large roasting tray with the olive oil, onion, garlic, half the parsley, half the dill, the chilli flakes, pine nuts, oregano, salt and pepper. Mix with your hands carefully, making sure it is all mixed well. Place in the oven and bake for 30–40 minutes. You want the top to be nice and brown, with the tomatoes soft and juicing. Stir around the halfway point.

To make the feta, drain and rinse the almonds. Ideally you'd use a high-speed blender for this. Put the almonds into a blender with the lemon juice and zest, salt, miso paste, oregano, garlic, vinegar, pepper, plant-based milk, nutritional yeast and some of the water. Blitz until it starts to reach a smoother consistency. You can add more water as you go for a smoother texture. This isn't super-smooth, there is some texture or 'bittiness' to it, helping to replicate a feta-like cheese. The mixture shouldn't be too thick, but should fall off a spoon rather than pour.

Transfer to a baking tray, greased with a dash of oil or lined with baking paper. You want it to be relatively thick and even, the shape doesn't matter. Sprinkle with extra salt, then put into the oven and bake for around 30–40 minutes. It will start to brown and crisp on top and be slightly firmer to the touch. Remove and allow to cool.

To serve, dish up the tomatoes and crumble the desired amount of almond feta on top. Sprinkle over the rest of the fresh parsley and dill and enjoy!

—

autumn

Autumn is probably my favourite time of the year. Don't get me wrong, the summer is dreamy, but often late September shines through, with its crisp morning air, beautiful warmth in the daytime and a cosy chill at night. I always look forward to the structure autumn brings and the exciting sense of new adventures. Perhaps because my birthday falls right at the start of the season, along with the new school year, the idea of it being a time of fresh beginnings is deeply ingrained in me. Autumn really is a thriving time . . . and I haven't even got started on the trees!

Cooking in autumn, in my opinion, is all about herbs and spices. I like to make the most of all those warming favourites: cinnamon, cloves, allspice, perfect in sweet and savoury recipes. These days we seem to get more 'Indian summers', so we're able to cling on to a lot of summer produce as it tends to continue its growth much later – the overlap of ingredients as the seasons cross over is incredible and allows for real creativity in the kitchen. Although I get a little sad about saying goodbye to plush summer tomatoes, the excitement about getting my hands on autumnal favourites quickly overrides it. I fantasize about picking blackberries on long meandering walks, eating the majority of them en route, while of course admiring the new warming colours on the trees. I have a fond autumnal memory from my childhood, not long after we moved up to London from Devon, of an afternoon spent conker-hunting with my dad before we headed home for a quick but delicious 'fridge pasta' supper. My dad was always extremely good at making a meal out of anything . . . consequently, and very happily, leading to me having a similar ability.

Autumn is a great time for a little spruce-up in the kitchen as we go into the early, milder months. Now's the time to move slowly away from raw salads and say hello to our ovens more frequently, and to new autumnal goods in the markets. The versatility of the produce is a real highlight. There is an abundance of recipes you can make with just a pumpkin, and no need to chuck away seeds or throw away those earthy beetroot tops.

star produce:

Blackberries

——

Beetroot

——

Parsnips

——

Kale

——

Pumpkins

——

Other seasonal produce: Kale family, cavolo nero, apples, persimmons, cauliflower, Swiss chard/spring greens, pomegranates, wild mushrooms, grapes, shallots, turnips, celeriac, coriander, figs, damsons.

——

You will of course notice some of these vegetables in other seasons as well. There is always a big overlap these days because of the climate and average temperatures we experience, regardless of where we are.

——

Grains harvested at this time of the year: Spelt, oats, amaranth, millet, freekeh, teff.

——

blackberries

One of my fondest childhood memories is of when my parents would suggest a long Sunday walk. Perhaps for most six-year-olds not the most exciting activity, but when blackberry-picking was thrown into the mix, my brother and I would be filled with glee. We'd pick as many of the berries, bittersweet, with a hint of sour, as we could so that my mum could make a crumble, usually with some apple thrown in and a giant helping of Devonshire custard. Naturally, leftover crumble for breakfast was the biggest treat at that innocent age. I've always been so impressed by how versatile blackberries are, especially once I realized just how good they are in savoury dishes too. That apple and blackberry crumble with a pinch of salt thrown in is a real game-changer. One of my favourite things to make in blackberry season is a huge batch of compote, as a porridge topping, for pancakes, crumbles (obviously) and, because I like to keep things quirky, as a sauce for grilled vegetables. Think of it as a sweet condiment to a savoury dish. Everyone loves sweet chilli sauce, right? Well, this is similar but more natural, glossy and vibrant in colour.

Waste tips:

If you're a blackberry lover like me, you'll know they don't keep for a huge amount of time once picked – a few days in and they start to slowly deteriorate or show small signs of mould. A little trick I picked up a few years ago in Spain (by the way, the blackberries there, oh my!) is to wash the blackberries in apple cider vinegar. It sounds odd but works a treat. Simply fill up a bowl with one part vinegar to three parts water, give the blackberries a quick soak for a minute or so, rinse, then drain well. Gently pat them dry with a tea towel and then put them into the fridge – I usually keep them in a Tupperware, as they last even longer this way. You can also put them between two pieces of kitchen roll, which helps to absorb any excess liquid. You can pretty much use this technique for any berry; apple cider vinegar really is a dream ingredient.

This is a somewhat romantic pancake, light, fluffy and crêpe-like with a little zing from the turmeric. I love using turmeric – it has a strong flavour and can easily become overpowering, but when used in a subtle way, it creates not only a beautiful colour but has an aroma that cannot be replicated. Sprinkled into these pancakes it adds a boost of nutrients and gives you that extra bit of flavour for the main event. Paired here with sweet spiced apples and tart blackberry coulis, it's the perfect balance of flavours. I love eating these on a slow weekend morning, adding a pinch of flaked salt on top for good measure.

TURMERIC PANCAKES

w/ spiced apple and blackberry coulis

Put the buckwheat and oat flour into a large mixing bowl along with the baking powder, cinnamon, turmeric and a pinch of salt. Mix with a wooden spoon. Make a hole in the middle of the ingredients to pour the liquids into.

First spoon the maple syrup into the hole in the dry ingredients, then slowly begin to pour in the milk, whisking as you go. You want this mixture to be smooth, not too runny, resembling a batter and with no lumps. Put to one side while you start your coulis and apple.

For the coulis, simply put the blackberries into a small saucepan with the lemon juice and zest, sugar and water. Add a small pinch of salt and slowly bring to the boil, then lower to a simmer until the blackberries become soft and form a compote or loose jam-type mixture. This shouldn't take more than 8–10 minutes. If it starts to look dry, add a dash more water. Once cooked, remove from the heat, set aside and cover.

For the apple, heat your tablespoon of coconut oil in a small pan. Once hot, over a low heat, go ahead and add the apple slivers, maple syrup, cinnamon, allspice,

For the pancakes (makes approx. 6 thin pancakes, depending on size)

60g buckwheat flour

40g oat flour (you can blitz oats in a processor to make this)

½ teaspoon baking powder

1 tsp ground cinnamon

2 tsp ground turmeric, plus a grind of black pepper

a pinch of salt

1 tbsp pure maple syrup

125–185ml plant-based milk

coconut oil, for frying (feel free to omit if you have a good non-stick pan)

For the coulis (may make more than you need)

200g blackberries, fresh or frozen

1 lemon, juiced, plus a dash of zest

½ tbsp sugar (coconut, palm, raw cane)

approx. 80ml water

salt

»

nutmeg and cardamom. Add a pinch of salt and toss the apple slivers in the liquid, making sure they are coated well. Allow to simmer for about 2–3 minutes, then flip over and cook the other side. They'll start to brown and the liquid will begin to caramelize. Once cooked, remove and place to one side, covering to keep them warm.

To make the pancakes, heat a drizzle of coconut oil in a large pan over a medium-low heat. If you are using a non-stick pan, you can omit the oil. Begin to ladle in the desired amount of batter – this will depend on how big or small, thin or chunky you'd like your pancakes and how big your pan is. Cook for a few minutes each side. You'll notice the pancakes will start to bubble on the top, which indicates the flipping time. They'll brown slightly as they cook.

Best served hot, with your coulis piled on top followed by the apple slivers. You can add any additional toppings you desire.

For the spiced apple (allow approx. ½ a medium apple per person)

1 tbsp coconut oil

1 apple, chopped in half, seeds removed, then cut into slivers, approx. ¾–1cm thick

2 tbsp pure maple syrup

1 tsp ground cinnamon

½ tsp ground allspice

½ tsp grated nutmeg

½ tsp ground cardamom

salt

Extra serving suggestions

granola

fresh fruit

crushed nuts/seeds

yoghurt of choice

Waste tips:

I love making an extra amount of this coulis, especially if I have a whole punnet of blackberries. Of course they are best fresh, but they don't always last long, so any on the turn are great for this recipe. You can keep the coulis in the fridge for adding to porridge in the morning or spreading on toast as you would with jam. The longer you leave it in the fridge, the thicker it will become. It will keep for about a week, sometimes a little less, so do make sure to keep an eye on it if you make a bigger batch, as it could turn easily and grow unwanted mould. If you do make a bigger quantity, go ahead and freeze it. It'll keep for a few months, so you can defrost your desired amount as you go. You could also use this coulis as a base for a crumble or mixed with other fruit. If you don't have blackberries, you can try this with raspberries or even blueberries or strawberries. The texture will be slightly different but it's a great alternative. Believe it or not, sweet potato and pumpkin are also amazing for this kind of dish. It's a great way to use them up if you have leftovers or fancy getting creative. Lightly steam them first, then follow the same steps as above, slicing them a little thicker to hold their shape. This gives a slightly more savoury twist to the dish, so if you fancy something less sweet in the morning, it's a great seasonal option!

As you've made your way through this book, by now you may have begun to understand that I'm a huge advocate of mixing sweet and savoury, using fruits not just in sweet recipes. This recipe is a great one for a warmer autumnal day, making you think back to the sunnier days of summer. The blackberries in the chimichurri give it an ever-so-tart taste, bringing to life the grilled vegetables and making what may seem a little boring into the complete opposite. I love serving homemade flatbreads with this dish, making them feel a little more 'taco' like, and inspiring another recipe further on in this chapter (see page 195).

Serves 3–4

GRILLED VEGETABLE SKEWERS

w/ smoked blackberry chimichurri

Preheat your grill to high. If you are using a barbecue, go ahead and set this up now. No grill – all good, just preheat your oven to 200°C fan, and they can be roasted.

Put your blackberries, parsley, capers, garlic, 2 table-spoons of olive oil, apple cider vinegar, lemon juice and zest, chilli flakes, smoked paprika, liquid smoke and a hefty seasoning of salt and pepper into a blender and blitz until it forms a paste-type mixture. You don't want this to be too wet, so wait before adding the final tablespoon of olive oil.

Take your skewers and start slotting on/threading the vegetables and apple one by one, alternating as you go. They don't have to be in any particular formation, but make sure to leave space at either end of the stick.

Lightly brush with olive oil and season with salt and pepper. Grill the skewers until the vegetables are lightly charred, rotating them every so often to cook on all sides. They should take around 10–15 minutes to cook through. Some vegetables will cook quicker than others and the onions will start to caramelize. If you are roasting, do the same but be careful when touching the sticks to rotate.

For the chimichurri (this recipe also features on page 197, in the beetroot tacos. You could use the beetroot tops as suggested in that and add the blackberries as below)

approx. 200g fresh blackberries

2 large handfuls of fresh parsley, finely chopped, stalks included (if you can't get parsley, coriander is also great)

2 tbsp capers

2 cloves of garlic, crushed or finely chopped

2–3 tbsp extra virgin olive oil

1 tsp apple cider vinegar

1 lemon, juiced, plus a dash of zest

a pinch of dried chilli flakes

1 heaped tsp smoked paprika

1 tsp liquid smoke (optional, see note)

salt and pepper

»

Once cooked, remove from the grill/barbecue/oven and brush between a third and a half of your chimichurri on to the skewers. Put back under the grill, on the barbecue or into the oven to crisp up for about 4–5 minutes.

To serve, simply plate up the skewers and drizzle over the extra chimichurri; you can heat the chimichurri up a little in a pan if you like, but I prefer it cold, as it complements the warm vegetables nicely. Serve with any extra fresh herbs, season with salt and pepper, and enjoy.

For the skewers
(I use 4 medium/ large metal skewers here as you can reuse them, vs disposable ones – however, if you are using wooden skewers, be sure to soak them first to prevent them splitting and burning when in the oven or on the grill)

———

1 small pumpkin/ squash, cut into bite-size chunks

8 chestnut or button mushrooms, quartered

4 small beetroots, washed thoroughly

1 large apple, cut into large cubes

2 red onions, cut into large slices

olive oil

salt and pepper

extra herbs of choice, finely chopped, to garnish

Waste tips:

These skewers are great made at any time of the year. You can replace the vegetables with the season's finest. Get creative, adding fruits or even some tofu if you have some. Thinly sliced potatoes are also great, and I love adding stone fruit in the spring. The chimichurri doubles up for many recipes, so you could make a bigger batch and keep it in the fridge in an airtight container. You can freeze it, but it can become a little watery over time, so add a dash more olive oil to help thicken it and balance the fats again. It's a nice little addition to jazz up a meal. Often, if I cook these skewers in the summer, I will throw some corn on the barbecue or into the oven, whole in the husk, and enjoy it on the side with a big leafy salad. You could save the cooked vegetables from the skewers in a Tupperware, too, for adding to salads or having as a snack when you like. The smoky charred flavours will start to develop, mixing up your roasted veggie routine.

Notes:

Liquid smoke is a great ingredient but not essential. Once you've got it in, it'll keep a long time. You can use an extra teaspoon of smoked paprika for a smoky hit if you don't have it in liquid form. It can sometimes be hard to source – check your local health food shop.

A wackier number, something different that'll soon have you committed to using fruits in some of your favourite dishes. Serve with your favourite brand of linguine . . . this is certainly one of my autumnal week-night go-tos! It's one of the easiest pasta dishes, somewhat resembling a traditional carbonara. It's rich and creamy, zesty, garlicky, with sweet little bursts of delight from the blackberries, which help to balance out the rich creaminess of the sauce. Lemons and blackberries are definitely a match made in heaven, so having them in a pasta dish is a real treat. The roasted shallots add a great depth to this dish and, you know, something a little different.

Serves 4–6

CREAMY LEMON LINGUINE

w/ roasted shallots, blackberries

Preheat your oven to 190°C fan. Put the shallots, whole, on a baking tray and roast for about 20 minutes. They will start to caramelize, the skins going crispy and the insides very soft. Once cooked, remove from the oven and allow to cool to room temperature.

In a saucepan, sauté your garlic in 1 tablespoon of the olive oil. This shouldn't take too long, and they will start to brown quickly. Lower the heat and add the lemon juice and half the zest, then simmer to reduce the liquid slightly.

Add your plant-based milk, nutritional yeast, three-quarters of the parsley and the nutmeg. Season with salt and pepper and allow to simmer on low for about 10 minutes, stirring occasionally. You want the liquid to reduce and for it to become slightly thicker.

Bring a pot of salted water to the boil and add your linguine. Cook for about 10–12 minutes, until al dente.

Your sauce should now be thicker, so go ahead and add the rest of the lemon zest, the other tablespoon of olive oil and any extra salt and pepper. Stir to combine. Your shallots should have cooked and cooled by now, so

4 medium shallots, whole, skins on

3 cloves of garlic, quartered, then cut into slivers

2 tbsp olive oil, plus extra for serving

2 lemons, both juiced, 1 zested

125ml plant-based milk (I like oat or cashew milk here, the thicker the better)

approx. 25g nutritional yeast

a small handful of fresh parsley, finely chopped

¼–½ tsp grated nutmeg

salt and pepper

approx. 350g dried linguine pasta

150g fresh blackberries, halved

carefully squeeze out the insides from the skins into the sauce. (You can then compost the skins.) Using a knife and the back of a wooden spoon, roughly break down the shallots, making sure you stir well.

Once your pasta has cooked, drain and pour straight into your creamy sauce. Fold carefully to coat all the pasta. Add the blackberry halves and the rest of the parsley, and season again with salt and pepper.

To serve, dish up, drizzling with a little extra olive oil and sprinkling over a pinch of nutmeg.

Waste tips:

You can swap the blackberries for another softer-type fruit, depending on the season you are in. You can add a pinch of chilli flakes to give this dish a kick, and even stir in some greens if you fancy. The shallots could also be subbed with regular brown onions, about 2–3 of them since they are a little bigger.

beetroot

Oh, the sweet beet plant, such an underrated vegetable in my opinion. It's delicate yet bold and boasts a subtle sweetness, and I think it's fair to say it has a very assertive 'vegetable-y' taste (as vegetables go, of course), plus an earthy unmatched flavour and texture. I could go on, which is why it is so versatile when it comes to cooking. I get a little bit over-excited when beet season comes into full swing. Chioggia, Pablo, Red Ace, Blankoma: with names like these it's hard not to be intrigued. The Chioggia beetroot in particular really gets me. With its soft orangey-pink skin and red and white rings on the inside, it's a food decor dream (albeit maybe just mine), and perfect for adding crunch to salads, making a statement on toast, or for roasting up and adding an additional somethin' somethin' to an ordinary hummus. Pickled beetroot is also a favourite. Now I could talk forever about the main root itself, but the leaves are equally important. With a texture similar to Swiss chard, when boiled they match any usual buttery greens flavour.

Waste tip:

For years I threw away the greens and only kept the root itself, but by now you'll understand that I have developed a strong love for using the whole vegetable. They add a great taste to a green salad, torn or chopped, raw or boiled, and, if time allows, letting them sit in your salad dressing is a real treat, to soften and lose any bitterness that they may have. Flicking to page 201, you'll see that one of my favourite renditions of a hummus is to chuck in a few roasted or boiled beetroots, adding a dash of cumin and whizzing up to probably the most vibrant hummus around.

Here's how to use the whole beet! I love using beetroot tops in salads – they add a beautiful colour and have a similar taste to chard. They are often thrown away, or you'll see beetroots sold without them in the shops, but they are very nutrient dense, full of vitamins *and* they taste delicious. For a summer addition, add some sliced avocado for an extra plant-based boost of healthy fats (and yes, I did just say that). Mostly because avocados are creamy and delicious and when paired with the thick dressing, the salad becomes a total summer fave.

Serves approx.
4 as a side, or
2 as a main

BEET-TOP AND MILLET CHOPPED SALAD

w/ a whipped tahini and dill dressing

Preheat the oven to 200°C fan. Prepare your beetroots by chopping the stalks and leaves off, as close to the top of the beetroot as possible. Place the leaves to one side while you prepare the roots. Scrub the beetroots well, removing any excess soil/dirt. Lightly brush them with the olive oil, seasoning with a pinch of salt and pepper. Pop them into the oven on the middle rack and cook for about 45–55 minutes. Depending on the size, the time will vary. You want them to be soft all the way through when you pierce them with a knife.

While the beetroots are roasting, wash the beetroot tops/greens thoroughly, again removing any soil/dirt. Finely chop them, along with the Swiss chard. Place both in a large mixing bowl and squeeze over the juice from your lemon. Add a good pinch of salt and pepper and begin to massage with your hands. This will help them to soften and also remove any bitterness. Put to one side and leave them to wilt further.

Put your millet grain into a pan with about 750ml of water and a pinch of salt. Bring to the boil, then lower to a simmer, cooking until the millet is soft and fluffy, about 12 minutes. Drain any remaining liquid

»

For the salad

4 small or 2 large beetroots, greens/tops included

1 tbsp olive oil

salt and pepper

1 bunch of Swiss chard, finely chopped

1 lemon, juiced

200g millet

4 spring/green onions, finely chopped

a large handful of fresh dill, finely chopped

1 apple, finely sliced into slivers

6 fresh figs, quartered

2 heaped tbsp sunflower seeds, lightly toasted

2 heaped tbsp sesame seeds, lightly toasted

For the dressing

4 tbsp tahini

1 lemon, juiced, ½ zested

½ tbsp apple cider vinegar

2 tbsp either coconut aminos or soy sauce/ tamari

1 tbsp pure maple syrup

1 heaped tbsp wholegrain mustard

a large handful of fresh dill

2 cloves of garlic, crushed or finely chopped

salt and pepper

through a fine sieve and add the cooked millet to the bowl of beetroot tops, greens and chard.

Add the green onions, chopped dill, apple, half the fig quarters, and half the sunflower and sesame seeds. Season with salt and pepper and gently mix to combine.

Once cooked, remove your beetroots from the oven and set aside to cool slightly.

To make the dressing, simply whisk together the tahini, lemon juice and zest, vinegar, coconut aminos/soy sauce, maple syrup, mustard, fresh dill and garlic. Season with salt and pepper. If your dressing is a little thick, add a dash of water. You can do this in a blender for a smoother consistency if you like, but I like mine a little more rustic.

Remove any overly charred areas of skin from the beetroots and chuck it on your compost. Chop the beetroots into bite-size pieces and add to the salad. Pour over three-quarters of the dressing and gently mix, coating everything nicely.

To serve, transfer to a salad bowl or dish and serve with the extra slices of figs, toasted seeds and a drizzle more dressing.

Waste tips:

This is a great way not only to get in some extra nutrients from the greens, but to use otherwise discarded parts of the vegetable. You can sauté the tops in a little oil to remove any bitterness, and they work great as a side like that, with salt and pepper and a dash of lemon. You could use dried figs or another dried fruit here if you don't have any fresh figs. If you're making this in a different season, stone fruits are also great. I love having this dish as a side with some kind of freshly baked bread or flatbread, adding a dollop of pesto or harissa on the side, occasionally some hummus for additional protein. Feel free to swap the grain for what you have in or prefer. This dressing is one of my favourites, and I often make a bigger batch of it, storing it in the fridge and adding it to salads when I fancy.

Inspired by my time spent in Sri Lanka, here's something a little less traditional but using ingredients that are very accessible there and indeed all over the world. Gram flour, also known as chickpea flour, is such a great flour to work with, especially for flatbreads. I first discovered it in Sri Lanka and have been hooked ever since. The flatbreads themselves have lots of spices to help bring out the flavours, and are paired with one of the finest autumnal vegetables, in my opinion: the pumpkin. The quick pickles will become a fridge favourite – I like to make a huge batch and love knowing that they are there ready, the perfect condiment for a dish like this.

Serves approx. 2

BEETROOT AND GRAM FLOUR FLATBREADS

w/ mashed pumpkin and quick pickles

To make the pickles, put your grated chosen vegetable into a bowl and add the sliced onion. Pour over enough vinegar to submerge the vegetables, leaving about ½ cm of liquid above, usually a couple of tablespoons. Add the sugar, coriander seeds, cumin seeds, salt and a pinch of pepper. Mix well to combine, then place in the fridge while you make the rest.

For the pumpkin, bring a pan of salted water to the boil. Add the cubed pumpkin and cook until tender, about 8–10 minutes. You could also steam this if you wish. Once cooked, drain and put back into the pan. Add the tahini, lime juice and zest, 1 tablespoon of soy sauce, 1 teaspoon of curry powder, and salt and pepper to taste. Using a fork, roughly mash the pumpkin down, mixing it with the other ingredients. I like this to be chunky and rustic, but feel free to mash more if you wish. Taste and add any extra soy, curry powder, salt and pepper if necessary. Cover while you make your flatbreads.

Put your grated beetroot, onion, gram flour, cumin seeds, coriander seeds, fennel seeds and salt and pepper into a

For the quick pickles

- 1 small cucumber/ 2 daikon radishes/1 large carrot, grated, the whole vegetable
- 1 small red onion, thinly sliced
- apple cider or white wine vinegar (or a combination), enough to submerge the vegetables
- approx. 1 tsp sugar of choice (coconut, palm, raw, etc.)
- 1 tsp coriander seeds
- 1 tsp cumin seeds
- a hefty pinch of salt
- a pinch of pepper

For the mashed pumpkin

- approx. 300g pumpkin, cut into bite-size pieces
- 2 heaped tbsp tahini
- 2 limes, juiced, plus a dash of zest
- 1–2 tsp soy sauce
- 1–2 tsp curry powder
- salt and pepper

»

bowl and mix to combine. Slowly add the water and stir until you have a smooth batter – you don't want any lumps of flour left. If your mixture is a little dry or thick, add a dash more water.

Put the coconut oil into a pan over a low-medium heat. Once hot, add equal ladlefuls of the batter to the pan. You can do several at a time or just one larger one, depending on the size of your pan. I like to make mine about ½–1cm thick, spreading the batter evenly as I pour. Cook each side for about 3–4 minutes, until a few bubbles start to appear and the bottom goes crispy and browns slightly but is not too dark. Flip and repeat until you have used all the batter.

To serve, quickly reheat your pumpkin mixture until it reaches the desired temperature. Place your flatbreads on a plate and add a few dollops of the pumpkin mash in the centre. Add a couple of teaspoons of pickles on top (as much as you desire) and sprinkle over some fresh herbs. Season with salt and pepper and enjoy. Depending on how big your flatbreads are or how loaded you've made them, you could roll or fold them as you wish, or eat taco style.

For the flatbreads

1 small beetroot, grated, skin on

1 small red onion, finely chopped

120g gram flour (chickpea flour)

1 tsp cumin seeds

1 tsp coriander seeds

¼ tsp fennel seeds

salt and pepper

190–250ml water

coconut oil, for frying

fresh herbs of choice, finely chopped, to garnish

Waste tips:

This recipe is extremely adaptable. You have a lot of vegetable options with the pickles already, but feel free to try other vegetables if you're in a different season: courgettes are great, or even just onions on their own. I love a salty, vinegary kick to most of my meals, so these are perfect to make and keep in the fridge. The same goes for the flatbread – you could grate carrot into it, sweet potato, radish, etc. . . . Adding a handful of freshly chopped herbs to the flatbread batter is also really nice and gives a lovely aroma. OK, OK, and the mash is adaptable too: use whichever pumpkin or squash you desire, or try potatoes if you don't have access to the others. It's really handy to have a reliable base of a recipe and be able to chop and change the fresh produce that goes into it.

Continuing my love affair with using both the beetroot and its tops, here's a recipe which is always a favourite in my house, along with a chimichurri like no other. If my boyfriend sees beetroots in the fridge, this recipe will no doubt come up in conversation. The whole roasted garlic creates an almost buttery consistency, so when smashed with the roasted beetroot and beans, it's a little like a chunky, deconstructed hummus.

Serves approx.
2–3

CHUNKY BEETROOT AND WHITE BEAN TACOS

w/ a beet green and caper chimichurri

Preheat your oven to approx. 200°C fan.

Wash and scrub your beetroots well, making sure to remove any dirt/soil. Remove the tops from the beetroots and place to one side.

Chop the beetroot into roughly bite-size pieces and place on a roasting tray along with the red onion and garlic. Season with salt and pepper and a drizzle of olive oil. Toss to combine and coat well, then put into the oven and roast for about 35–40 minutes.

Drain the beans and rinse thoroughly, then put them into a bowl with the lime juice and zest, tahini, chilli flakes and paprika, and season with salt and pepper. Add the nutritional yeast if using, then, using either a masher or a fork, begin to mash the bean mix until it's broken down and rough.

Once your beetroot has roasted, remove the garlic and place to one side. Add the beetroot and onion, plus any juice/oil left in the tray, to the beans. Squeeze out the garlic cloves from the bulbs and then mash and mix, combining well. Cover and set aside.

Now make your taco dough. Put the flour into a bowl, add the salt and stir. Add the oil, then slowly add the water. Knead into a dough, adding more water when needed and

For the beetroot filling

4 small or 2 large beetroots, washed thoroughly, leaves to be used below

1 red onion, cut into eighths

1 bulb of garlic, cut in half widthways

salt and pepper

olive oil, for roasting

1 × 400g tin of white beans, drained and rinsed thoroughly

2 limes or 1 large lemon, juiced, plus a dash of zest

2 heaped tbsp tahini

a pinch of dried chilli flakes

1–2 tsp smoked paprika

3 heaped tbsp nutritional yeast

sesame seeds, to garnish

For the tacos (makes approx. 8–10 smallish tacos, or fewer if you want to go slightly bigger)

240g plain flour, plus extra for rolling

½ tsp salt

2 tablespoons extra virgin olive oil, plus extra for cooking

190ml water

»

a little extra flour if your mixture is too wet. Set aside to rest for 8 minutes.

To make the chimichurri, put the chopped parsley, beetroot tops, capers, garlic, olive oil, apple cider vinegar, lemon juice and zest, chilli and salt and pepper into a blender and blitz until it forms a paste, seasoning with more salt and pepper if needed and adding a little extra olive oil if it's too dry. Remove from the blender and add between a quarter and a half of this mix to the bowl of beans and beetroot, mixing to combine. Put the rest of the paste to one side or into the fridge, ready for the tacos.

To make your tacos, flour a surface, your hands and a rolling pin. Split the dough into equal parts – you will usually make around 8 tacos, and the size will vary. Making sure your hands are floured, roll each piece of dough into a ball. Then, using the rolling pin on the floured surface, roll out to flatten. You can make them as thick and wide as you desire – the cooking time will just vary slightly.

Once you have made your tacos, lightly brush a pan with olive oil. Heat it up until it's nice and hot. Add the tacos (however many you can fit in at a time) and allow them to cook for about 2 minutes or so. You'll notice they start to puff or rise and brown underneath – flip them over at this point to cook the other side. Repeat until all your tacos are made, placing them on a plate when they are done.

Prepare any additional toppings as above, and put them into a little bowl ready for assembling/eating!

To assemble, take a taco from the plate and spread a nice layer of chimichurri over the base. Add about 2 tablespoons or so of the beetroot/bean mix, followed by any extra toppings you like, a drizzle of tahini and some salt and pepper. The eating part, well . . . that's up to you.

For the chimichurri
(if your beetroots have already had their greens removed, replace them with extra parsley or another herb of choice – coriander also works well, and dill or even basil)

---

2 large handfuls of fresh parsley, finely chopped, stalks included

beetroot tops from the filling above, or approx. 1 large handful more of herbs

2 heaped tbsp capers, drained

2 cloves of garlic, crushed or finely chopped

2–3 tablespoons extra virgin olive oil

1 teaspoon apple cider vinegar

1 lemon, juiced, plus a dash of zest (or 2 limes)

a pinch of chilli flakes

salt and pepper

Optional toppings
---

finely chopped tomatoes

sliced avocado

tahini, to drizzle

extra fresh herbs

sesame seeds

salt and pepper

Once you start making your own gnocchi, you'll never go back. It's a lot easier than you think, and adding beetroot to the mix creates the most amazing shade of deep pink. I'm keeping it simple in this recipe and serving it simply with kale pesto; it's a great one for a date night if you want to show off a little, I always think!

Serves 3–4

BEETROOT GNOCCHI

w/ kale pesto

Preheat your oven to 200°C fan. First make the pesto. Steam the kale for around 5–6 minutes, until it is a vibrant green and wilted. Remove from the heat and run it under a cold tap to stop the cooking process. Drain and allow to cool to room temperature or colder. Once cold enough, roughly chop.

Put the walnuts, garlic, fresh basil, lemon juice and zest and olive oil into a blender and blitz to a rough paste. Go ahead and add the chopped kale, nutritional yeast, chilli flakes and a hefty pinch of salt and pepper. Blitz again until the mix starts to form a smoother texture. If you want it a little looser, add a dash more olive oil. Test and add more salt and pepper if necessary. Transfer to a jar and set aside while you make your gnocchi.

Scrub and wash your potatoes and beetroots well. Lightly prick them with a sharp knife around the whole surface, then roast them in the oven, whole, for about 50–60 minutes. The timing will vary depending on their size, but you can check by slotting in a sharp knife to see if the insides have cooked through. The skins will be nice and crispy.

Once cooked, remove from the oven and leave until cool enough to touch. Slice the potatoes and beetroots in half, putting the beetroots to one side. Take your potatoes and one by one start scooping out the soft flesh (as close to the skin as possible) with a spoon, placing it in a bowl. Repeat

For the pesto (makes 10–12 servings)

approx. 200g kale (cavolo nero or any other dark leafy green will also work), stalks included

150g walnuts

2 cloves of garlic, crushed or finely chopped

2 large handfuls of fresh basil

2 lemons, both juiced, 1 zested

125–150ml olive oil

6–8 heaped tbsp nutritional yeast

a pinch of dried chilli flakes

salt and pepper

For the gnocchi (serves 3–4)

approx. 500g russet or King Edward potatoes

approx. 500g beetroots

1–2 tbsp olive oil

1½ tsp salt

240–360g plain flour, plus extra as needed and for dusting

until you have done this with all of the potatoes. Put the skins to one side, as we will use them later. Using a masher or ricer if you have one, mash the potatoes, removing any lumps.

The beetroot flesh is a little different, and it will need to be blended. Chop them roughly, then put them into a blender/processor and blend on high until smooth. I recommend adding a bit of oil, about a tablespoon, to help the beetroots to blend. This may take a few rounds, scraping down the sides if necessary. Once smooth, add to the mashed potatoes.

Add the salt and the other tablespoon of olive oil to the mashed vegetables and mix well. Slowly start adding the flour, working the mix into a dough. Make sure you have floured your hands to prevent sticking. If the mixture is a little sticky, go ahead and add a bit more flour, or a tad more oil if it is too dry. You want the dough to be soft but not sticky. It will form a nice dough that is pliable; it's neither hard nor soft, not dry or sticky.

Flour a surface and divide the dough into 4 equal pieces. Roll each one into a rope shape, 2–2.5cm in diameter. Using a sharp knife, cut the dough into approx. 2.5cm pieces. Use a fork to make small dents on the top and bottom of each piece.

Before you cook the gnocchi, quickly crisp up your potato skins. Roughly chop them, then toss them into a pan with a dash of olive oil, salt and pepper. Fry until crispy, placing them on kitchen paper to allow any excess oil to drain off.

To cook, bring a large pan of water to the boil. In batches, place the gnocchi in the boiling water, allowing them to cook for a couple of minutes. Timings will vary, but the gnocchi are cooked once they float to the top. It's important to do this in batches to prevent the gnocchi over-cooking and sticking together. Once cooked, remove and place on a tea towel or cloth to drain any liquid.

Heat a large pan with a dash of oil until hot. Add the gnocchi (making sure they don't still stick to

»

each other), crisping them up on each side for a few minutes or so. You may have to do this in batches. You can boil and crisp at the same time if you like – as each batch of gnocchi is boiled, let them dry, then crisp them up in the pan, repeating until you've cooked all of your dough.

Serve the gnocchi into bowls. Add a couple of dollops of pesto to each one, either stirring it through or leaving it as is, then sprinkle over the crispy skins, seasoning with any extra salt and pepper. You can also do this in one big pot, mixing the pesto well with the gnocchi and sprinkling the crispy skins on top.

Waste tips:

The pesto will last in the fridge for about a week, with a little olive oil on top to keep it moist. It can also be made with other vegetables. You can freeze the gnocchi in their uncooked form for around a month. Chop the dough into 2.5cm pieces and sprinkle with a little extra flour to prevent them sticking together. To cook, thaw the gnocchi until soft all the way through, then boil as above and lightly fry to crisp up.

In case you didn't love hummus enough already, here's one more, blended thick with roasted beets, gooey and almost caramelized shallots, and lots of caraway for good measure. The soy-glazed mushrooms add a lovely umami aroma, helping to complement the other flavours. I want to really celebrate the use of beetroot in the recipe, and by now you know about my love of hummus, so what better way than to combine the two?

ROASTED BEETROOT, CARAWAY AND SHALLOT HUMMUS

w/ soy-glazed mushroom topping

Preheat your oven to 200°C fan. Place your beetroot halves and shallots, whole, on some pieces of foil with the olive oil and a pinch of salt. Wrap them up to create little foil packets, making sure they are firmly closed. Roast in the oven for about 45–55 minutes. The shallots will cook quicker than the beetroots but will start to caramelize, becoming very soft on the inside. When cooked, remove from the oven and put to one side to cool.

Once cooled, squeeze the shallots out of their skins if they haven't completely fallen out already, composting the skins. Roughly chop with the beetroots and transfer both to a blender, along with any juice or residue left in the foil packets.

Add the tahini, lemon juice and zest, cumin seeds, caraway seeds, oregano and garlic to the blender and season with salt and pepper. Begin to blend, slowly adding the water until you reach the desired consistency. Feel free to add more water than stated if too thick, or olive oil if you wish. Transfer to a bowl and put into the fridge while you make the topping.

Put the sliced mushrooms into a shallow pan, along with the soy sauce or tamari, chilli flakes, lime juice and zest

For the hummus

2 large beetroots, washed thoroughly, halved (save the tops, see note below)

4 large shallots

1 tbsp olive oil

salt and pepper

4 heaped tablespoons tahini

1 large lemon, juiced, plus a dash of zest

1 tsp cumin seeds, toasted

2 tsp caraway seeds, toasted

1 tsp dried oregano/mixed dried herbs

2–3 cloves of garlic, crushed or finely chopped

approx. 65ml water

For the soy-glazed mushrooms

200g mushrooms (button, chestnut, etc.), sliced approx. 5mm thick

4 tablespoons soy sauce or tamari

a pinch of dried chilli flakes

1 lime, juiced, plus a dash of zest

salt and pepper

»

and a seasoning of salt and pepper. On a very low heat, simmer until the mushrooms start to caramelize and begin to 'shrivel' and become nice and tender.

Once cooked, remove the mushrooms from the pan, along with their juices, and set aside to cool to room temperature or below.

To serve, take the hummus from the fridge and top with the soy-glazed mushrooms and any additional toppings you desire. Add a sprinkle of toasted seeds, a little drizzle of olive oil, and of course any extra seasoning to taste.

To serve (all optional)

a handful of sesame/pumpkin/sunflower seeds, toasted

olive oil, to drizzle

fresh herbs of choice, roughly chopped

fresh bread/crackers or crudités of choice

Waste tips:

This recipe came about initially because I'd run out of chickpeas and other beans but I desperately wanted hummus – but then I spotted a couple of beetroots in the basket . . . The texture is slightly different, a little nuttier and more rustic but a really great alternative. You could, of course, add some pulses to the mix to achieve a more traditional hummus consistency. You can be quite creative with the quantities and types of spices here too, or add fresh herbs as you go. The hummus will keep in the fridge for about 5 days in an airtight container. The mushrooms double up as a great addition to many Asian recipes: a soup, a ramen, a broth, noodles. You could make the Asian stock from the basics section (see page 352), adding the mushrooms, a handful of greens and some noodles to serve. This vibrant dip, loaded with a variety of textures and flavours, is a great one to surprise guests with. Don't forget to save the beetroot tops. Use them for another recipe or store them in the fridge in a damp towel, then chop them into a salad or toss into a stew when in need of some extra greens. Any bits of onion or garlic you don't use when chopping, add to your freezer stock. See page 352 for more details.

parsnips

A clever little root vegetable, with an almost 'spiced' flavour, tones of cinnamon and nutmeg, and a cake-like texture when roasted. Parsnips are part of the parsley and celery family, which is where their subtle taste of both comes from. You'll usually see them without their tops/ leaves, which if cooked and used in the right way can be eaten in small doses. Everyone loves parsley, right? So why not the parsnip tops? I like to think of parsnips as posh carrots, or even herby potatoes: a little more grown-up and nuttier and richer in flavour. They are much less starchy than a potato and not as sweet as a carrot, so I suppose they sit somewhere in between. I remember seeing them on a menu when I was a kid, in chip form to be precise, which of course enticed me. While my parents were a little shocked at me choosing them over regular potatoes, I was nonetheless very smug at ordering such a 'grown-up' item. Nowadays, I love recreating that dish, partly as a memory, roasting them in the oven with a small amount of oil to help them crisp up entirely, a pinch of salt, a sprinkling of dried or fresh herbs, it's a real good 'un. A perfectly salted chip with a moist and 'cakey' inside . . . my mouth is watering just thinking of them.

Parsley roots are almost identical in texture and taste to parsnips, usually sitting next to them at markets when in season. They serve the same purpose, in my opinion, but can hold an even stronger flavour, so you may come across these beauties when on the hunt for parsnips – and either will of course work. Like pumpkin, parsnips truly remind me of autumn – perhaps it's those spice-like flavours and the common association of root veg with the season.

Waste tips:

As I said opposite, parsnips are the grown-up carrot (or perhaps grown-up French fry!), great to use instead of carrots, or even alongside, since often a combination of root vegetables is better than when they're cooked on their own. You get a little bit of everything you want that way. They're great to add to a regular potato mash, adding a herby hit (see page 211 for a real rooty version), and even for chucking into salads to bulk them out. I always keep my parsnips in the fridge, as it helps them keep a little longer. They can get soft quite quickly and may start to look a little sad, but they are still just as good to use and perfect in that week-night roast-whatever-you-have kinda dish.

Simple and effective, this chunky-style pesto can be served in any which way over these roasted parsnips. You can blitz the pesto or chop the ingredients with a sharp knife to reach a beautifully rustic version. I love these as a side on colder days in autumn, standing out among a veg-heavy spread.

Serves approx. 6–8 as a side

ROASTED PARSNIPS

w/ kale pesto

Preheat your oven to 200°C fan. Place your parsnips on a baking tray with the two garlic halves, olive oil and chilli. Season with salt and pepper and toss well to combine, making sure the parsnips are coated, then roast for about 30–40 minutes. You want them to be golden and slightly crispy on the outside, soft and 'cake-like' on the inside.

Meanwhile, make the pesto. Steam the kale for around 5–6 minutes, until it's a vibrant green and wilted. Remove from the heat and run it under a cold tap to stop the cooking process. Drain and allow to cool to room temperature or colder. Once cold enough, roughly chop.

Put the walnuts, garlic, fresh basil, lemon juice and zest and olive oil into a blender and blitz until you have a rough paste. Go ahead and add the chopped kale, nutritional yeast, chilli flakes and a hefty pinch of salt and pepper. Blitz again until the mix starts to form a smoother texture. If you want it a little looser, add a dash more olive oil. Taste and season if necessary.

Once your parsnips are almost ready, about 10 minutes or so to go, add a few tablespoons of the pesto, enough to cover the parsnips. Make sure they are coated, then continue to cook for the rest of the time. The pesto will turn slightly crispy as the parsnips cook.

To serve, spread a layer of pesto on a plate, followed by some yoghurt, and pile the parsnips on top. Best served hot.

1kg parsnips, washed thoroughly, quartered lengthways

1 bulb of garlic, sliced in half widthways, skin on

2–4 tbsp olive oil

1 small green chilli, seeds removed, finely chopped

salt and pepper

For the pesto

approx. 200g kale (cavolo nero or any other dark leafy green), stalks included

150g walnuts

2 cloves of garlic, crushed or finely chopped

2 large handfuls of fresh basil

2 lemons, both juiced, 1 zested

125–250ml olive oil

6–8 heaped tbsp nutritional yeast

a pinch of dried chilli flakes

salt and pepper

To serve

plant-based yoghurt of choice (see coconut yoghurt, page 284)

Waste tips:

I love adapting this recipe by adding a turnip or two, and a swede (my absolute favourite: full of flavour, slightly nutty, with a radishy aftertaste), to jazz up a Sunday roast, or as a side to a big leafy salad. Slice up and cook with the parsnips, as they take a similar time. This recipe also works well served simply with a grain of choice. It's super hearty and fulfilling.

I ate a few nut roasts while growing up, but none stood out to me. We didn't have 'Sunday roasts' that often, and if we did, my main priority was getting as much bread sauce on to my steamed carrots as possible. It was when I spent my first Christmas in Australia that our family friend Debbie rustled up a nut roast for the lunch spread, and it was everything a nut roast should be: textured, flavoursome, earthy but subtly sweet, moist from the parsnips . . . need I go on? In light of that memory, I couldn't help but re-create and adapt! This one's for you, Debbie!

PARSNIP NUT ROAST

Preheat your oven to 200°C fan. Grease a large loaf tin.

Put your parsnips on a baking tray and roast them dry for about 30–35 minutes, until they are browned slightly and soft on the inside. Roasting them dry prevents them losing any moisture. Remove from the oven and allow to cool. Once cooled, mash well and place to one side while you make the rest of your nut roast.

In a small bowl, combine your ground flax with the 8 tablespoons of water, creating a gloopyish paste. Put into the fridge to firm up.

In a frying pan, heat the olive oil over a low heat and sauté the onion until slightly translucent and fragrant. Add the garlic and sage leaves and continue to sauté until they start to slightly brown. Add the nutmeg and mushrooms plus a dash of water and continue to cook a little, stirring well. Season with a generous amount of salt and pepper.

Stir in the ground nuts, rosemary, thyme, miso paste, breadcrumbs, 2 tablespoons of wholemeal flour, the nutritional yeast and your flax mixture. Add the mashed parsnips and combine well, using your hands. Season again here if necessary. If your mixture is still a little wet, add the other 2 tablespoons of flour.

400g parsnips, thoroughly washed, roughly chopped, skins on

3 tbsp ground flax

8 tbsp water

1 tbsp olive oil

1 white or brown onion, finely chopped

4 cloves of garlic, crushed or finely chopped

approx. 6 fresh sage leaves, roughly chopped

½–1 tsp grated nutmeg

approx. 200g mushrooms, minced in a processor

salt and pepper

180g either cashews, almonds, or a combination (you could also use hazelnuts for a twist), ground in a processor

2 tsp fresh rosemary sprigs, 1 tsp if dried

2 tsp fresh thyme leaves, 1 tsp if dried

2 tsp miso paste

approx. 140g breadcrumbs (any kind, use leftover/stale bread)

2–4 tbsp wholemeal flour

3 tbsp nutritional yeast

»

Transfer the mixture to your loaf tin and pack it down tightly. Roast, on a low/middle rack, for about 30 minutes, checking it halfway through the cooking time. You want the top to become brown and crispy and the loaf to cook through. You can test it with a knife, making sure the mixture is not too loose.

Once cooked, remove from the oven and allow to cool in the tin for about 5 minutes, then place a serving plate over the tin and flip, giving the tin a little shake to help the nut roast fall out.

Serve with your desired sides, as part of a roast dinner, with fresh greens, grains, etc. (see page 293 for the ultimate mushroom gravy).

Waste tips:

Nut roasts are great fridge or freezer keepers. I often make a whole loaf knowing I can save it for another day to pair with other leftovers, or just make it ahead of time to serve with other 'roasted' items. There is a similar recipe for a chestnut version on page 278 – it's very adaptable. You could change things up with the parsnips – for example, try adding some carrot, or potato, swede, any vegetables of a similar texture. It's nice to have a combination of flavours and textures within the nut roast, and an orange vegetable of course adds great colour. Feel free to use any other flour you like or have in. I'd recommend using a coarser flour and avoiding finer ones such as coconut or buckwheat – they will still work, you may just need a tad more. I've also been known to add caramelized onions to this dish, either stirred in or on top, which adds a really great depth. Simply simmer a sliced onion in balsamic vinegar, with a dash of salt and sugar, and keep going until it becomes lovely and sticky.

You can't go wrong with a big batch of vegetables roasted to perfection, charred slightly on the outside, and those roots all soft on the inside. You don't need to think too much about this one – it can easily be adapted and is a great way to use up produce from your fridge for a quick weeknight meal.

Serves approx. 4

EVERYDAY ROASTED VEGGIES, FRESH HERBS AND TOASTED NUTS

Preheat your oven to 200°C fan. Bring a large pot of salted water to the boil, add your chosen grain, bring back to the boil, then lower to a simmer. Simmer for the time given on the packet instructions for the grain to cook through and become fluffy. Drain, then put back into the pot with a drizzle of olive oil to prevent sticking.

Place the chopped potato, pumpkin/squash, carrots and parsnips on a roasting tray. Drizzle 2 tablespoons of olive oil over them and mix to coat. Season with salt and pepper, then pop them into the oven and roast for about 20–25 minutes. They should be starting to become slightly tender by this point.

Remove from the oven, add the broccoli/cauliflower florets and mushrooms and mix. Drizzle over the other 2 tablespoons of olive oil if the vegetables are looking slightly dry. Add the sage leaves, dried oregano, fresh thyme and rosemary sprigs, crushed garlic cloves and dried chilli. Season again with salt and pepper, making sure to mix well to coat everything nicely and spread the herbs out evenly.

Roast for a further 15–20 minutes, until all the vegetables are tender and golden brown – some of them may be crispier than others.

To serve, portion up the vegetables along with your chosen grain, add a sprinkle of toasted nuts and season with salt and pepper to taste.

approx. 150–200g grain of choice (rice, millet, barley, etc.)

1 medium to large potato of choice (sweet, baking, red, etc.), chopped

½ small pumpkin/ squash, chopped

2 carrots, cut into thick slices

2 parsnips, cut into thick slices

2–4 tbsp olive oil

salt and pepper

½ a small broccoli/ cauliflower, cut into florets

200g mushrooms, halved

2–4 fresh sage leaves, chopped

2–4 tsp dried oregano

a few sprigs of fresh thyme and rosemary

1 bulb of garlic, cloves separated, crushed with the back of a knife, skins on and still relatively whole

a pinch of dried chilli flakes

small handful of nuts (pine nuts, almonds, cashews, hazelnuts, or a combination), lightly toasted, crushed

Waste tips:

This recipe can suit any season by varying the types of vegetables used and the grain. The herbs make the dish feel cosy, but use what you have and if you don't have fresh, simply use dried. You could add onions (red/ white/shallots) to roast in this dish. I love how they caramelize and add such flavour.

A combination of autumnal roots, spiced lightly with Dijon mustard and made ever so creamy with plant-based milk. The savoury granola is similar to a dukkha and adds a crunchy texture and a burst of flavour to jazz things up!

Serves approx. 6–8 as a side

GARLICKY PARSNIP, POTATO AND CELERIAC MASH, SAVOURY GRANOLA

Preheat your oven to 180°C fan. To make the granola, combine your oats, pumpkin seeds, crushed almonds, sesame seeds, coriander seeds, cumin seeds, oregano, garlic powder and nutritional yeast in a mixing bowl. Slowly add the olive oil and a good pinch of salt and pepper. Stir until it is 'wet' enough to stick to your hands.

Spread the mixture evenly on a baking tray, patting it down slightly as you go. Bake for 12–15 minutes, giving it a jiggle halfway through. It'll be golden and slightly crispy on top. Keep an eye on it, as the time will vary depending on your oven. Once baked, remove and allow to cool completely before breaking it up ready to sprinkle. (It will keep in a jar for a couple of weeks, a perfect topper for salads, vegetables, savoury pancakes or other breakfasts.)

Bring a large pot of salted water to the boil. Carefully add the potatoes, parsnips and celeriac and bring back to the boil, then lower to a rolling simmer and cook for about 12–15 minutes. Once all the vegetables are soft, remove from the heat and drain. Put back into the pot and add the olive oil, garlic, coriander seeds, mustard, 190ml of plant-based milk, paprika and nutmeg (start with the smaller amount of paprika and nutmeg and add according to taste). Season with salt and pepper and begin to mash with a masher. Go ahead and gradually add the rest of the milk if it is a little dry, seasoning again if necessary.

Serve up your desired amount of mash and sprinkle on the savoury granola, followed by a drizzle of olive oil. I love adding a drizzle of balsamic vinegar here too.

For the granola (makes extra)

45g jumbo oats (or normal are fine)

35g pumpkin seeds

35g almonds, lightly crushed

2 tbsp sesame seeds

2 tsp each of coriander seeds, cumin seeds and dried oregano

1–2 tsp garlic powder

1–2 tbsp nutritional yeast

4–6 tbsp olive oil

salt and pepper

For the mash

2 large russet or King Edward potatoes, washed thoroughly, quartered

3 medium/large parsnips, washed thoroughly, quartered

1 medium celeriac, chopped smaller than the potatoes

1 tbsp olive oil

5 cloves of garlic

1 tsp coriander seeds

2 heaped tbsp Dijon mustard

190–250ml plant-based milk

½–1 tsp smoked paprika

½–1 tsp ground nutmeg

salt and pepper

olive oil and/or balsamic vinegar, to serve

Waste tips:

This mash doubles up as a pie topper. You can vary the root veg used – try sweet potatoes, carrots, swede, etc.

kale

OK, so we all know we should eat our greens, but kale, I really would eat that any or every day of the week. I am that kind of gal, I love my greens, always have and always will. Without a doubt, if my mum ever asked, 'A side of salad with dinner?' or 'Broccoli?' it would be a firm yes. Like a lot of vegetables, kale comes in many shapes and sizes. Curly, lacinato (one of my favourites, similar to cavolo nero), red Russian, baby kale, they all serve a purpose. Kale is the ultimate autumn/winter green, in my opinion, delicious fresh or wilted into something a little warmer. It's a pet hate of mine that eating the stalks is often considered a no-go; sure, they're a little more bitter, but cooked or massaged with the rest of the dish, they are great and hold a lot of the nutrients that kale is so famous for. Part of the brassica family, types of kale vary in their silky texture and 'cabbagey' mustard-like taste.

Waste tips:

You'll see in this chapter that kale appears a whole lot of times, but with the climate now, it also crosses over into other seasons. Cavolo nero starts to appear as early as May, so is now known as more of a summer vegetable, curly kale being similar. Using the stalks is a great technique or habit to pick up, whether you toss them in with the rest or lightly fry them with seasonings of choice and use them as a topper. I almost always have some form of dark leafy green in the fridge, which I've washed and rinsed well prior to refrigeration, kept in a tea towel or Tupperware, and occasionally, if I'm feeling particularly prepared, pre-chopped so it's ready to use when I want.

For those who know me, this is the 'Soph' salad. It's my go-to, sometimes without barley if having it as a side, but I'm all for the salad-with-supper vibe. Massaging the kale is not only a therapeutic task, but helps to break it down, making it easier to digest but still keeping its raw freshness. The kale is paired with some crunch, some sweetness and a mighty grain!

MASSAGED KALE SALAD

w/ toasted walnuts, blackberries, barley

Bring a large pot of salted water to the boil and add the barley. Bring back to the boil, then allow to simmer and cook until tender, about 35–40 minutes. Once cooked, drain and set aside to cool.

Put your roughly chopped kale and leeks into a bowl. Add a good pinch of salt, 2 tablespoons of olive oil, the juice of 1 lemon and the zest. Using your hands, begin to massage the ingredients in the bowl, wilting the kale and removing the bitterness from it, about 3–4 minutes. The stalks will be a little tougher but add a nice texture to the salad.

Add the garlic, mustard and maple syrup and season again with salt and pepper. Massage once again to combine and coat the ingredients. Add the blackberries, apple or pear and the cooked barley. Carefully mix, trying not to squash the blackberries too much, adding the remainder of the lemon juice to loosen. Add half the walnuts and mix once more.

Serve sprinkled with the remaining walnuts and the nutritional yeast.

approx. 270g barley, dried, washed and rinsed thoroughly

1 large bunch of kale (cavolo nero is also good), washed thoroughly, roughly chopped

1 large leek, washed thoroughly, sliced in half lengthways, then finely chopped

salt and pepper

2 tbsp olive oil

1–1½ lemons, all juiced, ½ zested

2 cloves of garlic, crushed or finely chopped

1–2 tbsp Dijon mustard

1 tbsp pure maple syrup

approx. 125g fresh blackberries

1 small apple or pear

40g walnuts, lightly toasted

2–4 tbsp nutritional yeast (optional), to serve

Waste tips:

This is a great base recipe to vary with any additions you want. Leftover roasted veggies are great alongside or tossed in, and you could use any other onion, massaging it in replacement for the leek. The salad will keep in the fridge for a few days, continuing to marinate and soften in the oil, lemon and mustard. You could also heat it up quickly in a pan if you want something warming.

A few years back, my family got really into making a cavolo nero sauce for a quick midweek spaghetti dinner. I tried it a handful of times and loved the vibrancy so I've re-created my own. A pinch of chilli and lemon zest really brings it to life.

LAZY DAY PASTA AND GARLIC KALE SAUCE

Bring a pan of salted water to the boil. Add your chopped kale and cook for 5–7 minutes, until wilted and cooked through. You can also steam it. Once cooked, drain and blanch in cold water briefly to stop the cooking process.

Transfer the kale to a blender and add your chopped shallot/onion, the 4 crushed or finely chopped cloves of garlic, the olive oil, nutritional yeast, mustard, white wine, chilli flakes, lemon juice and zest. Season with salt and pepper and blend until you have a relatively smooth but thick sauce mixture. You can add water to loosen if necessary. Season to taste, then pop to one side while you make the rest of the dish.

Bring a large pot of salted water to the boil and add your desired pasta. Cook until al dente, about 10–12 minutes. Drain, then put back into the pot and cover.

While your pasta is cooking, heat up about 1 tablespoon of olive oil in a saucepan. Once hot, add the 2 sliced cloves of garlic and sauté until golden and fragrant. Make sure you stir frequently to prevent them burning.

Add your sliced mushrooms to the garlic and sweat until soft. You can add a dash more olive oil or water to the pan if it is a little dry. Season with salt and pepper. The mushrooms will sweat and wilt very quickly. Go ahead, pour in your kale sauce and heat up over a low heat, again stirring frequently. Heat until cooked through.

Pour the sauce over the pasta in the pot and stir well. You can do this over a low heat if your pasta has cooled too much. Season with extra salt and pepper, chilli flakes and olive oil to taste. Dish up accordingly and enjoy!

1 large bunch of kale, any variety, roughly chopped (cavolo nero is also great)

1 large shallot/ white onion, finely chopped

6 cloves of garlic: 4 crushed or finely chopped, 2 thinly sliced

2–4 tbsp olive oil

2–4 tbsp nutritional yeast

2 tbsp Dijon mustard

4 tbsp white wine

1 tsp dried chilli flakes

1 lemon, juiced, plus a dash of zest

salt and pepper

approx. 340g dried pasta of choice (penne, macaroni, rigatoni, cannelloni, fusilli, etc.)

200g mushrooms, sliced thin

Waste tips:

Any variety of greens works well in this sauce – it's super garlicky and creamy despite having no actual 'cream' in it. The white wine makes the dish feel like a real treat, but you can omit it or try adding soy sauce/tamari or vinegar – just go in with less initially. You could also roast any leftover veggies, or try adding another vegetable to the sauce if you don't have or like mushrooms. The sauce will keep in the fridge, if you find you have extra. You could also serve it differently by dishing up the pasta first, then pouring the sauce over – it's totally up to you.

pumpkin

My love affair with pumpkin is certainly a strong one. Such glee when my dad would tell us he was roasting one to turn into soup, made simply with fresh earthy herbs and a generous swirl of yoghurt for good measure, along with some fresh crusty bread. Pumpkins come in many shapes and sizes and, depending on the climate and your whereabouts in the world, a broad variety. Pumpkins tend to be known more commonly as squash, with only the larger ones being referred to as pumpkins, from the spaghetti squash to acorn, sweet dumpling, butternut, delicata, ambercup, sugar and (my all-time favourite name) golden nugget, followed closely by the green Hubbard squash – no wonder they're associated with Hallowe'en. Pumpkin and squash varieties make great purées: simply boil with water and a pinch of salt (just enough water to submerge them) for about 12 minutes, until soft and tender, then blitz until smooth. The perfect base for a creamy pumpkin pie (or a latte of that variety, see page 233), a thick béchamel, and of course endless baking possibilities.

Waste tips:

It's a common misconception that we shouldn't eat the skin of a pumpkin/squash, but pre-cooking, you can clean the skin with a dash of apple cider vinegar, salt and warm water and that baby is just as good as the rest, in fact, dare I say it, even better? And let's not forget about the seeds inside. When scooping them out, simply place them in a bowl of warm water to soak, remove any excess or surrounding pumpkin flesh that is left on the seeds, allow to dry and then roast/toast/fry for a crunchy topping for soups, salads or, better yet, a maple spiced granola. The seeds are incredibly high in both omega-3 and omega-6 fatty acids, as well as fibre, so they make a great addition to any diet.

I could eat granola any and every day. I don't load it with sugar but focus on there being a little bit of everything in it: nuts, seeds, oats, dried fruit. The mix of jumbo and fine oats allows clusters to form when cooking, especially when focusing on the 'patting down' part of the method. A dollop of coconut yoghurt and some fresh seasonal fruit . . . I'm always up for granola!

Makes enough for a 1-litre jar

PUMPKIN SEED AND NUT GRANOLA

Preheat your oven to 180°C fan. Line a large baking tray with baking paper, or an oven mat if you have one. If you are using pumpkin seeds from fresh, make sure they have been cleaned thoroughly and are dry.

Put the pumpkin seeds, jumbo and fine oats, chopped nuts, sesame seeds and desiccated coconut into a large bowl and quickly stir to combine. In a small bowl, whisk together your maple syrup (starting with 85ml first), coconut oil, cinnamon, cardamom, turmeric, nutmeg, ginger and a hefty pinch of salt. Whisk until well combined.

Slowly pour your spiced liquid mixture on to the bowl of dry ingredients, stirring continuously to combine. You want the mixture to be slightly sticky and for some clumps to be forming. I like to do this with my hands in order to create these clumps. If the mixture is a little dry, go ahead and add the rest of the maple syrup.

Spread your mix evenly on the baking tray, patting it slightly as you go. Place in the oven on the middle shelf and bake for about 15–20 minutes, until golden brown on top. Sometimes, depending on your oven, the granola can quickly burn on top, so I recommend checking on it halfway through, giving it a little jiggle.

Once cooked, remove from the oven and allow to cool entirely, then store in an airtight container/jar.

65g pumpkin seeds (either fresh from a pumpkin or store-bought)

180g jumbo oats

90g fine oats

approx. 120g nuts of choice (cashews, almonds, hazelnuts, or a combination), roughly chopped/crushed

2 tablespoons sesame seeds

4 tbsp desiccated coconut

85–125ml pure maple syrup

2 tbsp coconut oil

1 heaped tsp ground cinnamon

1 heaped tsp ground cardamom

1 tsp ground turmeric

½ tsp grated nutmeg

½ tsp ground ginger

1–2 tsp salt

Waste tips:

You can keep this granola in a jar for a few weeks in your
cupboard, perfect for breakfast or dessert toppings, or for a
handful when you're feeling peckish. As suggested, you can use
whichever nuts you have to hand, but you could also sub for
seeds too, whatever you like. I love adding raisins, especially
golden ones, to this granola right at the end, for a little burst
of chewy sweetness. They will burn quickly when being cooked,
so if you do want to include dried fruit, add it towards the end.
This recipe calls for jumbo and fine oats, but if you only have
one or the other, just use the sub for the same amount. For
a savoury twist, simply leave out the spices mentioned – add a
dash of cayenne, dried thyme, dried oregano and some fennel
seeds, and you've got the perfect crunch to a savoury dish, on
top of vegetables or even a morning-toast option.

These are in honour of one of the best and most unbelievable falafel wraps I ever had, at a cute roadside café in Sydney. I've tried and tested many falafels in my time but nothing has quite lived up to that one. I know it's not super traditional, but I loved that they weren't deep-fried and didn't leave you with dryness in your mouth. Roasting the pumpkin allows it to keep all of its water content, ready to be whizzed up with the other ingredients in this recipe. Great with a tahini dressing, flatbreads and some pickled cabbage if you're feeling fancy!

Serves approx. 4–6 (main or side depending)

PUMPKIN AND KALE FALAFELS

Preheat the oven to around 180°C fan. Line a baking tray with paper, or a mat if you have one. If you are using a whole pumpkin, chop it in half, scoop out the 'guts' and remove the seeds, reserving them to roast. Rub the cut side of the pumpkin halves with olive oil. Sprinkle equally with salt, pepper and smoked paprika. Set the halves cut side down on your baking tray and bake for about 20–25 minutes. If you are using just one half pumpkin, the same method applies. You want the inside to be nice and tender, and if you insert a knife it should be easily removed. Once cooked, set aside to cool.

To make the falafel, put about 350g of the maize flour or cornflour into a blender/processor along with the chickpeas, onion, garlic, oregano and coriander. Blitz for a few moments to grind this down a little to a wettish crumb consistency.

Roughly chop your cooked pumpkin (I love to leave the skins on, but you can remove and compost them if you wish) and add to the blender/processor, followed by the vinegar, olive oil, maple syrup and the kale. Season with salt and pepper to taste. Blitz again, this time until you start to get a paste-like mixture. If the mixture is a little crumbly, go ahead and slowly add some water or olive oil

For the pumpkin

1 small pumpkin of choice, 200–300g, or ½ a larger one, seeds removed and kept

1 tbsp olive oil

salt and pepper

1 tsp smoked paprika

For the falafel

the cooked pumpkin (see above)

350–450g maize flour or cornflour (or use plain flour – start with half the amount and add slowly)

1 × 400g tin of chickpeas, drained and rinsed well

1 small brown onion, finely chopped

2 cloves of garlic, crushed or finely chopped

3 heaped tsp dried oregano

a small handful of fresh coriander, finely chopped

1 tbsp apple cider vinegar/white wine vinegar

2 tbsp olive oil

2 tbsp pure maple syrup

2 handfuls of kale, stems removed and saved for topping, chopped small

salt and pepper

olive oil (or other oil of choice), for frying

»

to loosen, tablespoon by tablespoon. If it's too wet, you can slowly add the remainder of your flour. The consistency will vary depending on the processor you're using and any slight variety in the texture of the ingredients, so don't be alarmed.

Once a dough-like consistency has formed, flour your hands and work the mixture into even balls. If you want a more 'patty style', flatten the balls ever so slightly in the palms of your hands. Set to one side – you could put these into the fridge to firm up further if you like.

Make sure the pumpkin seeds have been cleaned and dried thoroughly, then put them into a bowl along with the kale stalks, soy sauce or tamari and oil of choice, mixing well to coat. You don't want them to be too wet but they should be nicely coated. Transfer to a baking tray and roast for about 15–20 minutes. They will be lovely and crispy, with some charring on top.

To cook the falafel, put some olive oil into a pan over a medium heat. Once hot, go ahead and add your falafel balls. You'll want to let them cook evenly on each side for about 4–5 minutes. This will vary depending on their size and your pan. They'll start to brown on the outside, so flip them once this has happened. The inside will be soft but cooked through.

To serve, sprinkle over the seeds and kale stalks. I love to serve mine on a bed of fresh seasonal greens with the occasional side of rice or millet, etc. You could add any other toppings of choice, or even have them in between some bread, similar to a sandwich or burger. You could drizzle over a dressing or sauce of choice. See optional sides, above, for recommendations.

For the seeds and kale stalks

the pumpkin seeds (see above), cleaned thoroughly

the kale stalks (see above)

2–4 tbsp soy sauce or tamari

2 tsp oil of choice

Optional sides

fresh greens

grain of choice

fresh tomatoes, herbs, etc.

dressings (see page 353)

pesto/harissa (see page 359/361)

Waste tips:

As mentioned in the recipe, these falafels are great to serve with a whole variety of sauces, dressings, fresh ingredients, types of bread, etc., and you could even go all out and make a toasted sandwich. I love to have a batch of these made, and I find this is also a great way to use pumpkin. Often, if it's just me at home, I find I have bought too much pumpkin and cooking it whole helps it to retain all its flavour, ready to go into the falafels. I've included a use for the seeds in this dish, but you'll also find a pumpkin seed recipe on page 220, another great way to make use of the whole vegetable. The falafels themselves will keep in the fridge for about 5–7 days and slightly longer in the freezer, making them great to pop into the oven and reheat for adding to salads or even as a snack. You also don't just have to stick to pumpkin – any squash will work, and even sweet potato for a more universal ingredient.

At weekend meals with family over, this one has always gone down a treat. I tried it in a few different ways before settling on this recipe. Black rice is great for jazzing up a dish and adding a sweet and earthy aroma. Once prepped, you can simply wait for it to cook in the oven. The flavours and juices from the pumpkin seep into the mix, making it feel very luxurious and of course, tasty.

Serves 4

BLACK RICE STUFFED PUMPKIN

Preheat your oven to 180°C fan. Cut your pumpkin/ squash lengthways so that you have two relatively equal halves. Place the halves on a baking tray, flesh side down, so that the skin is upwards. Lightly brush the skins with some coconut oil and season with salt and pepper. Put into the oven and roast for around 30–40 minutes. The time will vary depending on your oven and also on your chosen pumpkin/squash. You'll want the top to start darkening – be careful that it doesn't start to collapse in too much.

While your pumpkin/squash is roasting, prepare the rice. Put the stock and rice into a large pot, adding a pinch of salt. Bring to the boil, then lower the heat and simmer the rice until cooked, about 30–40 minutes. You can add a dash more water if need be. Once cooked, drain any excess water and put to one side.

In a saucepan over a medium heat, add about 1 table-spoon of the coconut oil and sauté the leeks until soft and fragrant. Add the garlic, ginger, turmeric, oregano and chilli flakes, and continue to sauté for another few minutes. Add the chopped kale, soy sauce or tamari, tahini, lemon juice and zest. Season with salt and pepper to taste. Stirring frequently, cook until the kale has cooked through and wilted. You may need to add a dash of water to help the kale on its way.

1 medium pumpkin/squash (butternut squash, delicata are great for this recipe)

1–2 tbsp coconut oil

salt and pepper

750ml–1 litre vegetable stock

300–400g black rice, rinsed thoroughly

1 leek, sliced in half lengthways, washed thoroughly, roughly chopped

2 cloves of garlic, crushed or finely chopped

a small knob of ginger, approx. 4cm, finely chopped or grated

2 tsp ground turmeric

2 tsp dried oregano

a pinch of dried chilli flakes

a large handful of kale, finely chopped, stems included

2 tbsp soy sauce or tamari

1 tbsp tahini

½ lemon, juice and zest

approx. 35g hazelnuts, or any other nut of choice

2 tbsp nutritional yeast

olive oil

Your pumpkin/squash should now be ready. Once you have removed it from the oven, scoop the seeds and about a quarter of the flesh from the inside. Add this to the pan of kale and stir, seasoning with extra salt and pepper. If you don't want to use the seeds in the mix, feel free to omit them. (See recipes on pages 220 and 363 for inspiration.)

Add the kale mix to the drained rice, once again stirring to combine. If the mixture is a little dry you can add the rest of the coconut oil, seasoning again if necessary.

Add your rice mixture to the pumpkin halves, patting it down lightly as you go, packing it in as much as you can. You may have extra rice left, depending on the pumpkin/ squash. Serve it with the pumpkin or pop it into a container. Sprinkle three-quarters of your hazelnuts and nutritional yeast over the two halves and pop back into the oven, inside up this time, to cook through and toast the top slightly.

To serve, slice the pumpkin as you wish. Serve with any extra leftover rice mixture, the rest of the crushed hazelnuts and a small drizzle of olive oil.

Harissa enhances so many dishes and here it not only does that, but works beautifully with the vegetables. I make some variation of this recipe at least once a week, swapping vegetables in and out according to the season but sticking to the foundations of the dish. A real 'Mexican' feeling dish that's easy to rustle up but still lives up to a taco feast, it's a great recipe for when you have friends over, served sharing-style.

CHUNKY PUMPKIN TACOS
—
w/ harissa and black bean purée

Chop your pumpkin in half and remove the guts and seeds. Clean the seeds thoroughly and place to one side. Chop the pumpkin into rough bite-size chunks. Put your cubed pumpkin into a large pot of salted water and bring to the boil. Lower to a simmer and cook until the pumpkin is very soft and tender, about 10–12 minutes. Drain immediately and put to one side, covered.

In a saucepan, sauté the onion in a little water until slightly translucent and fragrant. Add the garlic and cook for another minute or so. Add a dash more water along with the tomato purée, ground cumin, coriander seeds, soy sauce or tamari, half the coriander stalks and half the leaves. Season with salt and pepper and continue to fry until a chunky paste has formed and all the ingredients are well combined.

Add around 250ml of stock to the pan and stir in the black beans and cooked pumpkin. Mix well to combine and season again with salt and pepper. Add the harissa paste and chopped fresh tomatoes.

Using a fork or a hand masher, begin to carefully mash the contents of your pan. You want it to stay relatively chunky, so just break some bits down for a variety in texture. Slowly add the extra water (unless already relatively watery) and simmer to thicken and deepen

For the purée
—

1 small pumpkin/ squash (I like to use a Kent/ Kabocha variety), cubed, seeds saved and washed thoroughly

1 medium brown onion

2 cloves of garlic, crushed or finely chopped

2 tbsp tomato purée

2 tsp ground cumin

1 tsp coriander seeds

1–2 tbsp soy sauce or tamari

a large handful of fresh coriander, leaves and stems, finely chopped

salt and pepper

250–500ml vegetable stock (see page 352 for your own homemade stock recipe)

approx. 280g cooked black beans (usually drained weight of 1 tin if not using dried)

2 heaped tbsp harissa (see page 361 for homemade)

2 medium fresh tomatoes, roughly chopped

1–2 tbsp olive oil

1 tsp ground cumin or curry powder

»

in flavour. Season with salt and pepper to taste. You'll be simmering for about 15–20 minutes. Once cooked, cover and allow to sit.

While your pumpkin bean mixture is simmering, prepare your tacos. Sift the flour into a bowl, add the salt and stir. Add the oil, then slowly add the water. Knead into a dough, adding more water when needed and a little extra flour if your mixture is too wet. Set aside to rest for about 6–8 minutes.

You can now crisp up your pumpkin seeds. Place them in a pan along with the olive oil and cumin/curry powder. Fry on a low heat until they start to brown and become nice and crispy. Place to one side, ready for the taco building.

To make the tacos, flour a dry surface and divide your dough into approx. 8–10 pieces. Roll each one into a ball, then use a rolling pin to flatten it out to about 5mm or less thick.

Put a little olive oil into a flat pan and heat until it reaches its smoke point, then turn the heat down a little, add the rolled tacos (either one at a time or more, depending on the size of your pan) and allow to cook for about 2 minutes on each side. You want them to start to rise slightly, that's how you know when to flip them. They'll brown slightly once cooked. Repeat until you have cooked all your tacos, adding extra oil if you need it.

Reheat your pumpkin bean mixture if necessary and get ready to build your first taco. Place the taco on a plate, followed by a couple of spoonfuls of the pumpkin mixture. Sprinkle over the toasted seeds and eat it how you like. This can get a little messy, which in my opinion makes it more fun. Add any additional sides/toppings (see suggestions), and enjoy.

For the tacos

240g plain flour, plus extra for rolling

½ tsp sea salt

2 tbsp extra virgin olive oil, plus extra for cooking

approx. 85ml water

Optional additional sides/ toppings

fresh herbs, chopped

creamy sauce/ dressings (see basics section, page 356)

extra harissa

fresh vegetables of choice, roughly chopped

Waste tip:

You don't have to include the seeds with this dish – you could save them for another recipe such as granola or a savoury topper. But they do add great texture and I feel they enhance the 'pumpkin' flavour in this recipe – and, having said that, in many others, which is why they are great to keep and roast or dry. The dough will keep in the fridge for a few days, ready and waiting if you want to make more tacos. Just pop it into a bowl and cover. If you have any leftover purée, it can be a great side or mash to another dish/salad, and can even be turned into a hummus. You can use the base recipe in the basics section (see page 357), adding the purée and adjusting the seasoning and liquid content accordingly. If you can't find or don't have pumpkin, you could use squash or even sweet potato, as suggested. I've also done this recipe using carrots and parsnips, as I had a whole bunch left over from a veggie box, a great alternative option if you are without pumpkin.

I made this dessert for one of my first major catering jobs, served in tall glass ramekins I'd bought especially for the event and prepared really carefully. I'd seen something similar when roaming around the internet, and re-creating it at this time of the year seemed like a must. It's not too sweet but can be quite rich, so you don't need a lot of it, which is why it's a perfect sweet at any time of the day – dessert doesn't just have to be at dinner!

Serves approx. 2

PUMPKIN PIE PARFAIT

Remove the tinned coconut from the fridge. When you open the tin, you will see a thick layer of pure coconut cream at the top. (If you are using tinned coconut cream already, you won't have any liquid in the can.) Remove the cream and transfer it to a food processor, trying to avoid as much of the liquid as possible. You can save the liquid in the fridge; see waste tips for ideas.

Add the pumpkin, maple syrup, lemon juice and zest, 1 tablespoon of the arrowroot, the vanilla, cinnamon, nutmeg, ginger and salt to the processor. Blend on a high speed until you get a creamy smooth mousse-like texture. The arrowroot will help to thicken the mixture, and you'll notice as you blend that it will start to do so – add the other tablespoon for a thicker texture.

Once the mixture is thick, you're ready to serve. Place in a bowl or jar with any additional toppings you like. For a parfait style as suggested, place a couple of dollops in a jar, followed by some coconut yoghurt/cream, toasted nuts or granola.

1 × 400g tin of full-fat coconut milk, refrigerated overnight (you can also buy pure coconut cream – if you have access to this, go ahead and buy 1 tin, and use approx. half)

approx. 90g pumpkin purée (or see note for homemade)

approx. 60ml pure maple syrup

1 small lemon, juiced, plus a dash of zest

1–2 tbsp arrowroot powder

1 tsp pure vanilla extract

1 tsp ground cinnamon

½ tsp grated nutmeg

½ tsp ground ginger

a large pinch of salt

To serve

coconut yoghurt/cream

toasted nuts

granola (see page 220 for pumpkin seed granola)

Note:

If you want to use fresh pumpkin for this recipe, rather than ready-made purée, you can steam/boil or roast (plain) the amount you need and use it in place of the purée listed above. Occasionally I'll cook a whole load in advance so I'll be able to use it in a few different recipes as well as just having it left over for salads, soups, etc. Once you've cooked the pumpkin, just mash it with a fork or pulse it in a blender until smooth.

Any liquid you have left over from the tinned coconut can be kept in the fridge for a few days. It's great to drink as it is, served cold, or added to smoothies. Coconut milk is extremely hydrating and contains a lot of electrolytes, so when you have it left over, it's definitely one to keep. This recipe is perfect for pleasing crowds and serving to friends or at dinner parties. It's incredibly simple to make but the taste makes you think otherwise. Simply double, triple, or scale up the recipe as needed and you're good to go. You could even turn it into a DIY dessert, making the pumpkin mousse and serving it all in different dishes for your guests to build themselves.

My friend Franny and I spoke about this recipe for about ten months before I finally got into the kitchen to try it. We'd fantasize about sitting in her garden on a warm autumn day, sipping on a pumpkin spiced latte. It's definitely a treat but worth every sip. After making it that first time, it pretty much became a ritual through autumn and winter and we still remind each other of it every year.

PUMPKIN SPICED LATTE

Put the pumpkin purée, maple syrup, water, lemon juice and zest, vanilla extract, cinnamon, ground nutmeg, ground ginger and salt into a small saucepan over a low heat. Stir continuously to combine, and keep this going until a syrup starts to form. Be careful not to let it burn. The syrup should form after about 10–12 minutes. Remove from the heat and allow to cool. It will thicken as it cools, helping it to form a thick syrup mixture.

To make the latte, put your milk into a pan and slowly start to heat it up. Once the milk is lukewarm (you can test this by dipping your pinky finger into the pan), add about 2 tablespoons of the cooled syrup. Stir to combine and continue to heat. Test to see if you want to add more syrup, making sure it's well combined. You could use a whisk to do this too.

Once you've reached the desired temperature (be careful not to boil the milk), pour it into your mug and enjoy.

Notes:

If you are making more than one latte, simply put the amount of milk you'd like to use into a pan and add the heaped tablespoons of syrup according to how many you are making it for. You could also do half milk, half water should you prefer. I love to use oat or coconut milk here, it goes lovely and thick and brings out the spiced pumpkin flavours.

For the syrup

90g pumpkin purée (see notes in previous recipe for homemade)

60–90ml pure maple syrup (this entirely depends on how sweet you'd like this to be – you can add less when making the latte, so have a play about)

250ml water

1 lemon, juiced, plus a dash of zest

1 tsp pure vanilla extract

1–2 tsp cinnamon

½–1 tsp grated nutmeg

½–1 tsp ground ginger

a large pinch of salt

feel free to add any other additional spices you like, cloves, cardamom, etc., starting with ¼–½ tsp of each as you don't want it to be too powdery

For the latte

approx. 250ml or your favourite mug's worth of unsweetened plant-based milk of choice (if you are using a smaller than average mug, start with 2 heaped tablespoons of the syrup, then slowly add more for flavour as you desire)

2–3 heaped tbsp syrup (see above)

There are many dishes I could eat more than once in a week, and dal is very high on the list. I like to make it in big batches and serve it with different things each time I have it. This dal is particularly special, made in the way I'd jotted down after spending time with a local Sri Lankan family, with half of the pumpkin blended to make it even creamier. I love using yellow split peas, mostly for their texture, and they really enhance the dish, adding a bit more bite and an almost nutty taste.

Serves approx. 6–8

CREAMY CURRIED PUMPKIN SPLIT PEA DAL

Put about 1–2 teaspoons of your coconut oil into a large pot over a medium heat. Add the mustard seeds and cook until they start to pop – lower the heat when they do so and transfer them to a small bowl. Heat the rest of the coconut oil in the same pan, then add your onions. Sauté until they start to go translucent and fragrant, about 5–6 minutes on a low heat. Add the garlic, ginger, turmeric, coriander stalks, dried chilli flakes, ground cumin, curry powder and half your curry leaves. Stir continuously and keep frying until everything becomes nice and fragrant. Put your mustard seeds back into the pan. If it starts to dry up, you can add a dash of your stock to help continue the frying process.

Add the pumpkin, split peas, about half the fresh coriander and the rest of the stock to the pot. Stir and bring the mixture up to the boil, seasoning with salt and pepper. Once it reaches the boil, lower the heat to a simmer. Add the cinnamon stick and stir again. Cover and cook for about 45–55 minutes, until the split peas are cooked and the pumpkin is tender. Season again to taste.

Once cooked, transfer about a quarter of the mix to a blender. You may need it to cool slightly first, depending on your blender type. Add the coconut milk and blend until smooth and creamy. Pour back into the pot and stir, adding the lime juice and zest and seasoning again to taste.

2 tablespoons coconut oil

1 tbsp black or yellow mustard seeds

1 white or brown onion, finely chopped

4 cloves of garlic, crushed or finely chopped

2 tbsp freshly grated ginger

1 tbsp freshly grated turmeric

a large handful of fresh coriander, stems finely chopped, leaves roughly chopped

a pinch of dried chilli flakes

4 tsp ground cumin

2–3 tsp curry powder (without salt preferred)

a small handful of curry leaves, fresh or dried

1.5–2 litres vegetable stock

1 small pumpkin or squash, raw, any variety, skin on or off

550g dried yellow split peas, soaked for at least 4 hours

salt and pepper

1 cinnamon stick

250ml coconut milk

1 lime, juice and zest

»

Slowly heat back up, stirring continuously so that the dal does not burn on the bottom of the pan. Serve in bowls and sprinkle over the rest of the coriander to garnish.

Note:

Be sure not to blend the cinnamon stick. I tend to leave it in the big pot but you can remove it before serving up should you wish.

Waste tip:

I often pre-roast pumpkin for this recipe, as there is such a variety of other dishes it can also be used in and that it's useful for. If I have pre-roasted it I would add it after the split peas have cooked. Using pre-roasted pumpkin adds a different depth to the dal. You can also use squash, but if you can't find either, sweet potato or potatoes also work great. You could also use fresh chillies in this dish if you like a little more heat, or perhaps a bit more ginger or a pinch of cayenne pepper. The dal will keep for a week in the fridge, usually thickening up, so when reheating it you could add a dash of coconut milk or water to the pan to loosen. This also makes a great hummus. Add as much as you desire or have left over to the base recipe on page 357, a little more olive oil or lemon, and a creamy curried hummus just became your new best friend. You can of course also serve this dal with any desired sides: naan, chapatis, rotis, rice, salad . . . it's really up to you. If you want to pack in some extra greens, chuck in a handful of fresh spinach or kale when heating at the final stage, allowing it to wilt and cook through.

Two of the greatest things: rich fluffy baked pumpkin and dal, surely a match made in heaven. A creative take on a traditional Indian dish, transporting you to the delightfully overwhelming aromas of a local Indian kitchen.

When pumpkin season is in full swing, it seems obligatory to cook it just as it is. Roasting it whole obviously takes longer than it does when chopped, but the flavour is something really special. It's moist in all the right ways, the seeds develop a crunch, and the whole garlic becomes soft and buttery. I love to cook this and serve it with just a salad, enjoying every part of the star of the show.

Serves approx. 8–12 as a side

WHOLE ROASTED PUMPKIN, SEEDS IN, WHOLE GARLIC, ROSEMARY

Preheat your oven to 200°C fan. Put the vinegar into a small bowl and add a dash of boiling water. Using a cloth, wash your pumpkin using this. As we're leaving it whole and the skin can often be bitter, we want to tone that down and also remove any dirt or pesticides from the pumpkin.

Now roughly brush the olive oil over the whole surface of the pumpkin. Using a sharp knife, make pricks approx. 1–1.5cm deep, again around the whole surface. Put into a roasting tray and pour in about 1cm of water.

Place in the oven and roast for about 2–3 hours. This will totally vary depending on the type of oven you have. Often it can be quicker, but we want the pumpkin to be incredibly soft. Keep an eye on it, checking that there is enough water in the bottom for the first hour.

After about 1 hour, when the liquid has gone from the bottom of the tray, place your garlic cloves, bashed but left in their skins, around the tray, and season the pumpkin with some salt and pepper. Put back into the oven and continue to roast.

To test when your pumpkin is ready, use a sharp knife to pierce it. You should be able to pierce and remove it extremely easily – again the cooking time will vary.

approx. 1 large pumpkin (roughly 2.5kg in weight) – the Jap/Japanese or Kent varieties are my favourite for this

approx. 1 tsp white vinegar (for cleaning)

1–2 tbsp olive oil

2 bulbs of garlic, cloves separated, bashed with the back of a knife/ spoon, left whole

salt and pepper

approx. 15–20g fresh rosemary

»

Remove the pumpkin from the oven. The garlic will have also cooked and become lovely and caramelized. Using a sharp knife, carefully top the pumpkin, then start to slice downwards, creating thick wedges (8–10, or as many or few as desired). Take your garlic cloves and squeeze them out of the skins over the pumpkin slices (composting the garlic skins). Sprinkle over the rosemary and another good seasoning of salt and pepper.

Place your pumpkin wedges back in the oven for about 8 minutes, just to help cook the rosemary, as well as to crisp up the inner pumpkin. It'll look very rustic and doesn't have to be placed in any particular way.

Serve with your chosen sides, as a snack, or even on its own with some fresh herbs and a drizzle of tahini.

Waste tips:

Cooking it whole like this allows all the nutrients and moisture to stay within the pumpkin, allowing it to have that 'melt-in-the-mouth' feeling. Roasting it whole also means it's easier to save. You could save one half for another recipe on another night, keep it in the fridge and add it to salads and stews, or simply have it as a snack in the day. You could even try this recipe and blitz up some of the pumpkin flesh to create your own purée, making it perfect for one of the pumpkin purée recipes in this book.

winter
begins

Come the end of the year, in the UK we have no choice but to embrace winter, easing into what is usually, for us, a long season. It's definitely easiest to just throw yourself into it, to make the most of the time before December arrives and a hectic month of Christmas-related social events makes it feel too busy to think up or plan meals. So, the beginning of winter, before the festivities begin, is an ideal time to get a little craftier and more creative with all the new produce. I'm always looking for ways to generate and feel more warmth, whether that's via the decor in the house, the table, or the weekly menu. So, I can't pretend to entirely hate winter, especially when I am very easily pleased by the chance to cook my seasonal favourites. Some are a little heartier and more robust, like celeriac, others are a little more vibrant and can be paired with my favourite winter grain, farro. Despite the 'heavier', more earthy produce at this time of the year, I think it's important to keep things fresh as well as hearty. Just because the weather is colder doesn't mean we don't want refreshing and light suppers at times. Inspired by one of my favourite local restaurants, there's a treasured recipe in this chapter which I make often in winter, to enjoy the strange-looking but wonderful celeriac while it's in season. Elegant ribbons in a tangy vinaigrette, this salad pleases a crowd at my winter supper clubs. It cuts through the heavier dishes, adding a refreshing zing to the palate.

As well as some of my best-loved dishes making their way on to the table, in winter my decor gets a revamp as well. I'm heavily inspired by earthy tones, creating a moodier-looking table at my supper clubs and bringing it to life with tall candles, eucalyptus and a pop of burnt orange in the napkins. When the light is a little dimmer, everything else needs to work harder, so I like the food and table decor to look as inviting as possible.

You'll notice in this section a couple of Polish-inspired cabbage dishes, a vegetable truly in its prime at this time of year and a nice excuse for a nod to my heritage, plus my love for the fragrant bay leaf. Using cabbage in these ways (as wraps, pan-fried, etc.) is a nice addition to the repertoire.

star produce:

Celeriac

——

Cabbage (king, hispi, red)

——

Chestnuts

——

Pear

——

Mushrooms (including wild)

——

Other seasonal produce: Kale (variety), apples, beetroot, grapefruit, parsnips, celery, Jerusalem artichokes, sweet potatoes, leeks, winter squash, turnips, Swiss chard, chicory, onions, swede, cranberries, carrots, radicchio, tarragon, sage.

——

You will of course notice some of these fruits/vegetables in other seasons as well. There is always a big overlap these days because of the climate and average temperatures we experience, regardless of where we are.

——

Grains/pulses harvested at this time of the year: Farro, lentils, oats, winter barley, rye/cereal rye, wheat (variety), triticale seed (essentially a hybrid of wheat and rye combined).

——

celeriac

Underrated, unsung, but in my opinion a king of the root vegetable family, the slightly odd-looking celeriac is generally quite large, which is appropriate to its powerful flavour: nutty with a subtle celery-like taste. It often has a tough skin, which perhaps is another reason for it not being a vegetable of choice when it comes to cooking with it, but once you see and taste it in all its glory, this knobbly vegetable will hopefully become a favourite. There is a slightly bitter aftertaste to it, which is why I think it's perfect for adding variety to your average mashed potatoes (which, let's face it, in wintertime are definitely a staple); drenched in a rich mushroom gravy, you get the perfect balance of flavours and textures. Another dish I'm particularly fond of is grilled celeriac with a peanut satay. Who'd have thought these two very strong flavours would marry so well? But I promise you it's revolutionary.

Waste tips:

Too often overlooked at the bottom of the list of things to try, celeriac is great added to mash or stews, or slow-cooked whole, as it's so versatile and has an abnormal but delicious taste that makes a nice change. In the winter months at least one night of my week will involve a trayful of roasted root veggies. Celeriac in this form, batch-cooked in among the other veg with just a little seasoning, is lovely to have in the fridge, to reheat or use whenever you like. Uncooked celeriac does last a little while, so don't be alarmed if you've had one sitting with the potatoes for over a week. It'll start to sprout, similar to the potato, so you'll know when it's had its time. Its skin, like most veg, is exceptionally nutritious (and delicious), so be sure to make use of that, crisping it up as croutons or just making a habit not to remove it. Just be sure to give it a good scrub to remove any unwanted soil.

If this cosy, hearty recipe doesn't scream winter, I don't know what does. I love making this at the weekend, when I don't mind prepping a little earlier in the day. The cooking time for the celeriac is a few hours, but it's definitely worth the wait. While it's cooking you can make the gravy, allowing it to simmer and become rich and full of body. Pan-fried seasonal greens and a glass of wine are my favourites to pair with this!

WHOLE ROASTED CELERIAC

w/ mushroom gravy

Preheat your oven to 200°C fan. Wash and scrub your celeriac well, removing excess dirt. Using a sharp knife, pierce it all over its whole surface, about 1cm or so deep.

Place the celeriac on a baking tray. In a small bowl, combine your garlic, olive oil, thyme, turmeric and a good seasoning of salt and pepper. Using a pastry brush or your fingertips, cover the celeriac with the oil mixture, spreading the garlic pieces on the celeriac to roast too.

Place in the oven on a low shelf and roast for about 2½ hours. It may take slightly more or less depending on your oven. Check on the celeriac throughout, spooning over any juices that appear in the bottom of the tray. Once it's cooked you want a knife to be able to go through easily and for the outside to be a lovely golden brown. Once the celeriac has roasted, remove it from the oven and allow to cool slightly before serving.

While the celeriac is cooking, you can make your gravy. Drizzle a tablespoon or so of oil into a wide pan and start to fry your onions until soft and translucent.

Add the mushrooms and garlic and continue to fry for a few minutes – the mixture will become quite moist, due to the mushrooms. Once cooked and fragrant, add about 500ml of the stock, the thyme, rosemary and sage, and stir well. Bring to a gentle boil, then reduce to a simmer.

1 medium celeriac

2 cloves of garlic, skins removed, bashed with the back of a knife and roughly broken up

1–2 tbsp olive oil

a few sprigs of fresh thyme

1 tsp ground turmeric

salt and pepper

For the gravy

olive oil, for frying

1 medium onion, finely chopped or diced

250g mushrooms (chestnut, button, variety, etc.), sliced

3 cloves of garlic, crushed or finely chopped

approx. 500–750ml vegetable stock

2 tbsp fresh thyme, finely chopped

1½ tbsp fresh rosemary, finely chopped

a few fresh sage leaves, rubbed to release their flavour and roughly chopped

2–4 tbsp nutritional yeast

1 tbsp Dijon mustard

1 tbsp sherry or white wine vinegar

2 tbsp coconut aminos or soy sauce

2 tbsp plain flour

65ml unsweetened plant-based milk

salt and pepper

To serve

1 lemon, cut into wedges

»

Add the nutritional yeast, mustard, vinegar, coconut aminos, flour and plant-based milk. Season with salt and pepper to taste. Slowly stir on a low heat to get rid of any lumps, allowing the liquid to thicken. For a thinner gravy, you can go ahead and add the rest of the stock here.

Turn off the heat, then remove a third of the mushroom mixture and put to one side. Either pour the rest of the gravy into an upright blender, or use a hand blender to blitz it until smooth.

Season to taste, then put the blended liquid and the reserved mushrooms back into a saucepan. On a low-medium heat, begin to warm the mushroom gravy, stirring to combine.

To serve, place the celeriac, whole, on a serving plate. Score a cross on top and prise it open ever so slightly, pouring over the gravy and allowing it to seep through the gaps. Place the lemon wedges around the dish and season with extra salt and pepper if necessary. You could also plate up individually, cutting the celeriac into 'steaks' or any other way you like. Pour over the gravy and serve with lemon wedges, as above.

Waste tips:

This gravy is perfect for any vegetables. I love roasting a big batch of vegetables at the end of the week to pair with it. You could also pour the gravy over a mash or turn it into a pie. If you have any leftover gravy, you could create a 'meal for one' in a small pie dish or ramekin, placing some mash in the bottom, with a big handful of greens, and topping with the gravy. Bake in the oven for around 15 minutes to heat through and get a lovely crispy topping. You could add some nutritional yeast or another layer of mash – you can really be creative. If you don't have a celeriac, this recipe also works great with a cauliflower or a large, firm cabbage.

Chestnuts are not in season for very long, so using them any which way is always a ritual for me at this time of the year. I started playing around with this recipe out of curiosity, envisaging the soft, creamy texture of the risotto making the dish feel somewhat mischievous but very nutritious. It's served with lemon rind to cut through the creaminess and a good drizzle of olive oil at the end.

CELERIAC AND CHESTNUT RISOTTO

w/ olive oil, lemon rind

For the purée, scrub and wash your celeriac well, removing any excess dirt. I keep the skin on for the texture, but feel free to peel and compost. Chop the celeriac into chunks.

Bring a large pot of salted water to the boil and add the celeriac. Reduce the heat and simmer for approximately 15 minutes, until the celeriac is tender and an inserted knife can be removed easily. Once cooked, drain and transfer to a blender.

Add your cooked, de-shelled chestnuts to the blender, along with the tahini, and blend until smooth. Put to one side while you make the risotto.

Heat up 1 tablespoon of olive oil in a pan. Add the onion and leeks and cook until they start to turn brown and smell fragrant. Add your garlic and nutmeg and continue to fry for another minute or so, being careful not to burn the garlic.

Add the rice and stir well. You want to lightly cook this before adding your liquid – you will notice the outside of the rice start to go slightly translucent. Add the white wine and 'burn' off the alcohol. It'll have a strong smell at first and will then start to simmer nicely.

Start adding the stock, a ladle or two at a time, stirring frequently to prevent the rice sticking to the bottom of

For the celeriac and chestnut purée

1 small celeriac

approx. 250–300g chestnuts (unpeeled weight), cooked, then shells removed (see note below)

2 heaped tbsp tahini

For the risotto

2 tbsp olive oil (garlic-infused olive oil is great in this recipe), plus extra to garnish

1 large brown onion, finely chopped

1 small leek, sliced lengthways, washed, then roughly chopped

2 cloves of garlic, crushed or finely chopped

½ tsp grated nutmeg

350g risotto/ arborio rice

approx. 250ml white wine

approx 1 litre vegetable stock (see page 352 for homemade, or shop-bought)

salt and pepper

1½ lemons, 1 juiced and zested, rind peeled from ½

1 heaped tbsp miso (white or brown)

2 tbsp dried oregano, or other dried mixed herbs of choice

approx. 50g nutritional yeast, plus extra to garnish

the pan. Season with salt and pepper. Continue until you have added three-quarters of your stock, then turn the heat down to low.

Add three-quarters of the lemon juice and zest, the miso paste, oregano and nutritional yeast. Stir well and season if needed. Ensure the miso has broken down and dissolved.

Once your rice is almost done (after about 30 minutes of simmering), go ahead and add your celeriac and chestnut purée. The rice should have a little bit of bite, the Italian way. Stir well to combine, adding any remaining stock, lemon juice and zest to loosen and for taste. Warm through, again seasoning with salt and pepper should you need it.

Serve in bowls, adding the peeled lemon rind on top and a good drizzle of olive oil. Sprinkle over some nutritional yeast to garnish and for an extra 'cheesy' hit.

Notes:

When cooking your chestnuts from fresh, simply score crosses on the top and bottom of the outer shell. Roast at 200°C fan for about 10–15 minutes, until the shells start to crack and break away, showing the chestnuts inside. These will be soft. Leave to cool before removing the shells.

Waste tips:

One of my favourite variations on this risotto is to add seasonal mushrooms for amazing texture and depth of flavour. (See page 292 for an earthy mushroom risotto recipe.) Occasionally I'll omit the chestnuts and do the celeriac on its own, maybe adding a few tablespoons of plant-based yoghurt to give the purée some extra creaminess. You could also add a couple of handfuls of greens to boost the nutrients, and a handful of toasted nuts on top for a crunchy texture when serving.

A fresh number for when you want something a little lighter or perhaps a side to a more filling main, the celeriac in this recipe marinates beautifully in the dressing, softening and soaking up all the flavours. The toasted seeds add the necessary crunch to finish off the dish.

Serves 2 as a main, 4 as a side

CELERIAC RIBBON SALAD

w/ greens, toasted seeds

Using a sharp peeler or knife, start to peel around the circumference of the celeriac. You may not achieve full ribbons as such, but close to. Place the ribbons in a bowl as you go, and peel as far as you can get to the core of the celeriac. Thinly slice the remainder and add to the bowl.

Add the lemon juice and zest, vinegar and 2 tablespoons of olive oil. Mix well to make sure the celeriac is coated, then massage slightly with your hands and allow it to soften.

Add the garlic, parsley, seasonal greens, oregano and capers (and brine). Add the other 2 tablespoons of olive oil and season with salt and pepper. Again, using your hands, massage to help soften the greens. Leave to sit, covered, for about 10 minutes.

Serve individually or in one large bowl. Sprinkle over the toasted seeds, chilli flakes and a good pinch of salt and pepper.

1 small celeriac, skin peeled (then composted if you can)

1 large lemon, juice and zest

1 tbsp apple cider vinegar or white wine vinegar

2–4 tbsp olive oil

2 cloves of garlic, grated or finely chopped

a large handful of fresh parsley, finely chopped

2 large handfuls of seasonal greens of choice (chard, cavolo nero, kale)

2 heaped tsp dried oregano

2 heaped tbsp capers, plus a dash of the brine

salt and pepper

2 tbsp sesame seeds, toasted

2 tbsp pumpkin seeds, toasted

a pinch of dried chilli flakes, to serve

Waste tips:

This salad will keep well in the fridge – you'll find it will increase in flavour and the vegetables will soften, making them extremely easy to digest. You could replace the celeriac with any type of cabbage or even with turnips/radishes. You'll get a similar rich and mustardy flavour from these, as well as the bonus of them being seasonal. Often basil is harder to find at this time of the year, so occasionally I'll freeze some during the summer months. It's a great addition to this dish. Simply let it thaw slightly and add it alongside the parsley or instead of. If you want to serve this hot, you can boil the celeriac ribbons, as if you were cooking pasta. You can then add the greens to the boiling water and serve it as a hot side dish. Another nice way to vary this recipe is by adding the ribbons to your favourite pasta, along with some extra cracked pepper and nutritional yeast. Hot or cold, it's a real winner.

A wilder concoction, I know! Pickled pear became a regular affair for me after experimenting for an event, which in turn led to a lot more experimenting at home. The sourness from the pickle really helps to balance out the richness from the peanut satay; it's definitely one of those tastebud-tingling dishes.

Serves 4

GRIDDLED CELERIAC

w/ peanut satay, pickled pear

First make your pickles. Combine the vinegar, sugar, salt, ginger, peppercorns and red pepper powder in a small saucepan. Slowly add the water and bring to the boil, then reduce the heat and allow to simmer for about 5 minutes to allow the flavours to combine.

While on a very low heat, add the onion/shallot and green chilli. Simmer for a further few minutes, then remove from the heat and set aside until it's about room temperature.

Put the sliced pears into a jar or bowl and top with the pickling liquid. Allow to cool, then cover and place in the fridge to chill while you go ahead with the rest of the dish. You'll have more pickles than this dish calls for, but you can also make it a week or so ahead of time and that way the fermenting process of the pickles will have started.

Preheat your oven to 200°C fan, ready for the celeriac. For the satay sauce, put all the ingredients into a bowl or upright blender. Add the optional additions here if you are using them. Either using a whisk/fork or the blender, combine well until smooth. Loosen with water to reach your desired consistency, and season with salt and pepper. Allow to sit while you cook the celeriac.

Put the olive oil, peppercorns, thyme and a good pinch of salt into a bowl big enough to hold the celeriac sticks.

For the pickled pear (makes extra, approx. 6–8 servings)

approx. 600ml rice vinegar

2 heaped tbsp raw sugar (cane, coconut, etc.)

1–2 heaped tbsp salt

approx. 5cm piece of ginger, grated

½–1 tsp peppercorns

½ tsp Korean red pepper powder or flakes (if you don't have either, you can sub with paprika)

250ml water

1 small red onion or shallot, thinly sliced

1 small red or green chilli, thinly sliced (optional)

2 medium pears (any variety, quite firm – Corella, Anjou, Conference, etc.), sliced approx. 2.5cm thick, as close to the core as possible (seeds composted)

For the satay sauce

5 heaped tbsp peanut butter (smooth or crunchy)

2 tbsp soy sauce or tamari

2 tbsp maple syrup

1 small lime, juiced, plus a dash of zest

2 cloves of garlic, crushed or finely chopped

2 tbsp rice vinegar (or another relatively neutral vinegar)

»

Whisk to combine. Add the celeriac and toss – you may want to use your hands to do this.

Over a medium heat, place the coated celeriac on a griddle pan. (You can use a normal pan if you don't have a griddle pan, you'll just end up with a slightly different look.) Cook until the celeriac is nicely charred all over, making sure you turn the pieces as you go along. This will probably take about 10 minutes, and they should now be starting to soften. Once they are slightly soft, transfer the celeriac to a roasting tray and bake until completely tender, about 10–15 minutes.

While the celeriac is roasting, transfer the peanut sauce to a small saucepan and slowly warm it up over a low heat, stirring constantly and being careful not to let it burn.

To serve, dollop and spread a couple of tablespoons of the sauce on the bottom of each plate, with some of the celeriac on top, followed by the desired amount of pickles. Drizzle over some olive oil, salt and pepper and a sprinkling of fresh thyme. You could also serve this in one serving dish, combining the sauce and celeriac and garnishing accordingly, serving the pickles on the side.

2 tbsp nutritional yeast

salt and pepper

½ tsp onion powder (optional)

½ tsp chilli powder/flakes (optional)

For the celeriac

1–2 tbsp olive oil, plus extra for serving

2 tsp crushed peppercorns

a few sprigs of fresh thyme, plus extra for serving

salt

1 small/medium celeriac, washed thoroughly, chopped into thick sticks

Note:

If you have a barbecue and feel inclined to use it (even if the weather is a little colder), this recipe works great and it adds a lovely charred flavour and depth to the celeriac.

Waste tips:

Celeriac is a great earthy vegetable, and usually easy to get hold of, but this recipe can also be made with cauliflower, or you could try swede, turnips or parsley root for a similar 'celery' flavour. I often make a double batch of the sauce and use it when I fancy, as it keeps in the fridge for about 4 weeks in a jar. You can loosen it more with water, or even some lemon juice squeezed in. Another swap is to use almond butter instead of peanut butter. It's not as strong a taste but the consistency is lovely. Tahini also works well, so if you have either of these, you're in luck.

Cooking with celeriac can be daunting, as it looks pretty rough and unfamiliar. But these steaks are great for when you want to try something new but still with a sense of familiarity. The chimichurri gives a good kick to the steaks, and they're beautifully charred on the outside and soft in the middle once cooked. It's a recipe that I could never fall out of love with.

Serves approx. 4 as a side

CELERIAC STEAKS

w/ caper and parsley chimichurri

Preheat your oven to 180°C fan. Thoroughly wash the celeriac and cut it into approx 1.5/2cm 'steaks'. You should have roughly 6 steaks. Place them on a baking tray and rub the olive oil over both sides of each steak. Sprinkle with salt, then place in the oven and roast for around 30 minutes. They'll start to turn golden brown on top. Flip them over and roast for a further 20 minutes or so, allowing the other side to brown and the steak to become tender.

While your steaks are roasting, make the chimichurri. Put your parsley, capers, garlic, olive oil, apple cider vinegar, lemon juice and zest and chilli flakes into a blender and blitz until you have a paste-type mixture, seasoning with salt and pepper if needed and adding a little extra olive oil if it's too dry.

Remove your steaks from the oven and evenly spread about a quarter of the chimichurri over them. It will be quite rustic-looking. Put back into the oven for a further 5 minutes.

To serve, dish up each steak with a dollop of chimichurri. You could also make a bed of the chimichurri, serving the steak/s over the top. And feel free to add more than a quarter of the mix when putting the steaks back into the oven to warm through.

For the celeriac steaks

1 medium/large celeriac, washed thoroughly, sliced into approx. 1.5/2cm thick steaks

1–2 tbsp olive oil

salt

For the chimichurri

2 large handfuls of fresh parsley, finely chopped, stalks included, plus extra to garnish (if you can't get parsley, coriander is also great)

2 tbsp capers, drained

2 cloves of garlic, crushed or finely chopped

3–4 tablespoons extra virgin olive oil

1 teaspoon apple cider vinegar

1 lemon, juiced, plus a dash of zest

a pinch of dried chilli flakes

salt and pepper

Waste tips:

Chimichurri is such a delicious way to use up fresh herbs. You can try a combination of mint, dill, basil, depending on what you have in or what's in season. I love to keep a batch of chimichurri in the fridge – it's great with salads or other roasted vegetables. Simply put it into an airtight container with a drizzle of olive oil or lemon juice to help preserve it. For the steaks, you can replace the celeriac with cabbage, turnips, even cauliflower if you like.

cabbage (king, hispi, red)

Cabbage is a vegetable I find myself eating almost every day in the winter, whether I plan to or not. It's easy to cook, and to me it is always exciting because of the different varieties. One of my favourite snacks is cabbage (or fennel) dipped in mustard – it's not even a guilty habit, it's simply great. I'll never forget the time when, after spending a few days at my best friend Becs's house, she later texted me a picture of a cabbage leaf, a red one to be precise, wrapped tightly with not just one type of mustard in the middle but two. Her text read: 'You've changed me.' It always brings a smile to my face, and the thought of introducing more friends to this brilliant snack is quite joyous. One of my go-tos with cabbage is quite obviously a slaw, which, quelle surprise, features mustard in the dressing. The slaw itself is punchy and flavourful and works on its own, paired with a grain or perhaps as part of a bigger spread – or better yet, wedged in between two pieces of your favourite bread. It's a great way to make use of leftovers too, easily adaptable, with different end results each time.

Waste tips:

You might have seen tacos made with lettuce leaves – well, that is not where it stops because cabbage leaves are just as good, especially Savoy cabbage. Lightly steam just a few leaves and stuff them with whatever your heart desires. If you find yourself with a leftover cabbage and a lack of inspiration, actually one of the tastiest and easiest things to do is to simply fry it. Sauté some garlic in a little oil of choice, chuck in the cabbage, chopped any which way, with a bit of lemon juice and zest, and wilt it down until it's beautifully soft.

Perhaps you can relate to having just part of a cabbage still left in the fridge. I find that I don't always use the whole thing, so this recipe is a good solution, one of those 'let me see what's in my fridge' type dishes. With store-cupboard ingredients and paired with creamy chickpeas, having leftover cabbage may turn into not such a bad thing.

Serves 4–6

MAPLE-ROASTED CABBAGE

w/ creamy chickpeas

Preheat your oven to 180°C fan. Put your cabbage on a large roasting tray (don't throw away any of the stalk, it's often the best part). Put the olive oil, maple syrup, balsamic vinegar and a good pinch of salt and pepper into a small bowl and whisk to combine.

Drizzle the oil mixture as evenly as you can over the cabbage, reserving a little for a top-up halfway through. Using your fingertips, brush the oil mixture over the cabbage to help coat it further.

Roast in the oven on a lower shelf for about 40–60 minutes. This will totally depend on the size of your cabbage and also on your oven. You want the cabbage to be tender all the way through – you can test it by inserting a sharp knife from the outside through to the centre. After about 25 minutes, pour over the rest of the oil mixture and season with salt and pepper. Once cooked, remove from the oven and allow it to cool slightly. Make your chickpeas while the cabbage is roasting.

If you are cooking your chickpeas from dried, drain away the soaking water and rinse them. Place them in a large pan with a good heap of salt. Bring to the boil, then cover and simmer for around 30–40 minutes, or until cooked. You may notice the shells of the chickpeas starting to come away – this is normal.

For the cabbage

1 small/medium cabbage of choice, quartered

2 tbsp olive oil

4 tbsp maple syrup

1 tbsp balsamic vinegar

salt and pepper

For the chickpeas

approx. 250g dried chickpeas (pre-soaked for at least 10 hours), or 500g cooked chickpeas (from tins or jars)

350–500ml vegetable stock (either your homemade stock from page 352 or other stock of choice)

2 medium shallots, chopped in half lengthways, then thinly sliced

2 cloves of garlic, crushed or finely chopped

approx. 180g celery, washed, finely chopped, plus leaves

a small bunch of fresh parsley, stalks and leaves finely chopped

1 lemon, juice and zest

2 tbsp soy sauce or tamari

2 tbsp Dijon mustard

2 heaped tbsp tahini

2 tbsp dried oregano

a pinch of dried chilli flakes or chilli powder

salt and pepper

60g nutritional yeast

Once your chickpeas are cooked, drain and place them to one side while you make your base for the rest of the dish. If you are using tinned chickpeas, you can drain and rinse these now too.

Put a few tablespoons of your stock into a pan (non-stick if you can) and cook your shallots until soft. Once they have softened and turned a slightly golden colour, add the garlic and chopped celery. Cook for another 2 minutes.

Add about half the stock, the parsley, lemon zest and juice, soy sauce or tamari, Dijon mustard, tahini, oregano and chilli to the pot. Toss in your chickpeas and stir well. Season with salt and pepper to taste. Bring to the boil, then lower to a simmer.

As the liquid starts to reduce and becomes thicker, add the nutritional yeast and half of your remaining stock, seasoning again to taste. The chickpeas will continue to cook in the sauce, and you'll notice the texture becoming a little stew-like. You can go ahead and add the rest of your stock should you want more liquid in the dish.

Serve the chickpeas, topping each portion with a slice of cabbage. Sprinkle over some lemon zest and season with salt and pepper. Add any other additional toppings/serving suggestions here. If you are more than 4, slice the cabbage accordingly.

To serve (optional)

lemon zest

olive oil

balsamic vinegar

fresh herbs of choice

Waste tips:

This is an easy one to switch up and cook in different seasons, as it's a very simple recipe. You can play around with the herbs and you can use different varieties of cabbage in season. The cabbage gets better the next day, as the flavours deepen. You could add some 'winter' herbs when roasting the cabbage and even some finely chopped garlic for variety. You'll notice these creamy chickpeas also feature in the Depths of Winter chapter (see page 320), where I give a suggestion for how they can double up as a great hummus.

I've always been obsessed with ramen. Ever since I had my first bowl of the deliciousness that it is, I couldn't help but want to try making one myself. The broth is super simple, and the longer you leave it, the better it will be. It's more involved than other recipes purely because we're making the noodles from scratch, but once you get the hang of it, this one will definitely be a repeat.

Makes approx.
4 servings

CABBAGE RAMEN

w/ homemade ramen noodles

To make your own kansui, preheat your oven to approximately 150°C fan. Spread the baking powder on a foil-lined tray and bake for around 1 hour. Once cooked, allow to cool entirely and store in an airtight container/jar. Use accordingly.

To make the noodles, stir together the hot water, salt and kansui in a bowl. Wait until the kansui and salt have completely dissolved.

Sift in about three-quarters of the flour. Making sure your hands are floured, begin to carefully knead, slowly adding the rest of the flour and continuing to knead until you have a smooth dough with no lumps. If the mixture is a little dry, add water, 1 teaspoon at a time. You want the dough to form well without sticking to your hands. Shape it into a rough square and cover, then leave to rest for a minimum of 1 hour. If you want to use cling film here (and if you can find a compostable one) go ahead and use that to wrap the dough, or cover with a bowl.

While your dough is resting, make the broth. In a large pot over a low-medium heat, heat your oil and fry the onion until golden brown and fragrant, about 3–4 minutes. Add the garlic and continue to fry until this also turns golden, about another 1–2 minutes. Make sure you don't burn the garlic.

For the kansui (makes more than needed for the recipe: store in a jar for up to 6 months)

30g baking powder

For the noodles

125ml hot water (make sure this is not boiling)

½ tsp salt (high quality preferably)

1 tbsp kansui (see above)

210g plain flour, plus extra for dusting/kneading (00 flour is great here – you can also use bread flour, although the dough can be a bit harder to work with if you are hand kneading rather than using a processor, but you get a chewier noodle because the protein in the flour is higher than in plain)

For the ramen

1–2 tbsp olive oil (garlic or chilli infused oils are great)

1 medium white/brown onion, roughly chopped

4–6 cloves of garlic, thinly sliced

2 tbsp sesame seeds (black or white)

approx. thumb-sized piece of ginger, sliced thinly or grated

»

Stir in the sesame seeds and ginger and fry for a few seconds, then go ahead and add your stock, scraping the bottom of the pan with a wooden spoon to remove any of the ingredients that have stuck (don't worry if they are slightly charred, this will enhance the flavour).

Add the soy sauce or tamari, crushed red pepper flakes, spring onions, tomato purée, miso paste and soya milk. Bring to the boil, stirring frequently, then lower the heat to a simmer and add your cabbage and mushrooms. Allow to simmer until the cabbage and mushrooms have wilted and are very tender. The broth will start to thicken at this stage. Season with salt and pepper to taste.

To make the noodles, split the dough into 4 even pieces and sprinkle with a little extra flour. If you are not using a pasta maker/roller, you'll need to flour a surface and roll each piece approximately 1cm thick and as rectangular as you can get. Rub flour all over each one, then fold up until you reach the end, creating a smaller rectangular shape that's about 15cm wide. Using a sharp knife, carefully cut into the desired thickness for your noodles, placing them in a floured bowl while you do the rest. If you are using a pasta maker, start flattening the dough on the lowest setting, working your way up to achieve 1cm thin regular shapes. Then cover each flattened piece with flour and pass through either a noodle cutter or another cutter should you want thicker noodles. Again, place in a floured bowl while you make the rest.

This next stage is optional: you can remove about half or less of the solids from the broth and about 125–250ml of the liquid, add these to a blender and blitz until smooth. Add back to the broth. I like to cook the noodles separately, as you can pour the broth over when serving and don't have any residue starch in the broth. To cook the noodles, put them into a pot of salted boiling water and boil for about 3 minutes, then drain.

To serve, divide the noodles between bowls and ladle over the broth. You may have extra broth, which is why it's good to cook it separately. Serve with any extra or desired toppings. Note: if you are adding tofu, I'd go ahead and add this when the broth is simmering.

1.5–1.75 litres vegetable stock

2–4 tbsp soy sauce or tamari

1½ tsp crushed red pepper flakes, or 1 tbsp Korean red pepper powder if you have it

4 spring onions

1 tbsp tomato purée

1 tbsp miso paste (white, yellow, brown)

approx. 125ml soya milk (optional – if not using, you may need more stock/water)

½–1 small cabbage of choice (hispi, king, green, Savoy, etc. – start with half depending on how small your cabbage is and how hungry you are)

approx. 8 dried shiitake mushrooms or 150g fresh mushrooms (or you could use both for an extra 'mushroomy' ramen)

salt and pepper

noodles (see above), or approx. 350g bought ramen noodles if not making from scratch

Optional additions

dried seaweed/sea vegetables/nori sheets

sesame oil

chilli oil/sauce

fresh coriander, roughly chopped

tofu (any kind/preference)

Note:

If you are making the noodles from scratch as opposite, see instructions for making your own kansui. The kansui is just baked baking powder, very simple, but it does take an hour to cook in the oven, so make sure you're prepped. You'll also need to leave the noodle dough to rest for an hour, so make sure you allow time for this. You can make the broth while the noodle dough is resting.

Waste tips:

This broth can easily be made in a larger batch and put into the fridge or freezer. It's a great base to add to. Occasionally I'll add other vegetables if I fancy a more veggie-heavy ramen. Using cabbage of course is not traditional, but often pak choy and Asian-type vegetables are imported and not seasonal, so here you can achieve a similar taste with a seasonal vegetable. Making your own noodles is a relatively lengthy process, but definitely worth it. You can very easily double or multiply the quantities to make more. They keep well in the fridge for about 3–5 days and can also be frozen. I would recommend making sure they are well floured if you are putting them into the fridge or freezing them, to help prevent them sticking. The best thing about the noodles is that the dough can double up as pasta. See pages 186 and 216 for a few pasta ideas you could use with these noodles.

A tribute to my Polish heritage, this is a simple, almost buttery-tasting dish. I love having it as a side; it's full of flavour but not overpowering, and it's easy to rustle up, making the perfect accompaniment to a grain, or a more involved main.

CHUNKY POLISH-STYLE CABBAGE

pan-fried with garlic and bay

Put your olive and coconut oil into a pan over a medium heat. Add the onion and sauté for a few minutes, until soft and slightly translucent. Add the garlic and continue to sauté for another minute or so until fragrant.

Add the cabbage and 75ml of water. Add the bay leaves, 45g of nutritional yeast, the caraway seeds and paprika, and season with salt and pepper. Allow the cabbage to wilt and the liquid to disappear. Add the remaining water if necessary. You will notice that as it wilts the cabbage will become lovely and soft, so adding the extra water is not always necessary.

Once cooked, stir through the rest of your nutritional yeast. Serve with any extra seasoning, a sprinkle of paprika and a drizzle of olive oil.

Waste tips:

Feel free to use any type of cabbage you can find, especially if you're making this in a different season. For an extra Polish twist, you can add some fresh dill if you have access to it. Dried dill also works, but I always prefer fresh if possible! I love this recipe served with a fresh slice of sourdough, lightly toasted. The mix of olive and coconut oil adds a lovely buttery flavour to the cabbage. If I have a chilli or garlic infused oil, I love using that here to add an extra kick.

1 tbsp olive oil, plus an extra drizzle to serve

1 tbsp coconut oil

1 red onion, finely sliced

3 cloves of garlic, crushed or finely chopped

1 medium sized hispi/Savoy/green cabbage, shredded

approx. 150ml water

2–4 bay leaves, lightly crushed to release their flavour (use according to how strong you like this flavour)

45–60g nutritional yeast

1 tsp caraway seeds

1 tsp paprika, smoked or regular, plus a dash extra to garnish

salt and pepper

Salad-style dishes are not just for the summer months; often we still crave fresh things in the colder months too, so making use of this season's specialities in a slaw is a great solution. You can swap the vegetables and quantities based on what you have in, and the raisins in this dish become plump as they soak up the vinaigrette. I love adding a pinch of chilli to make it feel 'warmer'.

Serves 2–4
as a side or main

WARM WINTER VEGETABLE AND GRAIN SLAW

Preheat your oven to 200°C fan. Put your chopped or shredded vegetables into a roasting tray. Add the olive oil, soy sauce or tamari and oregano, then season with salt and pepper. Using your hands, mix well to make sure the vegetables are coated. Roast for about 20–25 minutes. Once cooked, remove from the oven and allow to cool for a few minutes.

In a saucepan, combine your freekeh with the vegetable stock. Bring to the boil, then lower to a simmer, cover and cook for about 20–25 minutes. The freekeh will be tender with a tiny bit of bite. Once cooked, fluff with a fork and allow to cool.

While your vegetables are roasting and the freekeh is cooking, make your vinaigrette. Either in a small bowl or using a blender, combine the Dijon and wholegrain mustard, maple syrup, vinegar, olive oil and oregano. Whisk/blend until smooth. Put to one side and allow to thicken.

Put the raisins/sultanas, shallot and fresh herbs into a bowl. Add your cooked cabbage and fluffy freekeh, followed by the lemon juice and zest. Season with salt and pepper and mix well to combine.

Add about half your vinaigrette to the slaw, mixing well to make sure everything is coated.

Serve individually or in one big bowl, drizzling over the rest of the vinaigrette and adding salt and pepper to taste.

For the salad

approx. 450g cruciferous vegetables (any variety of cabbage, kale, cauliflower, Brussels sprouts), roughly chopped or shredded

1 tbsp olive oil

1 tbsp soy sauce or tamari

2 tsp dried oregano

salt and pepper

200g freekeh (couscous, wheat berry, bulgur are also great here)

approx. 450g vegetable stock

70g raisins/sultanas (any variety – currants, golden, etc.)

1 shallot, finely chopped or sliced

a small handful of fresh seasonal herbs of choice (parsley, mint, etc.)

1 lemon, juiced, plus a dash of zest

For the vinaigrette

2 tsp Dijon mustard

2 tsp wholegrain mustard

2 tsp pure maple syrup, or any other sweetener of choice

85ml apple cider vinegar or white wine vinegar

125ml olive oil

1–2 tsp dried oregano (depending on taste)

My dad often talks about the variety of dishes he had when he was a kid. We used to get together with his family in a little authentic Polish restaurant in West London. I'd see these stuffed cabbage leaves flying around and always wanted to try them, but alas, to my disappointment they had meat in them. I attempted a few variations before landing on this recipe. The spelt creates a lovely chewy texture inside the leaves and the sauce brings it all together. A very colourful dish!

Serves 4–6

POLISH-STYLE STUFFED CABBAGE LEAVES

Preheat your oven to 200°C fan. Carefully separate the leaves of your cabbage from the base. Bring a large pot of salted water to the boil and blanch the cabbage leaves for around 2–3 minutes, just to cook them through, making them easy to handle when stuffing. Drain and place to one side while you make the filling.

Cook your grain according to the packet instructions in a large pot of salted boiling water. If using a slower-cooking grain, you can factor this into the overall cooking time. Once cooked, drain and set aside.

While your grain is cooking, make the sauce and filling. For the sauce, heat the olive oil in a shallow pan. Add the onion and sauté until slightly golden and fragrant, then add the garlic and continue to cook for another minute or so. Add the tomato purée, miso, chopped tomatoes, thyme, oregano and a dash of water to loosen. Season well with salt and pepper, stirring to combine.

Allow to simmer on a low heat, encouraging the tomatoes to soften and cook into a thick sauce. You can add a little more water if the sauce is sticking or too thick. When the desired consistency is reached, turn off the heat, ready for pouring over the cabbage leaves.

Over a low-medium heat, sauté your onions in the soy sauce or tamari. They will start to go brown quickly and

For the cabbage/filling

- 1 medium green or white cabbage, leaves separated
- approx. 120g grain of choice (pearled spelt, rice, barley)
- 1 brown or white onion, finely chopped
- 2 tbsp soy sauce or tamari
- 2 cloves of garlic, crushed or finely chopped
- a small handful of fresh parsley, finely chopped
- a small handful of fresh dill, finely chopped (optional)
- 6 medium button/chestnut mushrooms, very finely chopped
- 1 lemon, juiced, plus dash of zest
- 4 tsp smoked paprika
- 1 tsp ground allspice
- salt and pepper
- 1 heaped tbsp tahini
- 50g walnuts, roughly chopped
- 2 heaped tbsp raisins/sultanas/currants

For the tomato sauce

- ½–1 tbsp olive oil
- 1 small onion (any variety), finely chopped
- 2–4 cloves of garlic, crushed or finely chopped, depending on how garlicky you'd like the sauce

will caramelize ever so slightly. Add a dash of water if they dry up too much. Add the garlic and sauté for another minute or so, then add the parsley and dill, stirring to combine, and then the mushrooms. Mix well. Add the lemon juice and zest, along with the paprika and allspice. Season well with salt and pepper and add a dash of water to prevent the mixture sticking to the pan.

Transfer to a bowl and add the tahini, walnuts and sultanas, as well as your drained cooked grain. Season again with salt and pepper and stir well.

To build and serve, take your blanched cabbage leaves and place them flat on a surface. Divide your filling between the leaves (you can do as many leaves as you need in order to use up your filling) and roll them up carefully, starting from the bottom stem and tucking in the sides. Gently squeeze them to keep compact and place them in a baking dish. Continue until the dish is full and you have no mixture left.

Evenly pour over the tomato sauce, spreading it as you wish. Put into the oven to bake and warm through for about 20–25 minutes. They should be lovely and brown on top. Remove from the oven and serve on their own or with a simple side salad.

2 heaped tbsp tomato purée

½ tbsp miso paste

4 large or 8 small tomatoes (any variety), roughly chopped (see note)

1–2 tsp dried thyme

1–2 tsp dried oregano

salt and pepper

Note:

You can use a tin of tomatoes here if you can't find any fresh ones, depending on the season or what you want to use from your cupboard. Use tinned whole tomatoes, if you can.

Waste tips:

You can use any choice of grain in this dish, instead of the suggestions above, or feel free to use lentils or another cooked grain, depending on what you have in. Sometimes I'll add carrots and/or celery to the mix, or you can keep it very basic. Feel free to omit the mushrooms should you want to stick to cupboard ingredients, or add another vegetable of choice if you have leftovers. You can make big batches of the tomato sauce, as it keeps really well in the fridge or freezer. It's ideal for adding to pastas or rice dishes for something quick and hearty. This dish will keep in the fridge for a few days, so you could serve it cold with a plant-based

chestnuts

Oh, the sweet, sweet chestnut. Creamy, earthy and, believe it or not, a fruit. Once cooked, chestnuts are delicate and wholesome with a soft, velvety, slightly potatoey texture. When I was young I was always very keen on going for long walks through the countryside, but once we moved to London, that obviously became harder. To my surprise, we soon discovered many nice walks close to our house. One time we ended up on our local high street (the 'posher part', from what I remember), where, while waiting for my mum to stop chatting to a friend, my brother and I began collecting what we thought were conkers. We were a little confused, as we'd been told conkers were something you'd only see in autumn, but once we got home my dad told us what we'd collected were actually chestnuts, which we were excited about, knowing about them purely from a Christmas perspective. My dad roasted them for a little afternoon treat, then faced the 'challenge' of de-shelling them to reveal their delightful insides. They make great desserts, nut roasts, stuffings, purées: I'm wholeheartedly obsessed.

Waste tips:

Naturally it's easy to think that you have to chuck away the shells of the chestnuts once they're roasted or boiled. But a little trick is to add them to a milk of choice and let them sit for a few hours, to create a beautifully rich chestnut milk. Remove the shells from the milk and either serve it as it is, or warm it up with a few extra spices or perhaps even some cacao. If you've got any of the fruit itself left, you can add this along with the shells, let it sit as described, then blend to make it extra creamy (making sure to still remove the shells first). Depending on how many you use, you might have to strain it before drinking, but usually if it's just a few, you'll be fine.

I've expressed my love for chestnuts already (see page 272), and all my friends probably get just a little bit fed up with me cooking them when the season is upon us, as I'll have them with anything and everything. These ones are cooked, kept pretty much as they are once the shells have been removed, then seasoned with garlic, mustard seeds and a variety of oils to help create a 'buttery'-tasting sauce.

Serves approx.
4 as a side

TWICE-COOKED 'BUTTERY' GARLIC CHESTNUTS

w/ mustard seeds

Preheat your oven to 200°C fan. Using a sharp knife, make an X-shaped cut on both sides of each chestnut, making sure it goes pretty much the whole width and length. Place them on a baking tray and roast for about 15–20 minutes. The shells will start to pull back from where you've made the cuts, exposing the flesh inside. Allow to sit for a few minutes to cool, then peel the shells off.

Put the coconut oil into a large frying pan over a low heat. Once hot, add the mustard seeds and cook them until they start to pop, stirring occasionally. This should take a few minutes or so. Transfer them to a small bowl and set aside. Add the olive oil to the same pan, and heat. Add the garlic and fry until it starts to go golden and fragrant. Add the mustard seeds, 2 tablespoons of the milk, the nutmeg and a good seasoning of salt and pepper.

Add the chestnuts – you can break some of them up in the pan to give a variety of sizes. Stir to coat, then add the other 2 tablespoons of milk. Season again if necessary.

Serve hot, with sides of choice.

180g chestnuts

1 tbsp coconut oil

2 tsp mustard seeds

1 tbsp olive oil

4 cloves of garlic, finely sliced

4 tbsp unsweetened plant-based milk

½ tsp grated nutmeg

salt and pepper

Waste tips:

Often we neglect and forget about chestnuts, so this is a nice way to make them feel a little fancier. This recipe doubles up as a great creamy-style sauce. Simply follow the same process and blend at the end until smooth. You could add it to pasta, vegetables, risottos, even a very wintry curry. It also works well as a hummus or a pâté-style dip. If you have leftovers they will keep in the fridge for 2–3 days. Warm them up in a small saucepan and they're good as new! I occasionally add fresh herbs to this dish to jazz it up slightly, but it's a handy 'cupboard' recipe, simple but delicious.

This creamy pasta is one of my boyfriend Paul's favourites. The sage adds subtle crispness and a pop of colour, breaking up the shades of beige. You can use any pasta, but orecchiette is the winner for me here. The little hat-shaped pasta soaks up the sauce, surprising you with a burst of flavour. Rich and luxurious tasting, this is a real winter special.

Serves 4–6

CREAMED CHESTNUT AND SAGE PASTA

Preheat your oven to 200°C fan. Use a sharp knife to cut an X-shape on both sides of each chestnut, ensuring it goes pretty much the whole width and length. Place them on a baking tray and roast for 15–20 minutes. The shells will start to pull back from the cuts, exposing the flesh inside. Allow to cool for a few minutes, then peel the shells off.

Heat a tablespoon of olive oil in a saucepan and sauté the onions until soft and slightly browned. Add the garlic and fry for another minute or so. Season with salt and pepper, add the sage and thyme, stir to combine and fry slightly.

Add the cubed potato, stock, soy sauce or tamari, tahini, mustard and paprika. Season again with salt and pepper. Bring to the boil, then lower to a simmer and cook until the potato is totally tender, with less liquid in the pot.

Meanwhile, bring a pot of salted water to the boil, add your pasta and cook until al dente, about 10 minutes. Drain, reserving a little of the water, and put the pasta back into the same pot. Add the other tablespoon of olive oil and stir to prevent the pasta sticking together. Cover.

Remove the cooked potatoes from the heat, transfer the sauce mixture to a blender (or use a hand blender in the pan), add the cooked chestnuts, and blend until smooth.

Over a low heat, pour the sauce over the pasta and mix well to combine and heat through. Season with salt and pepper if needed. Serve hot with your favourite sides or vegan cheese (see pages 364 and 365 to make your own).

approx. 450g chestnuts
1–2 tbsp olive oil
1 medium brown or white onion, finely chopped
4 cloves of garlic, crushed or finely chopped
salt and pepper
3–5 fresh sage leaves, roughly chopped
1 tbsp dried thyme
1 medium potato, any variety, or
2 smaller potatoes, cubed
750ml–1 litre vegetable stock
2 tbsp soy sauce or tamari
2 tbsp tahini
1 tbsp Dijon mustard
½ tsp spicy paprika
approx. 250–400g orecchiette pasta (depending on how many you are serving)

Waste tips:

You can swap the potato for sweet potato, butternut squash or another squash variety. Chestnuts are delicious at this time of the year, and buying fresh is always better, but you can substitute ready-cooked ones if needed – look for ones sold in glass, so you can re-use the container. If you can't get chestnuts, omit them and use double the quantity of potato, plus 4 tablespoons of tahini to reach a similar consistency.

This is adapted from the parsnip nut roast on page 207. Adding chestnuts gives the loaf a creamier texture, while remaining still just as moist and just as tasty. When they're in season, chestnuts are a must here.

Serves approx. 6–8 as a side

CHESTNUT NUT ROAST

Preheat your oven to 200°C fan. Grease a large loaf tin and put to one side.

Place your parsnips on a baking tray and roast dry for about 30–35 minutes, until browned slightly and soft on the inside. Roasting them dry prevents them losing any moisture. Remove from the oven and allow to cool. Once cooled, mash well and put to one side.

In a small bowl, combine the flax with 8 tablespoons of water, creating a gloopyish paste. Set in the fridge to harden.

In a frying pan, heat the olive oil over a low heat and sauté the onion until slightly translucent and fragrant. Add the garlic and sage leaves and continue to sauté until they start to turn slightly brown. Add the nutmeg and the roughly ground cooked chestnuts plus a dash of water and cook a little, stirring well. Season with a generous amount of salt and pepper.

Stir through the ground nuts, rosemary, thyme, miso paste, breadcrumbs, 2 tablespoons of wholemeal flour, the nutritional yeast and your flax mixture. Add the mashed parsnip and combine well, using your hands. Season again if necessary. If your mixture is still a little wet, add the other 2 tablespoons of flour.

Transfer the mixture to your loaf tin and pack it down tightly. Roast, on a low/middle rack, for about 30 minutes, checking halfway through the cooking time. You want the top to become brown and crispy and the loaf to cook through. You can test it with a knife, making sure the mixture is not too loose.

400g parsnips, thoroughly washed, roughly chopped, skins on

3 tbsp ground flax

8 tbsp water

1 tbsp olive oil

1 white or brown onion, finely chopped

4 cloves of garlic, crushed or finely chopped

approx. 6 fresh sage leaves, roughly chopped

½–1 tsp grated nutmeg

approx. 200g cooked chestnuts, roughly/coarsely ground (you can do this in a processor; see notes for cooking chestnuts on page 251)

salt and pepper

185g cashews, almonds, or a combination (you could also use hazelnuts for a twist, ground in a processor)

2 heaped tsp fresh rosemary leaves, 1 tsp if dried

2 heaped tsp fresh thyme leaves, 1 tsp if dried

2 heaped tsp miso paste

approx. 140g breadcrumbs (any kind, use leftover/stale bread)

2–4 tbsp wholemeal flour

2–3 tbsp nutritional yeast

Once cooked, remove from the oven and allow to cool for about 5 minutes, then flip it over on to a serving plate. Place a plate on the open surface of the tin and flip, giving the tin a little shake to help the nut roast fall out.

Serve with your desired sides, as part of a roast dinner, with fresh greens, grains, etc. (See page 246 for the ultimate mushroom gravy.)

Waste tips:

You'll find a nut roast in the previous season too, but here I've adapted the recipe to use chestnuts, roasting them first to improve their texture and creaminess once ground. You could change things up with the parsnips, for example by adding some carrot, potato, swede, etc. – any vegetables of a similar texture. It's nice to have a combination, and adding an orange vegetable of course brings extra colour. Feel free to use any other flour you like or have in. I'd recommend using a thicker flour over a finer one such as coconut or buckwheat; they will still work, you may just need a tad more.

pears

To me, pears are the ultimate winter fruit. When they're good, they're good. I'll have them for breakfast, as a snack, or as part of a warm salad for a lighter supper or lunch in the winter months. Pears come in many varieties, from Bartlett to Bosc, Concorde, d'Anjou, nashi. They are mild but with a unique sweetness and an almost vanilla-like taste . . . and while we're on the subject, pears are in fact great paired with vanilla pods, for the real deal. One of the best combinations, loosely based on a childhood favourite of mine, is thinly sliced pears on toast that's been layered thickly with a nut-based ricotta. Serve it with toasted pine nuts, a drizzle of olive oil and salt and pepper, and you won't look back, I can promise. It's simple yet creative and actually quite the dish to impress, either as a savoury breakfast or perhaps at 3 p.m. when you're peckish but wanting something slightly different. Pears are a fruit that I would always recommend you buy organic if you can, otherwise they often contain a lot of pesticides, despite their easy growth.

Waste tips:

You can very easily replace pears with stone fruit in the summer, as their texture is quite similar, especially when cooked. Soft pears make the most delicious compote: add vanilla, spices and a pinch of salt and they won't disappoint. Apples are another great fruit to use either alongside or instead, should your pears not be ripe, as is quite often the case; and a hard, not-quite-ready pear is a little disappointing. Just like apples, pears tend to brown quite quickly, so when adding them fresh/raw, you'll want to dress them quickly, or squeeze a little lemon juice on them to prevent any browning.

I'm not usually one for desserts, or much into 'tea and cake', but this upside-down number is the exception. The pear becomes soft and gooey and the cake is light and fluffy, with nutty tones throughout, thanks to the buckwheat flour. It is delicious served with a dollop of coconut yoghurt and, yep, a cup of tea or coffee.

Makes 10–12 slices (size depending)

UPSIDE-DOWN PEAR CAKE

Preheat your oven to 180°C fan. Line a round cake tin (approx. 20cm) with some coconut oil or greaseproof paper. Sprinkle a dash of cinnamon and brown sugar evenly over the base of the tin.

Place the slices from two of your pears around the bottom of the tin, arranging them relatively neatly in a fan shape. You can overlap here too. Put the tin to one side.

In a mixing bowl, combine the buckwheat flour, coconut flour and baking powder. Add the rest of the brown sugar, the cinnamon/mixed spices and salt and mix well. Slowly pour in the coconut oil, plant-based milk and vanilla extract. Stir until you have a smooth batter, making sure not to over-beat. You want a 'dropping consistency', so if the batter is a little stiff, add a dribble more liquid.

Mix the diced pear into the batter and pour it into the lined tin, spreading it evenly. Remove any air pockets by carefully banging the tin a few times on a surface, then bake in the oven for about 50–55 minutes.

When done, the cake will be relatively spongy to touch and a lovely golden brown on top. Test the inside by using a sharp knife or skewer. It can be a little tricky if you hit a pear when testing, but you'll be able to tell if the batter is done.

Set aside to cool for 5–10 minutes. Once cool enough, turn the tin upside down on a cooling rack. Carefully remove the tin and greaseproof paper, if used. To serve, dust with a little extra spice.

3 ripe pears, 2 sliced into approx. eighths, 1 diced

240g buckwheat flour

120g coconut flour

2 tsp baking powder

165g brown sugar (coconut sugar will also work)

2 heaped tsp either cinnamon or mixed spices (nutmeg, cloves, cardamom, etc.), plus a little extra for dusting

a pinch of salt

125g coconut oil

approx. 500ml unsweetened plant-based milk of choice (I love to use coconut milk here)

2 tsp vanilla extract

Waste tips:

This is a good way to use up pears that are on the turn. You could swap in apples if you have some, or even a combination. My flour preference for this recipe is coconut because of the taste, but feel free to experiment with other fine flours, such as very fine oat flour, gram flour, etc., or whatever you have in. Vegan cakes are often easier to bake than normal cakes, as long as there is a raising agent, as they won't sink in the way that a regular cake can.

One of my first pear experiments, I have been making this recipe for longer than I can remember. Incorporating a savoury herb takes away any overpowering sweetness. My favourite way to enjoy these is with a sprinkle of extra cinnamon and some coconut cream or yoghurt, as suggested in the recipe.

Serves 3–6, depending on pear distribution/portioning

MAPLE AND THYME ROASTED PEARS

Preheat your oven to 200°C fan. Carefully remove the seeds from the sliced pears, keeping the halves intact.

Put the coconut oil into a heavy-bottomed/cast-iron pan, with 125ml of maple syrup, the vanilla extract, sugar, thyme, cinnamon, nutmeg, cloves and a big pinch of salt. Over a low heat, stirring frequently, let the mixture slowly come to a gentle rolling boil.

Add the pear halves, cut side down. Let them simmer and soften in the mixture for a few minutes. If you are using a cast-iron pan, you'll be able to transfer this straight into the oven, otherwise transfer it to an ovenproof dish here. Bake for 10–12 minutes, allowing the pears to cook, caramelize slightly and become soft all the way through.

While the pears are in the oven, you can quickly whip your coconut cream. Scoop out the cream from the refrigerated coconut milk tin and place in a bowl. Make sure you get as little liquid in the bowl as you can – you want as much cream as possible. (Save the coconut water/liquid, see waste tips.) Using a whisk (electric or hand) or a hand blender, beat until the cream starts to become a bit stiffer. Add the 2 tablespoons of maple syrup and a pinch of salt and beat for another minute or so.

To serve, remove the pears from the oven, and place either on separate plates or on a larger serving platter. Add a few small dollops of the whipped coconut cream on top, and an extra dusting of cinnamon. I like to decorate with sprigs of thyme, but this is up to you.

3 ripe pears (Bosc, Bartlett, Concorde), sliced in half lengthways

2 tbsp coconut oil (or a dairy-free butter)

125ml pure maple syrup, plus 2 tbsp for the cream (or other sweetener of choice)

1 tsp pure vanilla extract/essence

50g natural sugar (coconut, brown, cane, etc.)

approx. 2–4 tbsp fresh thyme sprigs

1 heaped tsp ground cinnamon

½ tsp grated nutmeg

½ tsp ground cloves

salt

1 × 400ml tin of coconut milk (refrigerated for 24 hours)

Waste tips:

These pears keep for 4–5 days in the fridge. They're great with granola, on porridge or even as a base for a crumble. To make a simple crumble for one, chop up a leftover pear, pop into a ramekin and top with a mixture of oats, coconut oil, spices, a tad of flour and sugar. The leftover coconut water will keep in the fridge, to use in smoothies, porridge, curries, etc. It's not always super creamy, but it adds a depth of flavour. Sometimes I use it instead of stock in chickpea recipes (see pages 260 and 320 for inspo).

I'll never forget the reaction I got when serving a 'cheese' platter for guests at a supper club. The magic of cashews, if you ask me. This gives you a bit of everything and can be served in a variety of ways, but of course the classic chutney pairing is a must, and some crackers or bread will never go amiss either.

Pear chutney makes approx. 30–32 servings of 2 tbsp

___

Baked cashew cheese makes 1 big batch, enough for approx. 20 servings

___

STOCK CUPBOARD PEAR AND ONION CHUTNEY

___

w/ smoked, baked cashew cheese

Preheat your oven to 160°C fan. For the chutney, dry fry your onions in a large pan over a medium heat for 1 minute or so, just until they start to brown. Add the coconut and olive oil and stir to combine. Lower the heat, add a dash of water and season with salt and pepper. Continue to cook the onions until they start to soften.

Once soft, go ahead and add the sugar, vinegar, half the water, the grated ginger and the diced pears. Stir to combine, and add an extra pinch of salt. Bring back to the boil, then lower to a simmer and let the mixture bubble for about 12–15 minutes. Your pears will start to soften and turn more golden.

Keeping it on a low heat, stir in the mustard, nutmeg, ground cloves, thyme and another seasoning of salt and pepper. Continue to simmer on low for another 20–25 minutes, stirring occasionally. You want the mixture to be thick and relatively glossy. The smaller your pears are, the quicker they'll cook, so be careful they don't start to 'mush' together. Once cooked, allow to cool to room temperature.

While your chutney is simmering, make the cheese. Drain your cashews and place them in a high-speed blender/processor. Add the lemon juice and zest, apple cider vinegar, nutritional yeast, thyme, smoked paprika (go in with less of the thyme and paprika first, then taste accordingly before adding more), chilli flakes, harissa if

For the pear chutney

___

3 red onions, halved, then thinly sliced

1 tbsp coconut oil

1 tbsp olive oil

salt and pepper

approx. 220g demerara sugar or light brown sugar

85–125ml vinegar (white wine, cider or white balsamic)

approx. 125ml water

approx. ½ tsp grated fresh ginger

5 medium ripe pears, any variety, diced small, seeds removed, skins left on

1 heaped tbsp wholegrain mustard

½–1 tsp grated nutmeg

½ tsp ground cloves

approx. 2 tbsp fresh thyme leaves

For the baked cashew cheese

___

240g cashews, soaked for at least 2 hours in boiling water, preferably overnight

1 lemon, juiced, plus a dash of zest

1 tsp apple cider vinegar

50–75g nutritional yeast

1–2 heaped tsp dried thyme

1–2 heaped tsp smoked paprika

a pinch of dried chilli flakes

using, mustard, garlic, milk and three-quarters of the water. Season with salt and pepper and blend. You want a smooth consistency, so it will take a few minutes or so. Depending on your blender/processor, you may have to scrape down the sides every so often. If your mixture is a little thick, add the remaining water. You want it to be smooth but thick enough so it doesn't fall or run off a spoon. Add your extra herbs/spices if necessary and blitz them in.

Line a flat baking tray with baking paper and start to scoop the cashew mix into the middle of the tray. I like to pour it all out first into a pile so that it forms a rough circular shape, then even out the top using a spatula or the back of a spoon. Sprinkle a good pinch of salt on top and add a light dusting of extra dried herbs.

Put into the oven on the middle shelf and bake for around 30–40 minutes. The time will vary depending on your oven. The top should start to crack and be a lovely golden brown. It will be crisp, but the inside will be a little softer. Once cooked, remove from the oven and allow to cool and harden slightly.

To serve, you could create portions, or a bigger platter/cheeseboard-style option. Slice the cheese and serve with a hefty dollop of chutney. The chutney will thicken over time, and once cooled and stored in the fridge.

1 tsp harissa (optional, see page 361 for homemade version)

1–2 tbsp Dijon mustard

2 cloves of garlic, crushed or finely chopped

125ml plant-based milk

approx. 500ml water

salt and pepper

Waste tips:

Both the cheese and the chutney keep well in the fridge; the chutney will thicken and develop more flavour. Often I add a pinch of dried chilli flakes when putting it into the jar, for a little kick. If you don't have pears, you can use apples, or even a combination, as well as playing around with the onions that you use, based on what you have in. This cheese variation is based on another recipe (see page 132), and you can easily alter the flavourings depending on taste.

When Sri Lanka meets India and then meets the Middle East. This is a recipe inspired by all of them, with lots of herbs and spices, a simple tahini sauce and another great use of cabbage!

Serves 2–3

CHICKPEA DOSA, ZA'ATAR SPICED PEAR AND CABBAGE, TAHINI SAUCE

Preheat your oven to 180°C fan. Make your tahini sauce first so that it can sit in the fridge and firm up slightly. In a small bowl whisk together the tahini, lemon juice and zest, vinegar, mustard, soy sauce or tamari, maple syrup, salt and pepper. Add a dash of water if you'd like the sauce to have a runnier consistency. Put into the fridge and leave to thicken.

Put the pears and cabbage on a baking tray and sprinkle over the za'atar spice blend. Drizzle over the olive oil and season with salt and pepper. Put into the oven and roast for about 20 minutes. They will cook quicker the softer they are, so be sure to keep an eye on them. Once cooked, remove from the oven and let them cool slightly.

To make the dosa, put the grated carrot, onion and garlic into a bowl and mix to combine. Add the gram flour, chopped herbs, cumin, turmeric, nutritional yeast and salt and pepper, and mix again. Slowly pour in the water and begin to mix. You want the batter to be runny, with no floury lumps. You can add a little more water or flour if need be.

Over a medium heat, add a small amount of oil to your frying pan and heat it up, swirling it around the whole pan. Using a ladle, gently pour in some of the batter. You can make the dosa as small or as big as you like, filling the whole pan with one dosa or making a few at a time (this will vary your frying time). Fry for a few minutes on one side, until the surface starts to show bubbles and the bottom is browning. Flip and repeat, frying for another couple of minutes.

For the tahini sauce

2 heaped tbsp tahini

1 large lemon, juiced, plus a dash of zest

½ tsp vinegar of choice

1 tbsp Dijon mustard

2 tsp soy sauce or tamari

1 tbsp pure maple syrup, or other sweetener of choice

salt and pepper

For the za'atar spiced pear and cabbage

2 medium pears (any variety/ available), sliced in half lengthways, then quartered, seeds removed

½ a small cabbage of choice, thinly sliced/shredded, lengthways

2 tsp za'atar spice blend

1–2 tsp olive oil

salt and pepper

For the dosa

1–2 small carrots, grated

1 small onion, finely chopped/grated

2 cloves of garlic, crushed or finely chopped

120g gram flour (chickpea flour)

1 large handful of fresh herbs of choice (parsley, dill, coriander, or a combination), finely chopped

1 tsp ground cumin

1 tsp ground turmeric

1 heaped tbsp nutritional yeast

salt and pepper

185–250ml water

oil of choice, for frying (coconut, olive, avocado, etc.)

approx. 2–4 spring onions,
  finely chopped
sesame seeds, lightly toasted
olive oil, to drizzle

To serve, place your dosa on a
plate and top with the desired
amount of pear and cabbage.
Drizzle over the tahini and
finish off with some sliced
onions, sesame seeds and
a drizzle of olive oil. Season
with additional salt and pepper
if necessary.

mushrooms

Portobello, cremini, button, shiitake, porcini, morel . . .
so many amazing names, all amazing mushrooms.
Mushrooms do have a bad reputation at times, something
that is quite foreign to me, as I have always loved them.
Even as a kid, while most children are averse to their
slimy texture, I loved them in everything: pasta dishes,
soups, roasted. My mum loved them too and was quite
experimental with them: she'd often roast them with a
little pesto and some crushed nuts on top and serve them
with a large leafy salad. It was simple, but we were very
fond of it. Mushrooms ooze a sort of 'wine' flavour to me,
which I think added to their appeal. Remember when
you always wanted to be older than you were, with an
acquired taste to fit the bill, trying to impress your
parents and their friends?

Mushrooms have a great meaty texture when cooked,
which is why they make an obvious meat replacement,
especially in burgers or bolognese-type dishes. You can
add them to curries and, if you're lucky enough to get your
hands on some large king oyster mushrooms, those are
ideal for recreating that 'pulled meat' style. When I lived
in Peckham we had a little grocer's close by where all
the produce was local and organic, store-cupboard items
as well as fresh produce. I wandered in there once and
spotted a little basket of fresh porcini mushrooms. Having
just bought a fresh loaf of bread from my favourite bakery,
I decided to snap up the last of these mushrooms, fry them
in a little garlic and have them on toast. Of course, because
they are so rare, they can be expensive. It's safe to say that
was an expensive lunch, but worth every penny.

Waste tips:

Mushrooms make great stock. You
can add a little twist with some
miso and dried mushrooms, boiling
them with the rest of your stock
ingredients. See page 352 for a
homemade stock recipe. Finely
chopped or minced mushrooms can
be added to dishes when you want
to replicate a meaty texture. You
can use them in falafel or burger-
type recipes, stuff them, roast them
. . . you name it, you'll always find
a use for mushrooms, whether
they're on the turn or you got a bit
mushroom-happy at the shops.

You can't go wrong with risotto, and my mum makes one of the best I've ever had. Her go-tos are mushrooms and seasonal greens. I think it was secretly one of her favourite meals to cook, due to the fact that we always devoured it!

Serves approx. 4–6

MUSHROOM AND TARRAGON RISOTTO

Heat 1 tablespoon of olive oil in a pan. Add the shallots and leeks and cook until they start to brown and smell fragrant. Add the garlic and nutmeg and cook for another minute or so, being careful not to burn the garlic.

Add your sliced mushrooms and a dash of water. You want them to soften but not cook entirely at this stage, as they will cook further with the rice. Once they've become a little tender, releasing some liquid, add the rice.

Stir constantly, to lightly cook/toast the rice before adding your stock – you'll notice the outside of the rice grains starting to go slightly translucent. Add the white wine and 'burn' off the alcohol. It'll have a strong smell at first, then will start to simmer nicely.

Start adding the stock, a ladle at a time, stirring often to prevent the rice sticking to the pan. Season with salt and pepper. Continue until you have added three-quarters of your stock, then leave on a low heat to simmer.

Add three-quarters of the lemon juice and zest, the dried and fresh tarragon, oregano and nutritional yeast. Stir well and season with salt and pepper if necessary.

Once your rice is almost done (after about 30 minutes of simmering), add the remaining stock, lemon juice and zest, and warm through. You want your rice to still have a little bit of bite. Season with salt and pepper to taste.

Serve in bowls with a pinch of lemon zest, the toasted hazelnuts and a good drizzle of olive oil on top. Sprinkle over some nutritional yeast for an extra 'cheesy' hit.

2 tbsp olive oil, plus extra for serving (garlic-infused olive oil is great in this recipe)

2 small shallots or 1 large white onion, finely chopped

1 small leek, sliced lengthways, washed and roughly chopped

4 cloves of garlic, crushed or finely chopped

½ tsp grated nutmeg

approx. 250–300g mushrooms of choice (wild, button, chestnut, cremini, etc.), sliced

350g risotto/arborio rice

approx. 250ml white wine

1 litre vegetable stock (for homemade see page 352)

salt and pepper

1½ lemons, juiced, zest from 1

1–2 heaped tsp dried tarragon

approx. 2 tbsp fresh tarragon, finely chopped

2 tsp dried oregano, or other dried mixed herbs

50g nutritional yeast, plus extra to garnish

approx. 50g hazelnuts, crushed, lightly toasted

Waste tips:

Mushrooms can start to look old and unhappy quite quickly, but this risotto is a great way to use them up. You can use any variety you want. The tarragon can easily be subbed with any other herb of choice, as can the dried herbs. Feel free to add more dried oregano if you like a stronger flavour.

Vegan gravy is one of those recipes that for me always brings the plate together. I love it poured right on top, soaking into all the vegetables. Not too rich, this gravy is beautifully smooth once blended, although I personally like to leave some mushroom chunks, but it works a treat either way.

Serves 4–6

MUSHROOM GRAVY

Put your olive oil into a wide pan over a low heat and sauté the onions until soft and slightly browned.

Add the mushrooms and garlic and continue to fry for a few minutes – the mixture will become quite moist, due to the mushrooms. Once cooked and fragrant, add 750ml of stock, the fresh thyme, rosemary and sage, and stir well. Bring to a gentle boil, then reduce to a simmer.

Add the nutritional yeast, mustard, vinegar, coconut aminos, flour, nutmeg, plant-based milk and chilli flakes, and season with salt and pepper to taste. Slowly stir on a low heat to get rid of any lumps, allowing the liquid to thicken. If it is too thick, add the rest of the stock.

Turn off the heat, then remove a third of the mushroom mix and set aside. Blitz the rest of the gravy in an upright blender, or use a hand blender, until smooth.

Check the seasoning and add extra salt and pepper if necessary. Transfer the blended liquid back to a pan, along with the reserved mushrooms. Stir over a low-medium heat, to warm the gravy. Serve hot, with sides of choice.

1–2 tbsp olive oil

1 medium onion, finely chopped/ diced

250g mushrooms (chestnut, button, a variety, etc.), sliced

3 cloves of garlic, crushed or finely chopped

approx. 750ml–1 litre vegetable stock

2 tbsp fresh thyme, finely chopped

1½ tbsp fresh rosemary, finely chopped

a few fresh sage leaves, rubbed to release their flavour and roughly chopped

2–4 tbsp nutritional yeast

1 tbsp Dijon mustard

1 tbsp sherry vinegar or white wine vinegar

2 tbsp coconut aminos or soy sauce

2 tbsp plain flour

½–1 tsp grated nutmeg

65ml unsweetened plant-based milk

a pinch of dried chilli flakes

salt and pepper

Waste tips:

This gravy is so versatile. You can serve it traditionally with a 'roast' style dinner, with vegetables, or even use it in a pie, pairing it with mashed potatoes and a lentil ragù (see page 249 for a pie suggestion). The gravy will keep in the fridge for about 5 days, or a lot longer in the freezer. You can blitz the whole thing if you'd rather have a looser gravy. You can also use the recipe above and add a choice of potatoes plus some extra stock for a nice, thick, soup-like consistency once blended, or else leave some parts whole for a more stew-type dish. It's a great way to use a recipe as a larger meal, especially if you're after something that's quick and easy but still cosy!

When wild mushrooms come out to play, I'm a sucker for them. My boyfriend, Paul, laughs at how over the top I am about them, but to me they are always worth the wait for their short-lived season. Served with a medium spiced harissa and a simple grain, here the mushrooms do all the talking.

WILD MUSHROOMS, MILLET AND GREEN HARISSA

Start by making the harissa. Put the garlic, jalapeño, coriander, mint, parsley, lemon juice and zest, cumin seeds, coriander seeds and vinegar into a blender (or put them into a bowl and use a hand blender). Season with salt and pepper and blitz for a minute or so, then add the olive oil and continue to blend until you have a rough paste. Taste and adjust, adding the chilli flakes if you like, and any extra oil to loosen. Transfer to a bowl and set aside.

Bring a pan of salted water to the boil. Add the millet, bring to a simmer, then cook until al dente, about 12 minutes. Once cooked, drain any excess water and cover to keep warm.

While your millet is cooking, heat 1 tablespoon of oil in a pan, then add the shallots and fry until they start to soften and brown. Add the garlic and sauté for another minute or so, being careful not to burn the garlic.

Go ahead and add the white wine, mustard, lemon juice, zest and mixed herbs/oregano. Season with salt and pepper and stir to combine. Bring to a low boil and add the mushrooms, stirring to coat them with the liquid.

Cook the mushrooms for about 10 minutes, until they soften and start to make the sauce a lot richer in colour, seasoning with salt and pepper if necessary. Add the chickpeas and stir. Add 2–4 tablespoons of the harissa, stirring to combine and heating through.

Serve the millet topped with the mushrooms and an extra dollop of the green harissa. Scatter over some freshly chopped herbs and enjoy.

For the harissa

2 cloves of garlic, crushed

1 large jalapeño, deseeded if you like

a large handful of fresh coriander, stalks included, roughly chopped

a large handful of fresh mint, leaves roughly chopped, stalks composted

a large handful of fresh parsley, stalks included, roughly chopped

1 large lemon, juiced, plus a dash of zest

1 tsp cumin seeds, toasted

1 tsp coriander seeds, toasted

1 tbsp white wine vinegar or apple cider vinegar

salt and pepper

approx. 125ml olive oil

¼ tsp dried chilli flakes (optional)

For the millet and mushrooms

approx. 350g dried millet grain

1–2 tbsp olive oil

2 small shallots, thinly sliced

2 cloves of garlic, thinly sliced

65ml white wine or 2 tbsp white wine vinegar (if you'd like to omit the alcohol)

1 tbsp Dijon mustard

1 small lemon, juiced, plus a dash of zest

2 heaped tsp dried mixed herbs/ oregano

salt and pepper

500g mixed wild mushrooms, roughly torn/ chopped (you can also use any other variety or combination)

1 × 400g tin of chickpeas, drained

Waste tips:

As above, you can use any type of mushrooms in this dish, making it really easy to adapt. You could also replace the mushrooms with aubergines for a similar consistency but a different outcome. I'd use about 2 medium aubergines in place of the mushrooms for the given serving suggestion here. See page 320 for cooking chickpeas from scratch if you are not using tinned ones. You could also use any other beans. Occasionally I make the harissa into a drizzle for this dish. Simply put a couple of tablespoons of harissa into a bowl, add a squeeze of lemon and about 1 tablespoon of tahini, mix with a fork to combine, then drizzle over the finished dish.

Mushrooms are so versatile – and wonderful for creating a 'meaty' taste and texture. This is a simple recipe that can be easily made ahead of time.

Serves approx. 4

MUSHROOM 'MEATBALLS' MARINARA

Preheat the oven to 200°C fan. In a small bowl, combine the chia/ground flax seeds and water. Put into the fridge to form a gel-type mixture.

Heat the oil in a pan and sauté your onions for a few minutes over a medium heat until they turn slightly golden and soften. Add the garlic and fry for a further minute or so.

Add the mushrooms and sauté until tender and slightly glistening. This won't take very long if they are very finely chopped. Take off the heat and transfer to a bowl.

Add the soy sauce or tamari, balsamic, miso, nutritional yeast, chopped parsley, oregano, thyme and chilli flakes to the bowl of mushrooms. Mix well to combine.

If you haven't already, blitz the oats, walnuts and pine nuts to a floury consistency and add to the bowl. Add your chia/flax gel and begin to mix into a chunky dough, using your hands. Season well with salt and pepper.

Form the dough into about 8–10 balls, depending on the size you'd like them to be. Once you've formed the balls, lightly brush them with a little olive oil, which will help to keep them in shape while they cook. Place the balls on a baking tray and put them into the oven for about 25 minutes. You want them to be brown all over and firmed up.

While the 'meatballs' are baking, make your marinara sauce. Heat the olive oil in a saucepan and add the onion. Sauté until brown and softened, then add the garlic and sauté for another minute or so, until fragrant.

For the 'meatballs'

1 tbsp chia or ground flax seeds

2–2½ tbsp water

1 tbsp olive oil

1 white or brown onion or large shallot, finely chopped/diced

4 cloves of garlic, crushed

approx. 225–250g mushrooms, any variety, very finely chopped

1 tbsp soy sauce or tamari

1 tbsp balsamic vinegar

½ tbsp miso paste (white, brown, yellow)

approx. 2 tbsp nutritional yeast

a small handful of fresh parsley, finely chopped, or 1 heaped tbsp dried

1 tbsp dried oregano

1 tsp dried thyme

1 tsp dried chilli flakes

approx. 65g oats, blitzed to flour

60g walnuts, lightly toasted, blitzed

2 tbsp pine nuts, lightly toasted

salt and pepper

olive oil, for brushing

For the marinara sauce

1 tbsp olive oil

1 brown onion, thinly sliced

3 cloves of garlic, crushed

2 × 400g tins of whole tomatoes

2 tbsp tomato purée

1 tbsp balsamic vinegar

½ tbsp raw sugar (cane, brown, coconut)

1–2 tsp dried mixed herbs

½ tsp grated nutmeg

salt and pepper

Add the tinned tomatoes, tomato purée, balsamic vinegar, sugar, mixed herbs and nutmeg, and season with salt and pepper. Bring to the boil, then reduce the heat to a simmer. Crush the tomatoes with the back of a wooden spoon as you go, reducing the liquid and thickening the sauce. When it is nice and thick, about 15–20 minutes, check the seasoning and add more salt and pepper if necessary.

To serve, you can either place your 'meatballs' in a dish and ladle over the steaming sauce, or serve it the other way round and have the 'meatballs' on top. The choice is yours. Add any extra fresh herbs you have, plus a drizzle of olive oil, and enjoy.

Waste tips:

A marinara sauce is a brilliant thing to batch cook and keep in the fridge or freezer. It's easy to add it to pasta dishes, rice, vegetables, etc., or even to use it to thicken a stew and add a bit more depth. You could also make these 'meatballs' using aubergines instead of mushrooms, perhaps for a summer supper rather than in winter. You'll need approximately the same amount of aubergine, chopped very small, then cooked in the same way. You'll achieve the same 'meaty' texture as you do with the mushrooms.

Note:

These 'meatballs' can also be fried in a little olive oil on the stove. Over a medium-high heat, cook on all sides until browned all over.

I don't often have noodles in – but they're one of those things I wish I remembered to buy regularly, because this recipe always springs to mind when a noodle craving arises. It's simple and tasty and can be adapted to the seasonal veggies you have. The kale is baked with coconut, adding an Asian twist to the dish, as does the addition of miso.

Serves approx. 4–6 as a side or main

NOODLES WITH CRISPY KALE, MISO MUSHROOMS

Preheat your oven to 180°C. Thoroughly wash your kale, then chop it and toss it into a large bowl. Add the coconut, nutritional yeast, garlic, 1 tablespoon of olive oil, half the lemon juice and all the zest. Using your hands, massage/mix thoroughly to make sure the kale is coated completely. If you need a little more liquid, add the other tablespoon of olive oil. Spread evenly on a baking tray and place on a middle shelf in the oven, baking for approx. 15 minutes. You don't want the kale or coconut to burn, so keep an eye on it. Remove from the oven to cool (as it cools, it will crisp up further).

While the kale is roasting, cook your mushrooms. Whisk together the balsamic vinegar, sesame oil, miso paste, garlic and mustard. Season with a little salt and pepper to taste and add your spring onions. Add the mushrooms, using a spoon to coat with the mixture, and leave for a few minutes to marinate.

Over a low-medium heat, put the mushrooms and their marinade into a frying pan or griddle pan. Cook for about 5 minutes, flipping them occasionally so they cook on all sides, until tender and slightly charred. You'll notice the spring onions will also start to caramelize and char, which will add a lovely flavour to the dish.

Bring a pot of salted water to the boil. Add the noodles and cook for about 12 minutes (this will vary depending on the noodles you are using). Once cooked, drain and quickly rinse under cold water to remove any excess starch. Put the noodles into a large bowl.

approx. 300g kale, roughly chopped, stalks/ribs included, any variety (curly, cavolo nero, etc.)

55g unsweetened desiccated coconut (try to get unsulphured)

20–30g nutritional yeast

1 clove of garlic, crushed

1–2 tbsp olive oil

1 lemon, juiced and zested

approx. 225g dried noodles (soba, udon, brown rice, etc.)

3 heaped tbsp tahini

2 tbsp soy sauce or tamari

2 tbsp sweet chilli sauce

dried chilli flakes (optional, to taste)

1 lime, juiced, plus a dash of zest

salt and pepper

For the miso mushrooms

4 tbsp balsamic vinegar

2–3 tbsp sesame oil, plus extra for serving

2 tbsp miso paste (white, yellow or brown)

1 clove of garlic, crushed or finely chopped

1 tbsp wholegrain mustard

salt and pepper

2 spring onions, finely chopped

4 large portobello mushrooms or 6–8 smaller mushrooms, thickly sliced

To serve

2–4 tbsp sesame seeds, lightly toasted

Whisk together the rest of your lemon juice, the tahini, soy sauce or tamari, sweet chilli sauce, chilli flakes if using, lime juice and zest. Season with a dash of salt and pepper.

Pour the tahini sauce over the noodles, and add the cooked mushrooms and roughly three-quarters of the cooked kale. Gently mix to combine, coating everything. Season with extra salt and pepper to taste if necessary.

Serve in dishes/bowls or on one larger platter, adding the rest of the crispy kale on top and a sprinkling of sesame seeds. You could add another drizzle of sesame oil here for serving, should you wish.

My friend Matilda had been raving about a restaurant that served garlic rice. We went in for some and it sent shivers down my spine. It certainly was garlicky but gave exactly what you'd want from a mouthful. The version I've made here is served with sautéed mushrooms, to jazz it up and make it into more of a meal.

Serves approx.
4 as a side,
2 as a main

GARLIC RICE

w/ caramelized onions, mushrooms

Put ½–1 tbsp of coconut oil into a saucepan over a low heat. Add the garlic and fry for a minute or so, stirring constantly to prevent the garlic burning. Add your rice and lightly dry fry.

Add about 1–1.5 litres of water to the pan (you may need more depending on the type of rice you are using), along with a large pinch of salt. Bring to the boil, then lower to a simmer and cover. Depending on your rice, the cooking time will vary. Longer for black, red, brown. Ideally keep the rice covered until cooked, about 12–15 minutes for white, about 30 minutes for brown and 35–40 for red or black. Once cooked, there should be little to no water left. Remove from the heat, let the rice sit for a few minutes, add the lemon then fluff with a fork.

While the rice is cooking, heat 1 tablespoon of coconut oil in a large flat pan or wok. Add the onion wedges and sauté for a couple of minutes, until fragrant and browned. Add the mushrooms plus a dash of water and sauté for a few minutes. Add the balsamic vinegar, thyme and chilli flakes, and season with salt and pepper. Continue to cook, allowing the liquid to reduce and the onions and mushrooms to begin to soften and caramelize, about 12–15 minutes. Season again with salt and pepper if necessary.

To serve, portion out the rice and ladle over the desired amount of mushrooms. Add any garnishes of choice: chilli flakes, thyme, etc., and enjoy.

1–2 tbsp coconut oil

5–6 cloves of garlic, crushed or finely chopped

approx. 250g dried rice of choice (brown, white, red, black, wild, etc.)

1 lemon, juice and zest

2 medium brown/white onions, cut into wedges

approx. 500g mushrooms of choice (mixed/variety, torn or roughly chopped)

2 tbsp balsamic vinegar (coconut aminos is also a great alternative here)

approx. 2 tbsp fresh thyme leaves

a pinch of dried chilli flakes

salt and pepper

Waste tips:

Any mushrooms will work for this dish – it's nice to mix them up and use a variety, but go with what you have or what's in season. It's a very simple dish that's full of flavour, quick to make, without compromising. You can use whichever rice you like, making the most of what's in your cupboard.

depths of
winter

Like most Brits, I usually claim to hate winter, and I find myself complaining about it often in the lead up, and again on any given dull day, which of course in the UK happens very frequently. However, if I'm being honest, it's not actually 'winter' that I dislike, it's more the grey skies and shorter evenings, and it often hits hard here come the start of the year. There are ways to stay positive in this climate, of course: one is to try not to be such a stereotypical Brit and to avoid moaning about the weather, and another is to make way for the best produce around, while cosying up and cocooning indoors, so that you don't even want to leave the house. Win–win, right? I'm definitely a homebody, despite travelling for a good part of the year, and I love to be at home, just pottering. Whether that's cleaning (mostly the kitchen – I really am my father's daughter, because cleaning the hob until it shines back in my face is for me pure glee), or testing new recipes, putting something on to cook all day or planning a dinner party. Winter dining is a real treat, with table decor in earthy tones and hearty food, as well as spiced, warming cocktails or a punchy glass of red. Hosting supper clubs in the winter never has the benefit of dining outside and basking in the sun, but warming up with good food and cosy surroundings is something I thrive on, so I look for any excuse to hold a dinner when we're all feeling a bit glum in the winter's depths.

Now here's the thing with this chapter: some of the most amazing seasonal winter produce is often completely overlooked, or has a bad rep, such as Brussels sprouts, yet they're all super adaptable, and when flavoured or seasoned with our favourite herbs and spices they can easily take on a star produce role. When winter is in full swing and we're in our little cocoons, I can't think of anything better to do than get experimental, impress friends and treat ourselves with some hearty recipes. Once I give up the pretence of hating winter, it becomes a pretty great time to romanticize about sitting in front of a fire with loved ones, a robust bottle of wine open and a stew on the stove. Call me old-school, but I know deep down you're probably thinking the same thing.

star produce:

Apples

———

Celery

———

Brussels sprouts

———

Jerusalem artichokes

———

Sweet potatoes

———

Other seasonal produce: Blood oranges, kale (a variety), parsnips, persimmons, cabbage, swede, turnips, squash/pumpkins, beetroot, onions, purple sprouting broccoli, celery root, parsley root, leeks, pears.

———

You will of course notice some of these vegetables in other seasons as well. There is a big overlap these days, because of the climate and average temperatures we experience, regardless of where you are.

———

Grains/pulses harvested at this time of the year: Farro, lentils, oats, barley, bulgur, rye.

———

apples

You'll probably think I'm exaggerating when I say that apples are, hands down, my favourite fruit. Always beautifully rustic and crisp, they're an absolute classic. Ever since I was young, I've been fond of them, and then I discovered a juicer . . . let's just say cloudy apple juice was pretty much my first love (I was a strange kid!). They're perfect in salads, as a snack with some form of nut butter or tahini, roasted (don't knock it until you try it), and of course in many peoples' favourite (or indeed first love), the apple crumble. I remember one year receiving a giant sack of apples that had come from a neighbour's tree. They were stuck with what to do with them but didn't want to let them just rot, so I gladly took them off their hands. Compote, crumbles, juice: I was in my element, and still to this day I will not turn down a silky, salty, cinnamony apple compote, oh so nostalgic. As we all know, there are so many varieties of apple, from Galas (my fave), to Pink Lady, Fuji, Honeycrisp, Granny Smith, Golden Delicious . . . the list really does go on.

Waste tips:

To prevent an apple going brown once you cut it open, a handy trick is to squeeze a little lemon or lime juice on to the cut flesh, and you can also dunk sliced/chopped apples into a mixture of honey and water for the same result. When using apples in salads, I either squeeze some lemon over first, or I'm pretty quick to dress the salad once I've sliced the apple. I'm sure you're used to having apples left in the fruit basket, for lack of appetite or imagination, but don't throw them away, because apples on the turn are great for compotes and sauces as well as for hearty crumbles. You can quickly chop them up, put them into a pan with a dash of water, a pinch of salt, and as many spices as you want, and simmer until soft. You can add a dash of sugar or syrup if you want extra sweetness, but often you don't need it.

You really can't go wrong with a crumble, especially with apples when they're in their absolute prime. I'm filled with warm nostalgia whenever I make this recipe. Perfectly spiced, soft, 'buttery' apples with a delicious crumble on top: the combination of all these elements, to me, is really special – like they were just meant to be put together.

Serves 4

SPICED APPLE CRUMBLE – THE LEFTOVER WAY

Preheat your oven to 180°C fan. Grease a glass dish or other dish of choice with a bit of coconut oil, just enough to stop any burning on the bottom when baking.

For the filling, slice your apples thinly lengthways, removing any pips and stalks. Chop the rest of the core slightly smaller. Put the apples in a mixing bowl with the lemon juice, mixed spice and sugar. Make sure there are no clumps of sugar and the apples are covered evenly.

For the topping, simply combine all the ingredients together – you can do this using your fingertips or a spoon in a bowl. You want the mix to be neither too dry nor too wet, so adjust with extra coconut oil or flour as needed. You'll get a better consistency if you use your hands for this.

Place the apples in the bottom of the dish and spread into an even layer. Add the topping, again as evenly as you can.

Bake for about 30 minutes, or until the topping is golden and the apples are tender. Serve hot, as is, or pair with some cashew/coconut yoghurt (see page 284).

For the filling

4 medium apples

1 tbsp lemon juice

2 tsp mixed spice

55g unrefined raw cane sugar (or coconut sugar, or a good-quality dark brown)

For the topping (or see waste tip for alternative)

2 heaped tbsp solid coconut oil, plus a little extra for the dish

1 tsp ground cinnamon

1 tsp grated nutmeg

½ tsp ground turmeric

a few cardamom pods, crushed

65ml maple syrup

1½ tbsp whole grain flour (spelt, kamut, wheat – whatever you may have in)

90g rolled oats (I use jumbo oats)

approx. 35g chopped nuts of choice

a pinch of sea salt

Waste tips:

The crumble will keep for a few days in the fridge – perfect leftovers for when you fancy something sweet. You could also have it for breakfast with extra seasonal fruits and toppings of choice. As an alternative crumble topping you can use a batch of nut pulp which you've recently saved – see page 363. Simply add the spices, maple syrup, coconut oil and salt to about 110–150g of pulp. You can toss in extra jumbo oats if you fancy, too.

I find these any-flour buns one of the most therapeutic things to make. They are an absolute staple in my house, whether this variation or ones with a twist. You pretty much can't go wrong when making them, so long as you don't overbeat the batter. They're fluffy, light, wholesome, and the crunch from the walnut surprises me every time, not to mention that little bit of sweetness from the apple. Inspired by many trips to Copenhagen, this recipe is a tribute to one of my wonderful friends, Faye, who first introduced me to these rolls, or, as they call them, Morgenboller (morning buns). However, as you'll soon discover, they are not just for the morning!

Makes approx. 10–12 buns

APPLE AND WALNUT ANY-FLOUR DANISH BUNS

In a mixing bowl, combine the white flour with the rye flour, salt and yeast. Make a hole or well in the middle of the flour and slowly pour in your warm water.

Using a wooden spoon, begin to mix the ingredients together. You don't have to be too gentle, but don't go overboard. The mixture should be relatively sticky. It doesn't form a solid dough, just a rough mix, so add a tad more water if your mixture is too dry, or a little of either flour if the mixture is too wet.

Cover with a tea towel and put to one side, preferably in a warmer space in your kitchen. Ideally you'd leave this overnight or for at least 8 hours, but if the space is warm enough, the mixture will have risen in 2 hours.

When you're ready to cook, preheat your oven to 250°C fan. When you remove the tea towel you'll notice that the mixture has risen – it will still be sticky and more air bubbles/streaks will have formed. Carefully add your apple and walnuts and gently fold into the mix. The mix can be quite rough.

Line a large baking tray with greaseproof paper or a silicone baking liner. Using two large spoons, begin to take sections of the dough to form bun-type shapes, again

(This recipe is best when you can leave the mix to prove overnight/for at least 8 hours, but will work after just 2 hours. The flour in the recipe is a base/starting point; see notes overleaf for flour subs explanation.)

400ml plain white flour/white bread flour (00 flour)

400ml rye flour

a generous pinch of salt

2 tsp dried instant yeast

approx. 400ml lukewarm water

1 small apple, cut into very small cubes, seeds discarded

a large handful of walnuts, roughly chopped

approx. 1 tbsp sesame seeds

coarse or cracked black pepper

»

quite rough. You can use the spoons to your advantage, moving them about to shape the dough. Repeat until all of the dough has been used up.

Sprinkle the rolls with the sesame seeds and some pepper. You could add some extra salt on top here too.

Bake in the oven on a middle shelf for about 20–30 minutes. The time may vary depending on your oven. The tops of the buns should be brown and they should be firm and crispy enough to feel solid when you tap them.

Remove the buns from the oven and allow to cool for a few moments before eating. Store any leftovers in an airtight container for about a week.

Notes:

I find these buns work best when at least a quarter of the flour in the mix is white. This is mostly down to the fact that the yeast can feed from the proteins that make up the gluten in the white flour. This being said, I've tried this recipe with wholemeal and rye and they still rise perfectly. You can cheat the method by using the warm water and also keeping the dough in a warm spot and proving it for a little longer – hence the 'any flour' title. As long as you stick to the ratios, you'll find it extremely easy to mix the flours. You could try wholemeal flour, buckwheat, a malted blend, dark or light rye, the list goes on. You could also stir through some whole oats, or another whole grain for some texture.

Waste tips:

As well as the varieties of flours you can change up in this recipe, depending on what you have in or can get your hands on, you can also mix up the nuts/seeds/fruit for the inside of the buns. Trying different combinations keeps it fresh and you can add whole spices such as caraway or cumin seeds to ring the changes. Nigella seeds also work really well in these buns, and a mix of sultanas too. How about multiseed buns, using whichever seeds you have, with some whole grains like spelt or oats for texture.

Some of my favourite recipes happen for no other reason than a love for a particular vegetable. This slaw actually came about from having more sprouts in my fridge than I knew what to do with. Given how well cruciferous vegetables and dark leafy greens soften when massaged, my instincts told me to do just that, to massage the sprouts until they wilted, or 'reduced' if you like. Paired with a punchy vinaigrette, this slaw is always a crowd-pleaser and, better still, a sprout-convert number!

Serves 4

APPLE AND SPROUT SLAW

First, make your vinaigrette so it has time to thicken slightly. Put all the ingredients into a blender and whiz to combine. If you don't have a blender, you can do this by hand, simply by placing the ingredients in a bowl and whisking with a hand whisk or fork. Whisk until thick, then season to taste.

For the slaw, using either a mandoline or a peeler (if you have a processor with this option, that will also work well), shave your Brussels thinly – any core left, simply chop small. Place in a large mixing or salad bowl.

Finely chop the kale, including the stalks, and add to the bowl of Brussels.

Finely chop the shallot and apple, adding them to the bowl. Lightly toast the walnuts, either in a pan on the stove or in the oven for about 5 minutes at 180°C fan. Add all these to the bowl.

Add around half the dressing and a good pinch of salt, and massage the kale and sprouts with your hands until they start to become soft. Add the rest of the dressing, along with the nutritional yeast/nut Parmesan, and loosely mix. Season again with salt and pepper if necessary.

Either serve in one big bowl, topped with the rest of the walnuts, or dish up individually.

For the vinaigrette

- 2 tsp Dijon mustard
- 2 tsp wholegrain mustard
- 2 tsp pure maple syrup
- 80ml apple cider vinegar
- 125ml olive oil
- 1–2 tsp dried oregano (depending on taste)

For the slaw

- approx. 450g Brussels sprouts
- 1 small bunch of kale, finely chopped, stems included
- 1 medium shallot, finely chopped
- 1 large apple, cored and diced small
- 50–70g walnut pieces
- 20g nutritional yeast/nut Parmesan (see page 365)
- salt and pepper

Waste tip:

Keeping the stalks and cores on the kale and sprouts is not only nutritionally beneficial but also prevents unnecessary wastage. However, if you don't want to use all the stalks, you can chop and freeze them, add them to smoothies or add them to your stock Tupperware in the freezer.

celery

With a distinct peppery flavour and crisp, refreshing texture, the long fibrous stalk vegetable that is celery really is a good 'un. The vegetable itself is actually part of the carrot family, a close relative that can range in vibrancy, some whiter, some more green. It's commonly thought that the lighter in colour, the less flavoursome the celery, but this totally depends on the variety, where it's grown and what the soil is like, and often the whiter stalks hold more flavour – it's really the luck of the draw. Celery and I have always got on, though I remember one of my best friends at school used to shudder at the thought of it and tease me for liking such a thing. Celery is delicious both raw and cooked. Apart from its obvious use as crudités, it's great in soups, or in slaw-type salads for that crisp crunch. It's perfect for adding texture to things, and often if I'm out of herbs and want to use something fresh, I will use the leaves in the same way I would coriander or parsley, finely chopped and added to salads, for a slight aniseed or liquorice taste. Celery generally first starts to appear in mid-winter, then sticks around into the depths of winter and continues until spring, a great contender! And given the cool climate in the UK, sometimes we're lucky enough even to be able to grow it in the late summer months, or at least early autumn, which explains why we can typically find it all year round. But let's celebrate it in its prime.

Waste tips:

When it comes to storing celery, I've found it does best when placed in a cup or bowl with a little water. You can keep it out of the fridge if you'll be using it within a day or two, just popping it into the fridge to cool before use. Otherwise wrapping it in a damp towel in the fridge always does the trick, keeping that unique texture. Celery is great for adding to juices or smoothies, and chuck in the leaves too, as they add more depth and are just as beneficial as the stalks themselves. You could add the leaves to a chimichurri (see page 361), using it as well as or instead of a particular herb should you not be able to find it.

I have a vivid memory from my childhood of my nan and grandad loving soup. Whether this was true or not, it's a thought I simply don't want to part with. Perhaps because we'd often go for a Sunday roast when we lived in Devon, and a soup for starters was always the favoured choice. Creamed potato, celery or mushroom were the usual suspects. So in light of this, with a slight Polish twist and coconut milk instead of dairy, this soup, every time, brings that childhood memory flooding back.

Serves 4–6 (depending on size of bowl)

COCONUT, WHITE BEAN AND CELERY SOUP

w/ sourdough croutons

Preheat your oven to 180°C fan, ready for making the croutons. Put the oil into a large pot over a medium heat, add the coriander and cumin seeds, and fry until fragrant. I like to bash the seeds slightly with the top of a wooden spoon to allow the flavours to deepen once you add the rest of your ingredients.

Add the chopped onion and cook until soft and slightly translucent. Add the sliced celery, celery leaves, garlic, apple and ginger, and continue to sauté until the vegetables become soft and fragrant.

Add your beans and stock and bring to the boil, then lower to a simmer, stirring occasionally. Season with salt and pepper to taste, adding a pinch of chilli flakes if you want a slight kick.

Once your soup starts to thicken, add the coconut milk and half your greens. Keep the heat low while the greens cook, adding the lime juice and zest as you go. Season with salt and pepper again to taste, and continue to simmer the soup to allow it to thicken even more.

While the soup is simmering, make your croutons. Simply toss the torn bread with the olive oil, garlic and some salt and pepper. If you are using any optional additions, add

For the soup

1 tsp oil of choice (coconut, sesame and olive oil all work well)

2 tsp coriander seeds

2 tsp cumin seeds

1 large white or brown onion, cut in half lengthways, then diced

1 bunch of celery, approx. 250g, thinly sliced, leaves included

3 cloves of garlic, crushed or finely chopped

1 apple, chopped, seeds removed, core included

approx. 2 tbsp grated fresh ginger

2 × 400g tins of white beans (cannellini, navy, lima), drained and rinsed well

1–1.5 litres vegetable stock

salt and pepper

dried chilli flakes (optional)

1 × 400ml tin of full-fat coconut milk

a large handful of fresh greens (kale, spinach, chard)

1 lime, juiced and zested

»

these now. Spread the bread on a baking tray and pop it into the oven for about 8–10 minutes, allowing it to crisp nicely. You can give the tray a shake about halfway through, to prevent burning. Once cooked, remove from the oven and place to one side to cool and crisp up further.

Once your soup is nice and thick, turn off the heat and use a ladle to remove half the contents of the pot to a bowl. You can either use a hand blender or, if you have a high-speed blender that can take heat, go ahead and use that here. Blend until smooth. I like to keep my soup with some additional texture, but feel free to blend all or less of the mix.

Add the purée back to the pot along with the rest of your greens and bring back to the boil, stirring to combine. To serve, ladle into bowls, and top with a squeeze of lime juice, any extra seasoning and the crispy garlic croutons.

For the croutons

3–4 slices of stale bread, torn into small chunks (I always slice and freeze half a sourdough loaf when making or buying so that it keeps for longer – feel free to use any bread of choice)

2 tbsp olive oil

2 cloves of garlic, crushed or finely chopped

salt and pepper

sesame seeds and lemon/lime zest (optional)

Waste tip:

If you don't have any beans or fancy swapping them for something else, potatoes are a great alternative, as they're pretty much an all-year-round root vegetable (of course with a few exceptions as to varieties). You can also play with the greens you throw into the soup: feel free to add more, for some extra iron, colour and an earthier taste. Occasionally, you'll buy celery without its leaves. If this is the case, you can use a handful of fresh coriander: chop finely and add with the other ingredients. Coriander is also a great garnish should you fancy an extra-citrusy refreshing taste.

A salad that's packed with textures, freshness and zing, in which tart flavours meet sweet, and crunchy meets soft and chewy. This is perfect on its own with your favourite bread, or as an almighty side for a winter spread. If you fancy a cooked element in this salad, the chicory is also great baked: quarter lengthways and roast with olive oil, salt and pepper.

Serves 6 as a main, 3–4 as a side

CELERY, CHICORY, WALNUT AND BULGUR SALAD

First cook your bulgur wheat. Put it into a pan with enough water to cover the bulgur, a good pinch of salt and a drizzle of oil. Bring to the boil, lower to a simmer, then cover and cook over a low heat until tender, about 12 minutes. Remove from the heat and leave to stand, covered, for 10 minutes. Fluff up with a fork and set aside while you make the rest of the salad.

For the dressing, simply put the orange juice, orange zest, lemon juice, tahini, balsamic vinegar, soy sauce or tamari and mustard into a bowl and whisk until well combined. You can also do this in a blender.

Wash and finely chop your celery, mint, parsley, tarragon, chilli and walnuts. Put into a large bowl and toss in the bulgur.

Carefully break off the outer leaves of the chicory, wash them individually and add to the bowl with the other ingredients. Once the chicory leaves become a little tougher and more tightly packed together, stop removing the leaves and finely chop, again adding to the mix.

Pour your dressing over the salad and mix. I like to use my hands to slightly massage the ingredients, to ensure they are coated and to help soften the chicory, removing any bitterness from the vegetable as well as aiding digestion. Season with salt and pepper.

Serve in bowls, adding extra fresh herbs if you like, and additional seasoning to taste.

For the salad

200g bulgur wheat

a pinch of sea salt

a drizzle of olive oil

1 bunch of celery, finely chopped

a small handful of fresh mint, finely chopped

a small handful of fresh parsley, finely chopped

a few sprigs of fresh tarragon, finely chopped

1 small red chilli, seeds removed, finely chopped

approx. 85g walnuts, toasted and crushed

4 chicory bulbs (any variety, red, white), larger leaves chopped, smaller ones left whole

salt and pepper

For the dressing

1 large orange, juiced and zested

1 lemon, juiced

2 heaped tbsp tahini

4 tsp balsamic vinegar

2 tbsp soy sauce or tamari

1 heaped tbsp Dijon mustard

Waste tip:

Bulgur is an easy grain to cook in bigger batches and keep in the fridge for adding to salads, soups and stews. It's an excellent source of B vitamins, protein, fibre and antioxidants, so it's a great addition for bulking out a meal with lots of nutrients.

This is a recipe that has become a real hero with me and my friends. With a few different renditions (see waste tips below), this dish is so simple but always show-stopping.

Serves 2 as a main, 4 as a side

CREAMY CELERY AND CHICKPEAS

If you are cooking your chickpeas from dried, drain them from the soaking water and rinse them. Place them in a large pan with a good heap of salt. Bring to the boil, then cover and simmer for around 30–40 minutes, or until cooked. You may notice the shells of the chickpeas starting to come away – this is normal.

Once your chickpeas are cooked, drain and place to one side while you make your base for the rest of the dish. If you are using tinned chickpeas, you can drain and rinse these now too.

Put a few tablespoons of your stock into a pan (non-stick if you can) and cook the shallots until soft. Once the shallots have softened and turned slightly golden, add your garlic and chopped celery. Cook for another 2 minutes.

Add the rest of the stock, the fresh parsley, lemon zest and juice, soy sauce or tamari, Dijon mustard, tahini, oregano and chilli. Toss in your chickpeas and stir well. Season with salt and pepper to taste. Bring to the boil, then lower to a simmer.

As the liquid starts to reduce and becomes thicker, add the nutritional yeast and 125ml of oat milk, seasoning again to taste. The chickpeas will continue to cook in the sauce, and you'll notice the texture becoming a little stew-like. If you prefer more texture you can serve it at this stage, or you can continue to simmer it on a very low heat to your desired consistency. If your liquid is disappearing quickly, or you want your chickpeas creamier, go ahead and add the remaining oat milk.

Serve sprinkled with fresh parsley, as a side or main.

approx. 250g dried chickpeas (pre-soaked for at least 10 hours), or 500g cooked chickpeas (tinned or jarred)

approx. 250ml vegetable stock (either your homemade stock from page 352 or preferred choice of cube dissolved in water)

2 medium shallots, cut in half lengthways, then thinly sliced

2 cloves of garlic, crushed or finely chopped

approx. 180g celery, washed and finely chopped, leaves on

a small bunch of fresh parsley, stalks and leaves finely chopped

1 lemon, juiced and zested

2 tbsp soy sauce or tamari

2 tbsp Dijon mustard

3 heaped tbsp tahini

2 tbsp dried oregano

a pinch of chilli flakes or powder

salt and pepper

60g nutritional yeast

125–250ml oat milk (any unsweetened plant-based milk is also fine)

Note:

You can use a variety of herbs in this dish, depending on what you have and what is in season. Fresh dill is great for a more Mediterranean style; fresh coriander for a slightly Asian variant. I love to eat this with some fresh crusty bread, but it's also great with rice, a salad, in tacos . . . the possibilities are endless.

Waste tip:

If you find yourself with leftovers, they can be blended into a hummus. Depending on the amount you have left, simply place in a blender with an additional 1–2 tablespoons of tahini, the juice of ½ –1 lemon and a dash of zest, and blend to your desired consistency. Add more chilli flakes, and salt and pepper to taste.

My mum, without fail, talks about this recipe a good few times a month. It's usually requested along with some home-made rye buns to help mop up the flavoursome residue that's left after gobbling down the rest.

Serves 4 as a main

ROOT VEGETABLE, CELERY, THYME AND BUTTER BEAN CHOWDER

Preheat your oven to 180°C fan. Line a baking tray with baking paper and set aside.

Heat a drizzle of olive oil in a medium to large pot, and sauté your onions over a medium heat until soft and translucent. Add your leeks, celery and celery leaves and continue to sauté until soft. You may want to add a dash of water if it starts to dry up. Add the garlic, thyme and oregano.

Once fragrant, add the parsnip, squash, sweet potato and cauliflower. Season and stir well, then add the mustard, nutritional yeast, oat milk and lemon juice. Add the vegetable stock and bring to the boil.

Once boiling, stir, then lower the heat to a simmer. Let the vegetables cook until tender – usually 15 minutes or so.

Once the parsnips, squash and potato are soft, remove from the heat. Ladle half the chowder into a separate bowl and set aside. Using a hand-held blender, carefully blitz the remaining chowder in the pot until smooth.

Put the unblended half of the chowder back into the pot, along with the drained and rinsed butter beans. Season if necessary.

Bring the chowder back to the boil to allow it to heat through.

To serve, ladle into bowls, and top with garnishes of choice and a thick slice of sourdough.

For the chowder

olive oil

1 medium white onion, cut into small dice

1 leek, cut into small dice (white and light green parts only)

5 stalks of celery, leaves included, finely chopped

3 cloves of garlic, crushed or finely chopped

4–5 thyme sprigs, leaves removed and chopped

4 tsp dried oregano

1 large parsnip, cut into bite-size pieces

½ a small butternut squash, peeled and cubed

1 small to medium sweet potato, cubed

1 small cauliflower, chopped small

salt and pepper

2–3 heaped tbsp Dijon mustard

2 tbsp nutritional yeast

4 tbsp oat milk

1 lemon, juiced

800ml–1 litre vegetable stock

1 × 400g tin of butter beans, drained, rinsed well

Optional sides

sourdough

savoury granola/ toasted nuts and seeds

coconut yoghurt

crispy kale (see page 298)

Waste tips:

This recipe is extremely adaptable. You can pretty much use any winter root vegetable you have in, or whatever's in season if you're cooking it perhaps for a rainy summer's evening instead. Yams and potatoes give an earthy taste, while turnips give more of a celery or radishy taste. Fennel works well too, and is also part of the humble root vegetable family, grown similarly to carrots. Batch cooking this recipe is a great idea, as it keeps well in the fridge and can be heated up on the stove whenever you want.

Brussels sprouts

A very noble, quirky vegetable with a distinct taste, but one which is not commonly liked (though I was an odd child who grew fond of them from an early age!). Something that brought me utter joy not so long ago was a message from a girl who had been at an event I'd cooked for. She said how much she'd enjoyed the Brussels sprouts I'd served, and asked for the recipe so that she could finally learn to enjoy them. When cooking particular vegetables, I think we too often stick to what we know, but the usual steaming of sprouts doesn't quite suffice. For this particular event I'd roasted them and added them to a salad with some other seasonal favourites. Sometimes I'll roast a batch in a little olive oil, salt and pepper, then keep them in the fridge to add to other dishes. One of my favourite discoveries with Brussels is plonking them into a kimchi, adding a whole new dimension to what in my opinion is one of the best condiments.

Waste tips:

Shredded, quartered, whole . . . sprouts are great in a variety of ways, and the core should definitely not be skipped. It's common for stalks and cores to be chucked, but give them a little scrub and they're just as good as the rest. Just like any vegetable that looks a little sad, Brussels are particularly delicious when roasted, simply, with minimal oil and seasonings of choice, and as mentioned above they keep well in the fridge, ready to chuck into dishes whenever you fancy. Don't be put off by the smell that may occur when they're cooked – that's what scares most people away, but it doesn't hinder their flavour.

A kimchi for everyone, the fermentalists or the newbies, this foolproof recipe makes the perfect side to so many dishes, be it a topping for a taco (see pages 195 and 228), or simply spread on toast – don't knock it until you try it.

Makes 1 large jar of kimchi

ANY-DAY BRUSSELS SPROUT KIMCHI

In a large mixing bowl, combine the cabbage, Brussels sprouts, apple and salt. Using your hands, gently massage, making sure not to mush the apple. Cover with a plate, allowing the mix to sit for around an hour to soften. If you have time, leaving it for up to 4 hours will help to ferment the cabbage at this first stage.

Drain the liquid fully, then rinse everything under cold water. Set aside in a colander to continue draining while you prep your other ingredients.

Using a hand-held blender or a processor, blitz together the onion, garlic, ginger and sugar until they form a paste. Add the Korean chilli flakes/red pepper powder and mix, then place to one side and allow to sit while you start the next step.

In a clean bowl, mix the cabbage, Brussels and apple with the paste, adding the coriander seeds and soy sauce. Mix well, making sure everything is coated and combined. You now need to transfer this mix into a clean jar, about 18cm tall. Mason jars or similar are ideal for this, as they have a tight screwtop lid.

Pour the water into the bowl and swirl it round to take up any remaining paste, then pour it into your jar. Pack down and screw on the lid, making sure it is sealed.

You'll now need to set this aside at room temperature for at least 3 days. The longer you leave it, the better the fermentation. You could pop the jar into a large bowl to catch any overspill that might occur as the mix ferments. The kimchi will keep in the fridge for around 6 months.

1 medium cabbage (Savoy, Chinese, hispi), thinly sliced

approx. 400g Brussels sprouts, quartered

1 small apple, thinly sliced (or julienned for a nice variety)

55g fine sea salt (high quality)

1 medium onion, thinly sliced

4 cloves of garlic, crushed or finely chopped

approx. 2 tsp ginger, grated or finely chopped

2 tsp raw cane/ brown sugar

2 tbsp dried Korean chilli flakes or Korean red pepper powder

2 tsp coriander seeds, crushed

1 tbsp soy sauce

65–125ml water (you may need a little more)

Waste tips:

If you want this kimchi to keep for a while in the fridge, be sure to use a clean fork any time you delve in, to avoid unwanted bacteria getting in and ruining the fermentation and thereby helping it to continue to be gut-friendly. You could put any other cruciferous vegetable in this kimchi, to use up leftovers or on-the-turn veggies. Another way to enjoy kimchi is in a fried-rice-type dish. Paired with your favourite seasonal veg, rice of choice, some soy sauce and chilli, it's a real winner.

Personally, I think blood oranges are a must at this time of the year. Their sweet but tangy flavour really finishes off certain dishes, this salad being one of them. The combination of buckwheat with the vegetables offers a variety of textures, the burst from the blood orange marrying it all together. It's a great dish to serve as a side along with something a little more robust, keeping the spread simple and fresh. Buckwheat is often overlooked as a salad grain, but it's one of my favourite things to use. It's versatile and gluten-free, great for when rice becomes boring or you're looking for something lighter than a pasta. And, a little fact to get you thinking, it's actually a seed, but acts like a grain. Pretty special if you ask me.

Serves 4
as a side,
2 as a main

SHAVED BRUSSELS SPROUTS AND BUCKWHEAT

w/ blood orange dressing

First prepare your buckwheat. If it is not already toasted, preheat your oven to 180°C fan. Rinse the buckwheat thoroughly until the liquid runs clear. Lightly dry with a clean cloth and spread evenly on a baking tray. Toast for about 20 minutes, or until golden brown.

In a pan, bring the 500ml of water to the boil. Add 1 teaspoon of salt, followed by the toasted buckwheat. Stir, cover and bring back to the boil. Reduce the heat and simmer, keeping the lid on without removing, for 10 minutes.

Once cooked (you may still have a little bit of liquid left – if so, carefully drain), remove from the heat and add the melted coconut oil. Fluff with a fork, then put the lid back on and place to one side.

To make your dressing, blend or whisk together all the ingredients, making sure to set aside half the orange zest for the salad. Place in the fridge while you make the salad.

For the salad

150g buckwheat groats, toasted if possible

500ml water

salt and pepper

1 tbsp melted coconut oil

400g Brussels sprouts, shredded

1 small or ½ a larger purple cabbage, shredded

1 apple (the firmer the better), shredded

2 stalks of celery, thinly sliced

a large handful of fresh coriander, roughly chopped

a few leaves of fresh mint, roughly chopped

4 spring onions, thinly sliced

zest of ½ a blood orange (use the zest of the other half in the dressing, see below)

2 tbsp sesame seeds, lightly toasted

Using a mandolin if you have one, or a sharp knife/peeler, shred the Brussels sprouts, cabbage and apple. Put them into a bowl along with your celery, coriander, mint, onions and orange zest. Add a good pinch of salt and gently massage with your hands. Add the cooked buckwheat, the dressing and additional salt and pepper to taste. Again use your hands to mix, combine and prevent the buckwheat from sticking together.

Serve with the toasted sesame seeds and any leftover fresh herbs.

For the dressing:

————

2 blood oranges, juiced, plus zest of ½ (regular oranges are also fine)

2 tbsp soy sauce or tamari

2 heaped tbsp tahini

1 tbsp rice vinegar

1 clove of garlic, crushed or finely chopped

a pinch of cayenne pepper (feel free to use as much as you like, depending on your spice preference)

salt and pepper

Note:

By toasting your buckwheat first, it allows the grains not only to retain their shape but also to become more nutrient-dense, as it makes it harder to overboil the seed, which can turn it mushy. Make sure you rinse the buckwheat beforehand to remove any lectins from the seed, making it easier to digest.

Waste tips:

The salad will keep in the fridge for about 3 days. It's great as a sandwich filler, with some additional lettuce for a different texture. The recipe also works well as a hot stir-fry if you don't fancy a raw dish. Before adding the buckwheat, toss the salad ingredients and dressing into a frying pan or wok and heat up, stirring as you would a normal stir-fry, wilting the vegetables to the desired texture. Either add the buckwheat and mix, or serve as a side instead.

Jerusalem artichokes

These beauties, believe it or not, are actually a species of sunflower, which is where they inherit their other names of sunroot or sunchoke. A nutty, savoury-tasting vegetable, they are like a cross between a creamy artichoke heart and the best potato you've tasted, but a little more alien-looking, like a big piece of ginger. They are very clean-tasting, fresh but earthy, and depending on how they are cooked, can have a subtle celery flavour. I wasn't really aware of this vegetable growing up, not until I started 'dining out' and spending my part-time job wages in new restaurants, whether I could afford it or not . . . yep, I was, and still am, that gal. I recall that one of my favourite places to eat in south-east London added them to their menu as a trial dish, which I very happily tried numerous times. Safe to say I was glad it stuck. With a Thai-inspired peanut and lemongrass dressing, they had perfected both the flavour of the sauce and the cooking time of the Jerusalem artichokes, which were creamy and soft on the inside, while light and delicately crispy on the outside. Naturally, over the years and inspired by this particular dish and one of my most-loved cuisines, the curry on page 334 has become a favourite of mine at home and on retreats when in season. Jerusalem artichokes have quite a long season, appearing around November and lasting all the way until March, and they remain in their prime the whole way through. I will add, which tickles me every time, that they can be known as 'fartichokes', a name I believe my dad once told me, so maybe don't overdo it (ha)!

Waste tips:

You can keep these in the same way you would potatoes, and often if I feel a little lost for inspiration, I'll use them in a similar way. They are incredible 'smashed', as the skins crisp up perfectly. Equally they are great when thinly sliced and lightly sautéed or roasted, added to salads, soups, or even used like croutons. They do vary in colour, so don't be put off if they look a little light or even purple-y at times. Chop them into chunks or keep them whole, after giving them a good scrub.

Always a winter favourite, or in fact, a year-round favourite, risotto is ideal for getting creative with, using new vegetables, trying different flavours, and pairing conventional ingredients with the unexpected. Jerusalem artichokes are incredibly aromatic and add a punchy, sweet, nutty taste to any dish, so they're perfect for jazzing up a risotto. I've always loved leeks, even from a young age, chopped chunky and steamed with a good helping of butter slathered over the top and a sprinkling of salt. Naturally I wanted to replicate this, with a fancier dairy-free twist: enter my 'buttered' leeks recipe, which has been a go-to of mine for a while. A combination of olive oil and coconut oil creates a beautiful, soft, buttery, melt-in-the-mouth taste. The leeks double up as a great toast topper, bruschetta-style, to impress not only yourself but guests and friends.

Serves 4

RISOTTO WITH JERUSALEM ARTICHOKES, 'BUTTERED' LEEKS

Preheat your oven to about 180°C fan. Put your Jerusalem artichokes on a lined baking tray and drizzle with 1–2 tablespoons of oil to coat. Season with salt and pepper and roast in the oven for about 20 minutes. They should start to crisp up and be a lovely golden brown on the outside and soft in the middle. While they are roasting, get started on your risotto. Once they are cooked, remove and place to one side.

Heat about a tablespoon of oil in a large frying pan. Once hot add the onion and fry until it starts to soften and brown. Add the celery and fry for another few minutes. Add the garlic and cook until fragrant, stirring as you go to prevent anything burning.

Add the grated nutmeg and risotto rice and stir until well coated and mixed with everything else. Lower the heat to a simmer and add the white wine. Once the wine has burnt off a little and the rice has started to absorb it, go ahead and start adding your stock, a ladle at a time,

For the risotto

200g Jerusalem artichokes, scrubbed well, quartered

olive or coconut oil

salt and pepper

1 large brown onion, finely chopped

1 stalk of celery, finely chopped

2 cloves of garlic, crushed or finely chopped

1 tsp grated nutmeg

350g risotto rice

approx. 250ml white wine

approx. 1.4 litres vegetable stock (either home-made, or shop-bought if you have not prepared your own – see page 352 for recipes)

1 lemon, juice and zest

60g nutritional yeast

2 heaped tbsp tahini

2 tbsp chopped nuts (hazelnuts, almonds, cashews)

»

stirring as you go to prevent the rice sticking to the pan. Keep the heat low.

Once you've used about half your stock, season with salt and pepper, add the lemon juice and zest and the nutritional yeast, and stir.

Keep adding the stock until the rice is tender with a little bit of bite. You may not need all the stock, but you want the risotto to be neither too dry nor too wet. Season again if necessary.

While your risotto is simmering, cook your leeks. Put the olive and coconut oils into a smaller pan, over a low-medium heat. Once hot, add your leeks and cook gently, adding the water gradually to allow the leeks to soften.

Add the turmeric, paprika and salt and continue to cook for a few more minutes, stirring to combine. The leeks will start to turn brown or yellow ever so slightly and will become very soft and broken down. Once cooked, remove from the heat and cover to keep hot.

When the risotto is ready, add the roasted artichokes and carefully stir until coated. If the risotto feels a little stiff, add any remaining stock or additional water to loosen.

Swirl in the tahini and half the buttered leeks.

Serve with the rest of the buttered leeks on top, sprinkled with the chopped nuts.

For the buttered leeks

2 tbsp olive oil

1 tbsp coconut oil

1 large or 2 smaller leeks, sliced in half lengthways and then into small slivers

2 tbsp water

¼ tsp ground turmeric

¼ tsp paprika (smoked paprika also works well)

a good pinch of salt

Waste tip:

Not only are these buttery leeks great on risotto but they make a nice bruschetta topping or even a 'something' on toast. Pile them on toasted sourdough or any other bread of choice, with an additional pinch of salt and pepper and some chilli flakes. You could also get creative and add a chopped seasonal fruit like apple or pear. A great way to make toast fancy, or just to add some variety.

I'm a big fan of 'less common' ingredients in dishes, and have a slight obsession for Jerusalem artichokes, so popping them into a curry has become somewhat of a ritual for me. Simple to make, with all the spices you could want during the colder months, it's simmered until thick and flavoursome, allowing all three show-stopping ingredients to come through.

Serves 4

JERUSALEM ARTICHOKE, PEANUT AND COCONUT CURRY

w/ basil and coriander

Cook your onions in a small amount of water in a frying pan until soft and fragrant. Add a dash more water, then chuck in the garlic, ginger, galangal, turmeric, pinch of pepper, cardamom seeds, coriander seeds, cumin seeds and coriander stalks. Make sure you do this over a low heat. Fry until no more water remains in the pan.

With the heat still low, add the red pepper, chilli, coconut milk, lime juice and zest, peanut butter, soy sauce or tamari, Jerusalem artichokes and chosen brassica vegetable/s. Stir well and bring to the boil, then lower to a simmer. Add a good pinch of salt and pepper.

Slowly add the water (for a thicker curry use less), stirring occasionally to allow the vegetables to cook and the sauce to thicken. Add half the basil, plus half the coriander leaves, and continue to simmer.

While your curry is simmering, cook your rice/grain.

Once the Jerusalem artichokes have cooked through (you can test by putting a knife through – if it goes through easily, they are ready), stir in the rest of the basil and season with salt and pepper.

To serve, simply ladle into bowls on top of your grain, adding the crushed peanuts and the rest of the coriander leaves on top.

1 brown onion, finely chopped

2 cloves of garlic, crushed or finely chopped

5cm fresh ginger, grated (and 5cm of galangal in addition to this is also great)

1 tbsp fresh turmeric or 1 tsp ground, plus a pinch of pepper to help activate

2 cardamom pods, seeds removed and crushed

2 tsp coriander seeds

2 tsp cumin seeds

a large handful of fresh coriander, stalks included, finely chopped

1 medium red pepper, finely chopped

2–4 red chillies (depending if you like it spicy)

1 × 400ml tin of full-fat coconut milk

1 lime, juice and zest

4 –6 heaped tbsp peanut butter, crunchy or smooth

2 tbsp soy sauce or tamari

approx. 350g Jerusalem artichokes, cut into bite-size pieces

1 small cauliflower/ broccoli/ romanesco/ cabbage, roughly chopped (or use 1–2 large handfuls of sprouts or collard greens – or any cruciferous vegetable you fancy!)

This curry has a fair number of components, and is packed with a variety of spices both fresh and ground. If you want a quicker or less involved curry, you could use the harissa recipe from page 361, adding the additional onion, ginger, galangal (if you have it) and fresh coriander, plus a little water. Then follow on with the coconut, peanut butter and vegetables.

If you want to switch this up a little, or make it in a different season, you have many options for vegetables (see above) and can switch the Jerusalem artichokes for another starchy vegetable such as potatoes.

salt and pepper

125–250ml water (for extra flavour you can also use stock)

1 large handful of fresh basil, carefully chopped

To serve

approx. 250–350g rice of choice, or other grain

2–4 tbsp peanuts, lightly toasted, crushed

Sage always reminds me of a work trip to Tuscany, where I went a bit crazy for it and ended up putting it in the majority of the evening dishes, using almost an entire small plant from out the back, only to discover another few round the corner. Crispy sage is the best. A little indulgent, sure, but so worth it. I've kept this recipe super simple, balancing the strong flavour of artichokes with hints of citrus, garlic and the earthy warming sage. It works perfectly as a winter side to a dark leafy green salad, or as a little twist for a weekend roast.

Serves 4–5
as a side

ROASTED ARTICHOKES AND POTATOES

w/ whole garlic, crispy sage

Preheat your oven to 200°C fan. Line a baking tray with a mat if you have one, or with greaseproof paper.

In a large mixing bowl, toss your potatoes and Jerusalem artichokes with 2 tablespoons of water. Make sure they are all wet, then add the garlic, lemon juice and zest, smoked paprika and the chopped half of the sage. Season with salt and pepper.

Put on your lined tray, spreading evenly, and roast in the oven for about 20 minutes.

Remove the tray from the oven and pour over the olive oil. Adding it at this stage will allow the potatoes and artichokes to crisp up beautifully. Season again with salt and pepper and put back into the oven for a further 20 minutes.

Remove the potatoes and artichokes from the oven. They should be a golden brown colour, crispy on the outside but soft through the middle. You can test them by seeing how easily a sharp knife goes through.

Heat 2 teaspoons of olive oil in a small frying pan and add a pinch of salt. Put in the whole sage leaves and crisp them up over a medium heat. This will only take a few moments, so watch that the leaves don't start to burn.

To serve, place the potatoes and artichokes in a bowl. Top with the crispy sage and enjoy.

3 medium baking potatoes, scrubbed/washed, cut into bite-size pieces

approx. 500g Jerusalem artichokes, scrubbed/washed, cut into bite-size pieces

8 cloves of garlic, smashed but left whole, skins removed

1 lemon, juice and zest

1 tsp smoked paprika

1 bunch of fresh sage, approx. 35g, half the leaves finely chopped, the other half left whole

salt and pepper

2 tbsp olive oil, plus 2 tsp

Waste tips:

This dish is also great served cold: add a little more lemon juice and zest and 1–2 tablespoons of tahini, mix well and serve as a salad. You could also have the vegetables crushed – use a fork or potato masher to lightly crush. They are great to use as leftovers, adding to cosy winter stews, such as the one on page 342.

Cooked until golden and crispy, spiced with homemade harissa, this simple yet effective dish acts as the perfect side to a fresh wintery salad and is great even on its own with a garlicky hummus.

SMASHED JERUSALEM ARTICHOKES

w/ homemade harissa

Preheat your oven to 180°C fan. To make your harissa, put the dried chillies (both kinds if you are opting for both) into a bowl, pour over hot water, and let them soak for around 15 minutes. Make sure they are submerged.

Over a medium heat, lightly (dry) toast your coriander seeds, caraway seeds and cumin seeds until they are fragrant and start to pop. Transfer to a mortar and pestle or a small processor and grind/crush into a powder.

To the powder add the garlic, ginger, paprika and salt. Briefly blitz or grind, then add the lemon juice, zest, vinegar and tomato purée and mix again until you have an even paste. If you are making this using a mortar and pestle, the paste will be a little more rustic.

Once the chillies have rehydrated, drain them and remove the stems (if any) and seeds. Add to the food processor or mortar along with some more salt and pepper. Blend or mash well until combined. If you were using a mortar and pestle initially, you can also transfer to a blender now to finish it off.

Slowly add the oil or water, mixing as you go. You may need a little more or a little less, depending on the desired consistency. I like to keep mine nice and thick, to add to other dishes later on. Season to taste – you can squeeze in a little more lemon juice here for a bit more of an acidy or citrusy taste.

The harissa will keep in a jar in the fridge for about a month, and longer in the freezer.

For the harissa (makes approx. 1 medium jar/ 16 tbsp)

10 large dried chillies, mild to medium heat

5–7 dried chiles de arbol (a Mexican variety, widely stocked – these are very spicy, so depending on how you want your harissa, use less or use additional ordinary dried chillies, as above)

2 tsp coriander seeds

1 tsp caraway seeds

1 heaped tbsp cumin seeds

3–5 cloves of garlic, crushed or finely chopped

a thumb-size piece of ginger, finely grated

2 tsp smoked paprika

a hefty pinch of sea salt (tailored to your salt preference)

½ a lemon, juice and zest

1 tbsp apple cider vinegar (white wine vinegar is also fine)

1 tbsp tomato purée/paste

salt and pepper

approx. 65ml good-quality olive oil, or water for an oil-free option (I prefer using oil in this recipe, as I'd then omit when using on or in a dish, but it's totally up to you – the oil will also help to create a richer or deeper flavour)

»

Put the Jerusalem artichokes into a pan of cold water and add the salt. Cover and bring to the boil, then lower the heat and simmer until tender, about 15 minutes or so. Drain, then place on a baking tray.

Using the back of a spoon or the bottom of a glass or cup, flatten the artichokes with a little bit of pressure. Add about 1 teaspoon of the harissa to each artichoke, spreading it to cover the surface. Sprinkle on some nutritional yeast and flip them over, adding harissa to the other side.

Bake the artichokes until they have browned on one side, flipping them to bake the other. They'll start to crisp up nicely. This usually takes around 10 minutes.

Serve, adding a drizzle of your chosen dressing, with nuts or sesame seeds.

For the smashed Jerusalem artichokes (serves 4–6, depending on main or sides)

- approx. 450g Jerusalem artichokes, scrubbed and washed well
- 1 heaped tsp salt
- 2 tbsp nutritional yeast (not essential but a great addition)

Optional additions

- creamy dressings from basics section, page 356 (silken tofu based, tahini, etc.)
- toasted crushed nuts
- sesame seeds

Waste tips:

If you are freezing the harissa, a tip is to pour it into an ice cube tray. This will allow it to keep longer and you can easily add it in cubes to different dishes. Harissa is great for adding to pasta sauces, soups, stews, Mexican food, even to the base of a hummus recipe or dressings (see page 361 for guidance). This recipe is lovely with a giant green salad, or served with some hummus for extra dipping.

sweet potatoes

In case you've started to think I don't like 'normal' vegetables, well, let us not forget the understated beauty that is the sweet potato. Despite its basic appearance, the sweet potato, once cooked, is more than appealing, with its sticky, sweet, yet rich flesh. Both white and orange versions of this noble and earthy root vegetable are sweet, the white ones with a slightly more fragrant taste. Sweet potatoes are pretty much all-year-round these days, but in their prime in the depths of winter. Due to their purée-type flesh when cooked, they are great for a variety of dishes, so you really can get experimental in the kitchen. Cakes, burgers/patties, twice-baked, roasted, fries: I just can't get enough. Although, having said that, I once went through a phase of consuming far too many in too short a period of time and had to take a break from them for a while, using other ingredients in their place and revisiting a regular baked potato. I think I managed two months without a sweet potato in my life, then my craving resurfaced. It's safe to say that the recipe on page 348, in which they are baked whole and topped with delicate crispy chickpeas and a creamy dressing, was the best welcome back.

My love for textures and combinations of ingredients certainly gets going when cooking with sweet potatoes. They're versatile, filling, incredibly good for you and can add a whole new dimension to dishes. As they are quite sweet, the key is to balance them out with fats, citrus, salt, crunch . . . no element is more important than another! And if you haven't ever 'twice-baked' them, you're in for a treat. Imagine the creamiest and most delicious mashed potatoes you've ever had, inside a perfectly salted crispy skin. Sometimes normal potatoes just don't cut it!

Waste tips:

Sweet potatoes are great for roasting in batches. Simply roast them whole for about 40 minutes, remove them from the oven, allow to cool, then refrigerate. You can keep them in the fridge in a Tupperware for around 4–5 days. You can then have them when you like, as a snack, or added to other dishes, even using them in a sweet dish. Their unique flavour tends to get a little stronger and sweeter the longer they are left after cooking, while the caramelization stays just as good. Whether you're purposely cooking the sweet potatoes in advance or have maybe cooked one too many the previous day, they are one of the best leftover vegetables going. You can make them into breads or bakes, add them to porridge for a twist, have them as a savoury breakfast, or, the best one, make them into sweet potato toasts! Char the top a little under the grill or slice them to fit your toaster, then top with your savoury favourites and you've got a little winner.

This recipe was born a few years back, when I spent a little more time in the UK over the winter period, and combines two loves: stews, and all things baked. My dad was a traybake fanatic, usually when we had minimal things left in the fridge, or sometimes just for ease, and it stuck with me. This recipe goes against the grain, quite literally, by baking split peas with nourishing sweet potatoes and a subtle umami hit from the mushrooms. I always so fondly think of my dad every time I make this dish and question as to why I haven't yet made it for him.

BAKED SPLIT PEA, SWEET POTATO AND ROSEMARY STEW

Preheat your oven to 190°C fan. Place the split peas in a pot along with 750ml of your vegetable stock. Bring to the boil, then lower to a simmer to allow the split peas to become tender. This should take around 20 minutes. Once cooked, season with salt and pepper and set aside.

Drizzle a dash of oil into a medium pan over a medium heat, and cook your onion, carrot, celery and leeks until soft and fragrant. In a separate pan, over a low heat, cook your mushrooms in 2 tablespoons of soy sauce or tamari. They'll start to soften and become a slightly darker brown. Remove from the heat and set aside.

To the onions, carrot, celery and leeks, add your rosemary, thyme, oregano and garlic. Continue to cook for a further few minutes. You can add a dash of water if your pan is drying up. Once fragrant, add the aminos/balsamic vinegar, and season with salt and pepper to taste.

Mix together your split peas, mushrooms and onion mixture, then put into a large baking dish with another 50ml of the stock.

To prepare the sweet potatoes, wash them well, then, using a sharp knife, peeler or mandolin, create thin slices (no larger than 1cm thick).

200g dried split peas, soaked for at least 2–4 hours

approx. 800ml–1litre vegetable stock

salt and pepper

1 large brown or white onion, finely chopped

1 large carrot, finely chopped

2 stalks of celery, leaves included, finely chopped

1 large leek, sliced lengthways, roughly chopped

approx. 500g button mushrooms, thinly sliced

2 tbsp soy sauce or tamari, plus 1 tbsp

1 large sprig of fresh rosemary, finely chopped, or 2 heaped tsp dried plus a tad extra for sprinkling

1 small/medium sprig of fresh thyme, finely chopped, or 1 heaped tsp dried

2 tsp dried oregano

4 cloves of garlic, crushed or finely chopped

2 tbsp coconut aminos, liquid aminos or balsamic vinegar (or a combination)

2 medium sweet potatoes

a pinch of dried chilli flakes

Start to layer your sweet potatoes on top of the split pea mixture, season again with salt and pepper if necessary, and add the chilli flakes and remaining rosemary.

Put into the oven on a middle shelf and bake for about 40–50 minutes. The liquid will start to disappear and the split peas will become even softer. The top will start to brown and the potatoes will cook through. You can use the remainder of your stock (approx. 200ml) to add gradually to the dish if it's starting to look a little dry, and to prevent the potatoes on top from burning.

Remove from the oven and allow to sit for a few moments before serving.

Waste tips:

As mentioned, you can use any variety of sweet potato in this dish, or, if you only have regular potatoes, they will also work, though they may take slightly longer to cook. This dish is also great with a creamy sauce or vegan cheese. Check the basic sections (pages 356 and 364) for ideas, and pair with some fresh greens or even your favourite bread for mopping up the juicier bits on the plate.

Cashew-based sauces have been a total game-changer for me since I first discovered them. I am a lover of simple dishes, with an oomph from a sauce or even just from herbs, and this dish definitely hits all the spots. The recipe calls for dried oregano, but let your heart run wild. This mash also works well on bakes or pies or even in quesadillas (see page 346).

Serves 4–6 as a side

SWEET POTATO, GREENS AND GARLIC MASH

w/ herbed cashew sauce

First, prep your sauce. Place all the ingredients in a blender (high-speed if possible) and blend until smooth. You can add more water if you want the sauce to be looser. Season with salt and pepper.

Place your kale or greens in a large pan of cold salted water. Bring to the boil and cook until the leaves are a vibrant green and the stalks have softened slightly. Once cooked, drain and set aside.

Place the cubed sweet potatoes, the 2 whole garlic cloves and 2 teaspoons of salt in a saucepan. Cover with cold water and bring to the boil, then lower to a simmer until the potatoes are soft and tender. Once cooked, drain and put back into the pan.

Add the cooked greens along with the olive oil, crushed garlic, Dijon mustard, non-dairy milk, oregano and spring onions. Mash to combine the ingredients and reach your desired consistency. I like mine slightly textured, but you can make it as smooth as you like. Season with salt and pepper. If it's too dry, add a dash more milk.

Serve drizzled with a hefty dollop of the cashew sauce. The sauce can be served hot or cold. To heat it up, simply pour it into a small pan with a little extra water and heat over a low heat, stirring as you go. It will start to thicken when you do this. Extra sauce can be kept in the fridge for up to 5 days, to add to salads or grilled vegetables.

For the sauce (makes approx. 450g)

240g raw cashews, soaked overnight

a large handful of fresh mixed herbs (parsley, coriander, dill, basil, oregano . . . whatever tickles your fancy and is available – if dried, use approx. 2 heaped tbsp)

1–2 tsp apple cider vinegar or white wine vinegar

approx. 180ml water

2 cloves of garlic, crushed or finely chopped

1 lemon, juice and zest

1 tbsp sea salt

fine or coarse black pepper

For the mash

7–8 stems of kale or any dark leafy green of choice, leaves roughly chopped, stems separated and finely chopped

5 small to medium sweet potatoes, washed well and cut into cubes

5 cloves of garlic: 2 whole, 3 crushed or finely chopped

2 tsp salt

2 tbsp olive oil

2 tbsp Dijon mustard

125ml non-dairy milk, plus extra if too dry

1 heaped tbsp dried oregano

1 bunch of spring onions (approx. 6), finely chopped

salt and pepper

This recipe really is about using what you have, a mish-mash of flavours, produce, grains, pulses and seeds. The dressing is suitably sweet, with a little chilli kick to polish it off. As the title suggests, you can make easy subs to use what you have, for an extremely adaptable salad that is far from boring!

Serves 4–6

MOROCCAN-SPICED SWEET POTATO SALAD (USE-WHAT-YOU-HAVE-STYLE)

First make your dressing. Place all the ingredients in a blender and blitz for a few minutes until well combined. If you don't have a blender, feel free to do this by hand using a fork or whisk. Add a little water if you prefer a runnier dressing.

Cook your millet or other grain according to the packet instructions. Bring to the boil in salted water and simmer until cooked. Depending on what you are using, the time can vary. For millet, it's about 20 minutes.

Place the sweet potatoes in a large pan of cold water and add a pinch of salt. Bring to the boil, then lower to a simmer for about 20 minutes. You want the potatoes to be soft and tender but not overcooked. Drain and set aside. I like this salad warm, but feel free to place them in a bowl of cold water to cool them down quicker.

Put the carrots, celery, leeks and kale into a separate bowl. Add the apple cider or white wine vinegar and 1 teaspoon of salt. Using your hands, gently mix and massage the vegetables to soften them slightly.

Add your cooked millet (or other grain), sweet potatoes, beans/chickpeas, fresh herbs, nuts and toasted cumin seeds. Season with salt and pepper and pour over your dressing, mixing gently as you go.

Serve as is, or with anything else you like. I often squeeze on some extra lemon or lime, and a pinch of dried chilli flakes if I feel like adding a touch more spice.

For the dressing

2 tbsp date syrup

2 tbsp olive oil

1 lemon, juiced

2 tsp Dijon mustard

1–2cm fresh ginger, grated

2 small cloves of garlic, crushed

½ tsp each of ground coriander, cumin and cayenne pepper

¼ tsp ground cinnamon

For the salad

100g millet (or any grain, or omit for a lighter salad)

2 medium sweet potatoes, well washed, cubed

2 carrots, ribboned (any variety, i.e. purple, orange, yellow)

1 bunch of celery, ribboned or thinly sliced, leaves included

2 medium leeks, sliced down the middle, washed, roughly chopped

a few stalks of kale, roughly chopped (also use stalks or add to your stock box)

1 tsp apple cider or white wine vinegar

salt and pepper

1 × 400g tin of beans/chickpeas (any variety, or omit for a lighter salad)

a large handful of freshly chopped herbs (coriander, mint, parsley)

50g chopped and lightly toasted nuts (pistachios, almonds, hazelnuts, etc.)

1 tbsp cumin seeds, lightly toasted

A favourite among my friends, event/retreat guests and at home, these are a pretty good store-cupboard recipe to keep in mind, as you will more than likely have most of the ingredients in. Quesadillas are one of my favourite Mexican recipes – they're quite show-stopping but incredibly easy to make, so they're a great option if you feel like showing off a little, as they pretty much do all the talking.

Serves 2
as a main,
4 as a side/snack

SWEET POTATO AND CANNELLINI BEAN QUESADILLAS

Bring a medium sized pot of water to the boil. Add a good pinch of salt and your cubed sweet potato. Bring back to the boil, then lower to a simmer and cook until soft and tender, about 10–12 minutes. Once cooked, drain and put back into the pot. Using a fork or a potato masher, roughly mash until almost smooth. Place to one side.

In a frying pan, heat the coconut oil. Once hot, add your onion and fry until slightly brown and fragrant. Season with salt and pepper. Lower the heat and add your miso paste, maple syrup, chilli flakes, garlic and coriander stalks, stirring all the time to prevent the garlic burning.

Add the paprika, cumin and ground coriander and sauté for another minute or so. Once cooked, transfer to a bowl and add the beans and your mashed sweet potato. Season again with salt and pepper. You could add a pinch more chilli here if you like it spicy.

Using a fork, start to combine the mixture. It won't be entirely smooth but will combine into a textured mix.

Once combined, add the fresh coriander leaves, nutritional yeast, lime juice and zest and mix well. If your mixture is a little dry, add a little olive oil or water to loosen.

Now make your quesadillas. Heat a dash of oil in a pan, then add a tortilla and lightly fry each side. Turn the heat

4 tortillas (see page 370 for homemade, but if you have leftover or store-bought, these will also be fine)

For the filling

1 large sweet potato, cubed, skin left on

1–2 tbsp coconut oil

1 small red onion, finely chopped

salt and pepper

1 tbsp miso paste

1 tbsp pure maple syrup or other sweetener of choice

1 small red chilli, finely chopped

2 cloves of garlic, crushed or finely chopped

a small handful of fresh coriander, roughly chopped, stalks included

2 tsp smoked paprika

2 tsp ground cumin

2 tsp ground coriander

1 × 400g tin of cannellini beans, drained and rinsed well (if using dried beans, approx. 125g, soaked overnight and boiled until tender)

4 heaped tbsp nutritional yeast

1 lime, juice and zest

olive oil, to loosen

to its lowest and add about half the filling mixture to the tortilla. Spread it out evenly, and add another fried tortilla on top. Depending on how large or small your tortillas are, use an appropriate amount of filling mixture. Carefully cook until the tortilla begins to brown and blister slightly on the bottom. Flip and do the same on the other side. Repeat for the second quesadilla, keeping the first one warm by either placing it in the oven with the light on, or putting it on a plate and covering it with a saucepan lid or tea towel.

Once both quesadillas are cooked, simply use a sharp knife or pizza cutter and cut into quarters. Don't worry if some of the filling spills out each side.

Best served warm. Serve with your chosen condiments or additions, or just as they are!

Waste tips:

If you don't have cannellini beans, you can use any other soft white beans, or, if you fancy a very Mexican twist, you could try black beans. You can serve these with fresh corn, salsa and salad for the ultimate Mexican feast. They work nicely as a savoury breakfast or brunch too, if you want something a little different.

Baking a sweet potato whole is, in my opinion, one of the greatest ways to cook it. The skin caramelizes so perfectly, the insides soft and sweet yet earthy at the same time. This recipe is simple but effective, with a subtle crunch from the chickpeas that really lifts the dish, and a creamy dressing to finish it off, creating the perfect balance of textures and flavours. A handy week-night dish that also makes great leftovers!

Serves 4

BAKED SWEET POTATO, CRISPY CHICKPEAS

w/ tahini dressing

If you are cooking chickpeas from dried, you'll need to soak them overnight in water with a pinch of salt beforehand. Once soaked, drain and rinse well, then put them into a pot of cold water. Make sure they are submerged in the water. Typically when cooking chickpeas from dried you'll want double the amount of water to chickpeas. Add a large pinch of salt, cover, and bring to the boil. Once boiling, lower to a simmer and cook until soft. This usually takes around 40 minutes but can be longer. Once cooked, drain, rinse and set aside to dry.

Preheat your oven to 200°C fan. Wash your sweet potatoes well, scrubbing them if necessary. Using a sharp knife or fork, prick the potatoes a few times (over the whole surface) about 1cm deep.

Place on a baking tray and put into the oven to roast. They will take around 30–40 minutes, the outside becoming golden brown, the inside soft. Occasionally the potatoes will start to 'ooze' a slightly caramel-type liquid. This is normal and is due to the sweetness of the potato.

Put the cooked chickpeas into a large mixing bowl and toss with the olive oil, cumin, coriander, smoked paprika, ground cloves, turmeric, garlic, salt, pepper and the stalks from the fresh coriander. Add the lemon juice and mix until the chickpeas are well coated.

4 medium sweet potatoes

approx. 600g cooked chickpeas (2 × 400g tins, drained, or 300g dried – see method, left)

2–4 tbsp olive oil

4 heaped tsp ground cumin

2 heaped tsp ground coriander

2 tsp smoked paprika

1 tsp ground cloves

1 tsp ground turmeric

5 cloves of garlic, crushed or finely chopped

a hefty pinch of salt

2 tsp fine or coarse black pepper

a small handful of fresh coriander, finely chopped, stalks included

1 lemon, juiced, ½ zested

3 spring onions, finely chopped

fresh chives (optional – if in season, these are great with this dish)

For the dressing

2 lemons, juiced, ½ zested

2–4 tbsp tahini (depending how thick you want your dressing)

2 level tbsp Dijon mustard

1 tbsp chilli sauce (optional)

2 tbsp soy sauce or tamari

2 tsp apple cider vinegar

2 tsp dried oregano

water, or plant-based milk for a creamier option

Spread on a baking tray and put into the oven to roast. They will take around 20–30 minutes, depending on how crispy you want them. After 15 minutes, take out the chickpeas, sprinkle the lemon zest over and mix well, freeing up any chickpeas that may have got stuck to the bottom of the tray.

For the dressing, simply place all the ingredients apart from the water in a blender and blitz. If you don't have a blender you can do this by hand, using a fork or whisk. To loosen, slowly pour in a little water (or plant-based milk) and continue to whisk until the dressing reaches the desired consistency. Set aside.

To serve, slice your potatoes lengthways. Top with the crispy chickpeas and drizzle over the tahini dressing. Sprinkle over the fresh coriander leaves and spring onions. If you have chives, scatter those over as well.

Waste tips:

You can get a variety of different sweet potatoes, some with a purple skin and white inside, some orange and again white inside. Use any type or a variety, especially if you are not in the UK and different ones are available. You could also try adding a harissa or pesto to this dish, serving it in a dollop on top or perhaps adding it to the chickpeas when roasting.

The basics

As a true condiment queen, a prepper, a planner, a lover of ease, I've devoted this section of the book to my trusty staple recipes. Many of these are used in the recipes throughout the main chapters, and others you may have seen mentioned. You'll learn how to whip up homemade stock, pesto, harissa and even vegan cheese, discover the fundamentals of hummus, what to do with leftover vegetable tops, make an any-fruit compote and – one of my favourite summer go-tos – homemade flatbreads, any which way. The beauty of the recipes in this section is they can be made during any season. You can adapt them easily to suit your needs and to whatever produce or cupboard essentials you have in. Once you know each base, you can run wild with other flavours and variations.

As a bonus, you don't have to worry about leftovers either. A lot of these recipes will make more than you need for a meal, but you'll find a tip with each one for how to carry it further, turning a harissa into a creamy salad dressing, or using leftover nut butter to make a quick nut milk. By making your everyday or favourite sauces/condiments at home, you avoid unnecessary packaging from the shops and of course can have a little fun in the kitchen, playing with variations based on your tastes and needs.

Use your scraps for stock

Making your own stock is one of the best ways to reduce food waste, eliminate packaging and ensure you use the whole vegetable. And in my opinion, homemade stock tastes a whole load better. You can pretty much use whatever you want in it – celery ends, carrots, cauliflower, veg tops, tomato cores, etc., boiling it down with garlic and dried herbs.

It's very simple to start collecting your scraps for stock. I keep a Tupperware in my freezer, or a jar if I have fewer scraps and want to make stock sooner rather than later. When it comes to making the stock, you chuck it all into a pot, fill to the brim with water, then season as you wish. As well as salt and pepper (or omit the salt and remember to salt your dish later), you can add old herbs or spices, bay leaves, herb sprigs, whole garlic, and additional onion.

Here are two of my go-to stocks: one is a standard base with suggested extras, and the other is an Asian-style base which I use for noodle dishes. Stock isn't just a base for soup or stew, it's also great for risottos, as a flavour enhancer, in dressings, sauces and so on.

——

SCRAP STOCK

Standard base:

as many scraps as you've saved (but not less than around 2 mugfuls)

salt and pepper

optional additions: fresh or dried herbs and spices (thyme, rosemary, oregano, chilli, bay leaves), whole garlic (smashed), extra onion

Asian base:

as many scraps as you've saved (but not less than around 2 mugfuls)

2–4 tbsp soy sauce or 1–2 tbsp miso paste

15g dried mushrooms, any variety (or more if you like)

1 small knob of ginger, thinly sliced

cloves of garlic (as many as you like)

salt and pepper

optional additions: tomato purée, dulse flakes or dried seaweed, chilli, cloves

For both varieties, simply place all the ingredients in a saucepan (don't worry about thawing frozen vegetables). Pour in enough water to almost cover the contents and season as desired. Simmer for half an hour to an hour, depending on how much is in the pan and how strong you want the stock to be. You'll notice the water start to turn yellowy-brown; the darker the colour, the stronger the stock. Remove from the heat and pour the stock through a sieve or colander into a bowl. Compost the scraps. For the Asian variety, you could leave the dried mushrooms in the broth if you fancy an extra 'mushroomy' hit.

Depending on how smooth you want the stock, you could strain it again. Funnel it into a jar or Tupperware and store it in the fridge or freezer. If I make a big batch, I tend to keep a big jar in the fridge and the rest in the freezer, so I can use it as I go. You could also pour some into ice cube trays for adding to dishes as you need them.

> **Note:**
>
> You needn't stop at vegetables, you can also use fruits, especially the cores of apples or pears, etc. They will add a slight sweetness, similar to carrots or beans.
>
> ——

Dressings

The key to dressings is mostly intuition . . . trusting your taste buds will help you to build the perfect dressing to accompany a dish, dress a salad or add a drizzle to a flatbread. I tend to separate dressings into two categories, vinaigrette types and creamy types. Once you get to grips with the basic principles, you'll find it easy to build your own dressings freely and creatively, based on your preferences or what you need for a dish. It's important to remember a few key tastes: salt, acids/vinegars, a fat and a sweetener. You don't always need to include all of these, as you may get some tastes through the dish itself, but if the balance doesn't seem right, refer back to these principles and go from there. You also don't have to stick to just one of each component; for example, my two main base ingredients for dressings are usually lemon juice and a mustard. They are technically both acids but have different purposes. Of course, you'd then need to add other tastes to complement and balance them out.

Opposite are some examples of things you might use for each component, then overleaf we'll move on to combining them for the two main dressing types I mentioned above. You'll notice the addition of heat, which is another great component if you want a bit of spice in a dressing. You can of course jazz any dressing up with herbs/spices as you desire.

———

Salt: salt, soy sauce/tamari, aminos, miso paste.

———

Acids (vinegars/citrus): lemon, orange, lime, garlic, mustard (any variety), vinegars (any variety), pickle or caper juice, ginger, shallots or onions (finely chopped).

———

Fats/natural creamy types: oils (any variety), tahini, nut butter, vegan butter, yoghurt, silken tofu, plant-based milk, avocado, hummus.

———

Sweeteners: maple syrup, date syrup, agave, honey, any granulated sugar, molasses, soft fruits.

———

Heat: dried or fresh chilli, chilli sauce, sweet chilli sauce (also part acid/vinegar category).

———

Herbs/spices: any fresh herbs (finely chopped), oregano, cumin (seeds or ground), coriander (seeds or ground).

———

VINAIGRETTES

A vinaigrette typically contains an acid (vinegar, citrus, or a combination), some salt and a fat, usually in oil form. Occasionally, I'll add a sweetener such as maple syrup, and I also love adding oregano if the salad is very simple. Vinaigrettes are great for keeping in the fridge for salad dressings, vegetables, grains such as couscous, or even for dipping fresh bread into. I like to start with a simple ratio of 1 part acid, 1 part oil, but you can also play about with the ratios. If you are adding a sweetener, go in tablespoon by tablespoon. It's good to have a couple of tried and tested combinations in the bag and then spruce up if necessary.

When it comes to combining the ingredients, begin with your acid, then slowly add your oil and build it up, whisking as you go, to check the consistency and taste. That way you avoid it becoming too heavy, keeping it light and fresh. You can use a hand whisk, or, if you have a small blender, this can help to emulsify and incorporate the ingredients. For additions like onion or garlic, a blender is a good option. You could also put the ingredients into a jar and shake it aggressively to combine. See what works best for you.

When you begin to add other components, start slow. You want the dressing to have a good balance and not be too overpowering (unless it's deliberate). If you're adding herbs and spices, the longer you leave the dressing for, the more it will infuse, and the same goes for garlic and chilli. Remember that caper and pickle juice can be salty, so use before salting.

Here are a few of my go-tos. You'll see some include more than one acid, but the 1:1 rule still applies.

DIJON AND MAPLE SYRUP

Makes approx. 250–315ml

—

85ml apple cider vinegar

125ml olive oil

2 tbsp pure maple syrup

1 heaped tbsp Dijon mustard

approx. ½ tsp sea salt

a grind of black pepper

—

LEMON AND GARLIC

Makes approx. 250–315ml

—

125ml lemon juice, plus a dash of zest

125ml olive oil

2 tsp pure maple syrup or honey

approx. ½ tsp sea salt

1 large clove of garlic, crushed or finely chopped

a grind of black pepper

—

BALSAMIC VINAIGRETTE

Makes approx. 250–315ml

—

125ml balsamic vinegar

125ml olive oil, plus 1 tbsp

1 tsp pure maple syrup

2 tbsp lemon juice

approx. ½ tsp sea salt

a grind of black pepper

2 tbsp dried oregano

For all these dressings, simply whisk, blend or shake in a jar. If you want the garlic in the lemon dressing to be smooth, I'd recommend blending it.

—

CREAMY DRESSINGS

Creamy dressings tend to have a base of a fat and an acid, again with the relevant additions: salt, sweeteners, herbs/spices, etc. As before, you can combine a few fats, or a fat and a 'cream', such as silken tofu or a plant-based milk. Despite the dressing having a creamy texture and including a 'fat' as a base, that doesn't mean it's overly fatty or not good for you. These dressings serve a great purpose, for example bringing to life a very simple salad that you might want to be a bit more filling, therefore adding a creamy, 'fattier' part to it, as a sauce for a taco, a pasta salad, or even on the side, as a condiment.

Creamy dressings keep well in the fridge, and are always great to add to, starting slow with additions and adjusting to your desired texture and flavour. They do tend to get thicker in the fridge, so if you want to loosen them, just add water or a little extra lemon juice for more of a punch.

Unlike the vinaigrettes, there isn't a ratio I follow too strictly here. I tend to mix 1:1 as a foundation, but once everything else is added (sweeteners/salts/herbs, etc.) it tends to become 1:1:1. In terms of how you combine the ingredients, the same applies as for the vinaigrettes. Your options depend on what equipment you have and how much washing up you want to do.

Here are a few of my favourites. Tahini is usually the start of my base – it's easy to jazz up and instantly provides a perfect creamy texture. There is also a recipe on page 371 for a silken tofu dressing which can be adapted easily and which I often use as a dressing for tacos or as a 'Caesar' or 'ranch' dressing.

—

BASIC TAHINI DRESSING

Makes approx. 250–280ml

—

125ml tahini (smooth/ runny if available)

65ml water (extra for loosening)

65ml lemon juice

salt and pepper

¼ tsp garlic powder

—

TAHINI DRESSING AND THEN SOME

Makes approx. 200ml

—

125ml tahini (smooth/ runny if available)

2–4 tbsp water or plant-based milk

1–2 tbsp soy sauce/ tamari/aminos

1 lemon, juiced, plus a dash of zest

1–2 tbsp pure maple syrup or sweet chilli sauce

1 clove of garlic, crushed or chopped

1 tbsp dried oregano

salt and pepper

—

TAHINI, GINGER, MISO DRESSING

Makes approx. 200ml

—

125ml tahini (smooth/ runny if available)

a small knob of ginger, finely chopped or grated

1–2 cloves of garlic, crushed

1 heaped tbsp miso (any variety)

1 tbsp soy sauce/tamari/ aminos

1 tbsp vinegar of choice

1 tbsp sweetener of choice

water, to loosen

pepper

—

NUT BUTTER DRESSING

Makes approx. 200–250ml

—

approx. 125–150g nut
  butter of choice
  (peanut, almond, etc.)

1 lemon or 2 smaller
  limes, juiced, plus
  a dash of zest

1–2 tbsp soy sauce/
  tamari

1–2 tbsp sweetener
  of choice

a pinch of dried chilli
  flakes or a dash of
  chilli sauce

water or plant-based
  milk, to loosen

salt and pepper

For all these dressings, either hand whisk,
blend or shake in a jar to combine. Use water
to loosen where necessary, and feel free to jazz
up or pimp in your own way.

——

HUMMUS: FOUNDATIONS AND THEN SOME

For the hummus variations which follow,
simply use this base recipe as the foundation.
Some of the recipes need extra olive oil/water
or lemon, so this is noted, as are other changes.
The blending method is the same each time.

Makes 6–10 servings, depending on size/use

—

The base

240g cooked chickpeas
  (120g dried or 1 tin),
  rinsed well

2 cloves of garlic,
  crushed

1 large lemon, juiced,
  plus a dash of zest

2 heaped tbsp tahini

2–4 tbsp olive oil/water,
  or a combination

a pinch of dried chilli
  flakes

salt and pepper

Rinse and drain your chickpeas, then place
in a blender/processor. You can also use a
hand-held blender.

Add the garlic, lemon juice and zest, tahini,
olive oil/water (start with less, as you can
add more to reach your desired texture),
chilli flakes and a hefty seasoning of salt
and pepper. Blitz until smooth and creamy.
If you like your hummus chunkier, feel free
to stop when you wish.

Either serve straight away or put into a
Tupperware and store in the fridge. You could
drizzle over a little olive oil to keep it moist.
This keeps in the fridge for about 5 days.

You can pretty much add any spice or herb
that you like to this recipe. Over the page
are a few of my favourite variations. When
fresh ingredients are not in season, it's still
very easy to jazz it up with spices such as
ground or whole coriander/cumin seeds,
paprika (smoked or not), fennel seeds,
caraway, oregano, and so on. As a bonus,
 you could mix it with another recipe from
this section – harissa or a pesto – to create a
hybrid. Use what you have and what you like.

Tip:

Depending on how sensitive your digestive system
is, a great hack when making hummus is to reserve
some of the water from the chickpeas, either from
the pan you've cooked them in or from the tin –
whatever you are using – and add a few tablespoons
of that instead of tap water. This creates an
exceptionally smooth, creamy hummus. You also
don't have to stick to chickpeas for hummus;
butterbeans are great, or pinto, or cannellini . . .
you get the idea.

——

BEETROOT AND CUMIN HUMMUS

base recipe ingredients, as previous page

approx. 150g beetroot, cooked

1–2 tsp cumin seeds

1 tsp ground cumin

2–4 tbsp olive oil/water

an extra pinch of chilli flakes, for more of a kick

How you cook your beetroot depends on how much time you have. Either cut into chunks and cook in boiling water for about 15 minutes, until tender and a sharp knife inserted is easily removed, or wrap the beetroot in foil and roast it in the oven at 200°C fan, for about 40 minutes. In both cases, allow to cool.

Put your base ingredients into a blender, followed by the rest of the ingredients above. Blitz to your desired consistency. Store as per the base recipe.

—

BASIL AND SPINACH HUMMUS

base recipe ingredients, as previous page

approx. 20–25g fresh basil (for this variation, you could instead add 2 heaped

tbsp of pesto from the opposite page if you don't have fresh basil)

100g fresh spinach

2–4 tbsp olive oil/water

Put your base ingredients into a blender, followed by the rest of the ingredients above, adding the olive oil/water slowly at first. Blitz until you reach your desired consistency. Store as per the base recipe.

—

LEMON AND CORIANDER HUMMUS

base recipe ingredients, as previous page

20–40g fresh coriander (depending on how strong you'd like it)

1 lemon, juiced, plus an extra dash of zest

½ tbsp soy sauce

Put your base ingredients into a blender, followed by the rest of the ingredients above. Blitz until you reach your desired consistency. Store as per the base recipe.

—

SQUASH/PUMPKIN HUMMUS

base recipe ingredients, as previous page

approx. 250–350g squash/pumpkin, any variety (amount depends on whether you'd rather it is

more chickpea-heavy vs squash/pumpkin)

½–1 lemon, juiced

2–4 tbsp olive oil/ water/a combination

How you cook your squash/pumpkin depends on how much time you have. Either cut into chunks and cook in boiling water for 12–15 minutes, until tender and a sharp knife inserted can easily be removed, or roast in the oven, preheated to 200°C fan, for about 25 minutes, until tender. In both cases, allow to cool.

Put your base ingredients into a blender, followed by the rest of the ingredients above. Blitz until you reach your desired consistency. Store as per the base recipe.

—

PESTO: WALNUT BASE AND SEASONAL ADDITIONS

Who said pesto has to be just basil-based? I love to experiment with other vegetables and herbs, depending on season. For the variations which follow, simply use this base recipe as the foundation. Some of the recipes need extra olive oil/water or lemon, and this is noted as well as any other changes. The blending method is the same each time and it couldn't be easier to whiz up, blended smooth or keeping a little texture for a more rustic feel.

Serves 6–8

—

The base

150g walnuts

4 cloves of garlic, crushed or finely chopped

1–2 large handfuls of fresh basil

2 lemons, both juiced, 1 zested

approx. 125–250ml olive oil

approx. 6 heaped tbsp nutritional yeast

a pinch of dried chilli flakes

salt and pepper

a pinch of nutmeg

a pinch of cayenne pepper (for extra spice)

Put all the ingredients into a blender. Blitz to a paste, adding extra olive oil to loosen if needed.

The simple additions: you'll find the following variations used throughout the book according to the seasons, but you can vary further. You could make the carrot top pesto but substitute your chosen veg top, e.g. beetroot tops or celery tops. If you have extra fresh herbs, why not toss in for a slightly different outcome.

Tips:

I'd always recommend using less of the olive oil first – you can easily add more as you need. There can be a slight variation in weight of different veg tops and you may like a chunkier pesto. To preserve it a little longer, drizzle more oil on top each time you store.

—

KALE PESTO

roughly 200g kale (cavolo nero or any dark leafy green), stalks included

150g walnuts

2 cloves of garlic, crushed or finely chopped

1–2 large handfuls of fresh basil

2 lemons, both juiced, 1 zested

approx. 250–350ml olive oil

6–8 heaped tbsp nutritional yeast

a pinch of dried chilli flakes

salt and pepper

Steam the kale for 5–6 minutes, until a vibrant green and wilted. Remove from the heat and run it under a cold tap to stop the cooking process. Drain and allow to cool to room temperature or colder. Roughly chop.

Put the walnuts, garlic, fresh basil, lemon juice and zest and olive oil into a blender and blitz to a rough paste. Add the chopped kale, nutritional yeast, chilli and a hefty pinch of salt and pepper. Blitz again until the mix starts to get smoother. If you want it looser, add a dash more olive oil. Test and season if necessary.

Transfer to a jar and set aside. Use immediately as desired, or store in the fridge with a little olive oil on top to keep it moist.

—

CARROT TOP PESTO

the tops from a 1kg bunch of carrots

1 large handful of fresh basil (or parsley if you can't get basil, or a combination)

50g walnuts (almonds, cashews or hazelnuts are also great, or a combination)

4 heaped tbsp nutritional yeast

4 small cloves of garlic, crushed or finely chopped

approx. 125–250ml olive oil

1 lemon, juice and zest

a pinch of dried chilli flakes

salt and pepper

Wash and chop the carrot tops. These can be quite tough, so chopping them smaller helps them to blend and not get stuck in the blade.

Place in a blender with the basil, walnuts, nutritional yeast, garlic, olive oil, lemon juice and zest, chilli flakes, salt and pepper. Blend to a relatively smooth paste, adjusting with extra olive oil if needed. Remove from the blender and put into a bowl or airtight container.

—

BROCCOLI PESTO

1 small/medium broccoli, 180–225g, roughly chopped, stalks included (you may need to cut them smaller, or they take a while to cook)

150g walnuts

4 cloves of garlic, crushed or finely chopped

approx. 1–2 large handfuls of fresh basil

2 lemons, both juiced, 1 zested

250–350ml olive oil

6–8 heaped tbsp nutritional yeast

a pinch of dried chilli flakes

salt and pepper

Steam the broccoli for around 6 minutes, until a vibrant green and tender. Remove from the heat and run under a cold tap to stop the cooking process. Drain and allow to cool completely.

Put the walnuts, garlic, fresh basil, lemon juice and zest and olive oil into a blender and blitz to a rough paste. Add the broccoli, nutritional yeast, chilli flakes and a hefty pinch of salt and pepper. Blitz again until the mix starts to get smoother. If you want it looser, add a dash more olive oil. Test and season if necessary.

Transfer the pesto to a jar for serving/storing. It will keep in the fridge for about a week. You can drizzle some additional olive oil on the top to help keep it moist.

—

CHIMICHURRI

This herby sauce is great in dressings for adding a slight tang, on toast, over grilled veggies, in a bake, on a pizza or, a personal favourite, in a pasta salad. It keeps in the fridge just like any other condiment, and I'd suggest using it within a month, making sure it's in an airtight container/jar. Making seasonal adjustments to the recipe is easy. You can sub the fresh parsley with coriander or any other fresh herb of choice, or a combination. A little mint is also great for a summery twist. As well as fresh herbs, you can add vegetables too, for some variety and earthiness. On page 197 you'll see a beetroot top variation for autumn.

Makes 1 medium jar (12 heaped tbsp)
—

2 large handfuls of fresh parsley, finely chopped, stalks included

2 tbsp capers, drained

2 cloves of garlic, crushed or finely chopped

2–3 tablespoons extra virgin olive oil

1 teaspoon apple cider vinegar

1 lemon, juiced, plus a dash of zest

a pinch of chilli flakes

salt and pepper

Put your chopped parsley, capers, garlic, olive oil, apple cider vinegar, lemon juice and zest, chilli and salt and pepper into a blender. Blitz until you have a paste type mixture, seasoning with more salt and pepper if needed and adding a little extra olive oil if too dry.

The chimichurri is a pretty rustic sauce, but you can add more oil or blend until you reach your desired consistency.

—

HARISSA

Harissa is handy to keep in the fridge for adding when you're roasting vegetables, or to dressings, hummus, baked cheeses, or even to a sauce to add some spice and depth. If you've made a milder version, it's easy to spice up, and blending with a large handful of fresh coriander or parsley is a great variation.

Makes 1 medium jar (16 tbsp)
—

10 large dried chillies, mild to medium heat

5–7 dried chiles de arbol (a Mexican variety, widely stocked – these are very spicy, so use fewer if you prefer, or omit and just use more of the ordinary dried chillies above)

2 tsp coriander seeds

1 tsp caraway seeds

1 heaped tbsp cumin seeds

3–5 cloves of garlic, crushed or finely chopped

1cm ginger, finely grated or chopped

2 tsp smoked paprika

a hefty pinch of sea salt

½ a lemon, juice and zest

1 tbsp apple cider vinegar (or white wine vinegar)

1 tbsp tomato purée/paste

1 tsp pepper

approx. 65–85ml good-quality olive oil, or water for an oil-free option (I prefer using oil here, and omitting from the dish I'm cooking, the fat does help create a richer or deeper flavour)

Put the dried chillies (both kinds if you are using) into a bowl, pour hot water over them, and leave to soak for around 15 minutes. Make sure they are submerged.

Over a medium heat, lightly (dry) toast your coriander, caraway and cumin seeds until fragrant and starting to pop. Transfer to a mortar and pestle or a small processor and grind/crush into a powder.

—

To the powder add the garlic, ginger, paprika and salt. Briefly blitz or grind, then add the lemon juice, zest, vinegar and tomato purée. Mix again until you have an even paste. If you are using a mortar and pestle, the paste will be a little more rustic.

Once the chillies have rehydrated, drain and remove the stems (if any) and seeds. Add to the food processor or the mortar, along with some more salt and pepper. Blend or mash well until combined. If you were using a mortar and pestle initially, you can also transfer everything to a blender to finish it off.

Slowly add the oil or water, mixing as you go. You may need a little more or a little less, depending on the desired consistency. I like to keep mine nice and thick for adding to other dishes later on. Season to taste – option to squeeze in a little more lemon juice here for a bit more of an acidy or citrusy taste.

The harissa will keep in a jar in the fridge for about a month, and longer in the freezer.

—

ANY-NUT BUTTER

Perhaps one of the easiest things you'll ever make, with a catch: a high-speed blender/processor is needed. Bullet-type blenders are ideal. You can use a smaller, less powerful model, but it may take more time as they can overheat easily. Below is a basic recipe, which you can easily spruce up with different nuts and additions, such as the ones suggested, and don't feel confined to a single type of nut. The nuts produce their own oil, so it's not necessary to add extra; however, if you have a less powerful blender, you could add a drizzle to get it going.

Makes approx. 500g nut butter

—

500g nuts of choice (almonds, peanuts without skins, macadamias, pecans, cashews, Brazils, hazelnuts, etc., or a combination)

a large pinch of salt

optional additions: cacao powder, cinnamon, nutmeg, cardamom (mixed if you like), desiccated coconut, coconut oil, sesame oil, tahini, maple or date syrup, extra salt

The key to getting nuts to blend easily and for the ultimate flavour is to roast them first. Preheat your oven to 180°C fan. Spread the nuts on a large baking tray and roast for 8–12 minutes, until they start to turn golden brown. Smaller nuts will cook fast, so make sure they don't burn. Shake the tray halfway through to make sure each nut roasts fully. Remove from the oven. Allow to cool to room temperature.

Transfer the nuts to a blender/processor, add the salt and get blending. You may have to pause to scrape down the sides. Blitz until you reach your desired consistency. The longer you blend, the smoother the nut butter will be. Transfer to a jar and allow to cool to room temperature before you put the lid on.

Variations: sometimes I add lots of salt for a salted variation. You could also add a drizzle of maple syrup or date syrup for a salted caramel version. Go in slow when adding spices, as you don't want it powdery.

Tips:

The same method applies for seeds, if you want to add in or make a seed-only butter. For a 'crunchy' outcome, remove a handful of nuts after roasting and crush. Blend the rest and then, before storing, add the crushed nuts and mix well.

NUT/SEED MILK

Believe it or not, nut and seed milks are really simple to make. A high-speed or bullet-style blender isn't essential but is a great tool to have, as well as a nut milk bag or muslin cloth. You don't need to invest in anything fancy or expensive, but once you've got it, you've got it. A little tip if you don't have a high-speed blender is to use a couple of heaped tablespoons of nut butter to replace the whole nuts, blending with water (the amount depends on how thick you want the milk). Typically, I'd use around 2–3 heaped tablespoons for 500ml of water to reach a creamy consistency, not too thick, not too thin.

When it comes to the nuts/seeds themselves, I always try to get unsalted, raw ones. Occasionally I lightly roast/toast them for a different flavour, but more often I just keep them raw. My next tip for the nuts/seeds is to soak them, ideally overnight, or at least 2 hours in almost boiling water will do the trick. Seeds don't need as long, so 2 hours will suffice. This helps them to blend, as they soften in the soaking process, and I think it enhances the flavour. You just need enough water to submerge them, so put them into a bowl and cover with water. If you're soaking overnight, put them into the fridge. Lastly, when it comes to straining your milk, if you don't have a nut milk bag you can fashion one yourself using a cheesecloth, muslin cloth, or other material that the milk can seep through. Not every nut needs to be strained, especially after soaking. I don't usually strain cashews or macadamias, as they tend to go creamier, but nuts like almonds have a 'bittiness' to them, so are better strained. Pumpkin seeds and hemp seeds don't tend to need straining either.

When it comes to leftover pulp, there's a recipe on page 367 for a nut-pulp granola, for which the seed pulp will also work, and you can play around with the quantities and spices. You could also experiment with making cookies following the base recipe on page 369, or raw balls, blending with a dried fruit and any other additions you'd like. You can of course freeze the pulp for later and use it as you desire: breadcrumbs, or a savoury crispy topping, etc.

Makes approx. 1.5 litres of milk (depending on amount of nuts used and thickness)

—

70–140g nuts or seeds of choice (the more nuts, the creamier and thicker the milk), soaked overnight or for 2 hours at least in almost boiling water	1 litre filtered water a pinch of salt optional additions: pitted medjool dates, maple syrup, date syrup, agave, cinnamon or other spice, vanilla extract

Drain and rinse your soaked nuts/seeds and place in a high-speed blender. Add the water and salt. Add any additions here, starting with a smaller amount and going in with more after you've tasted.

Blend on a high speed for about 1½–2 minutes. You want the nuts/seeds to be fully blended, creamy and frothy.

With your nut milk bag or cloth suspended over a glass bowl, slowly start to pour your blended mix through the cloth. Depending on how much mix there is, you can do it in one or two batches. Grasp the bag or cloth with one hand and slide your hand down, squeezing gently, so the liquid strains through the cloth/bag. You could also gently twist the bag to help the liquid on its way.

Once you've squeezed out all the liquid, you'll be left with a relatively dry mixture. You can either compost it or use as part of a granola (page 367) or as other suggestions above.

Pour the liquid from the bowl into a large jar or glass container. Seal and store in the fridge.

Notes:

Be sure to give your milk a little shake before you use it, as it tends to separate when stored. It will keep for 3–5 days, depending on additions. I always add a pinch of salt, and I find when I add a date or sweetener, it lasts a little longer. Occasionally, I'll freeze some of the milk in an ice cube tray and use in smoothies or iced coffees. If you want a super-thick milk (which I like to make for, say, a batch curry), use about 200–250g of nuts. It's also pretty good as a creamer or for froth on a coffee, LA style.

NUT-BASED CHEESE

These nut-based cheeses are great for topping dishes, as well as for stuffing vegetables. All three versions are easy to jazz up with any dried herbs or spices you want in the mix, even a dollop of pesto or harissa in the baked ones. You could also use fresh herbs, but the texture will be a little different and may require an extra bit of blending. I love adding smoked paprika to the cashew base and serving it up on a cheese board at a dinner party. If you want to create a béchamel-style cheese for a lasagne or other type of bake, you could use the baked cashew or baked almond recipe, but instead of baking, use the mixture, blended to your desired consistency, and you're good to go.

All these cheeses will keep in the fridge for up to 2 weeks so long as they are in an airtight container. The Parmesan will keep a little longer, but check it before eating.

BAKED CASHEW CHEESE

Makes 1 big batch, approx. 20 servings

240g cashews (soaked for at least 2 hours in boiling water, preferably overnight)

1 lemon, juiced, plus a dash of zest

1 tsp apple cider vinegar

60–90g nutritional yeast

2–4 heaped tsp dried oregano/thyme/

rosemary or combination

1–2 tbsp Dijon mustard

2 cloves of garlic, crushed or finely chopped

125ml plant-based milk

125–250ml water (or more, to loosen)

salt and pepper

Preheat your oven to 160°C fan. Drain and rinse the cashews, then put them into a high-speed blender/processor. Add the lemon juice and zest, apple cider vinegar, nutritional yeast, dried herbs, mustard, garlic, milk and water. Season with salt and pepper and blend. You want this to have a smooth consistency, so it will take a few minutes or so. Depending on your blender/processor, you may have to scrape down the sides every so often. If your mixture is a little thick, add a dash more water. You want it to be smooth but thick enough, so it doesn't fall or run off a spoon.

Line a flat baking tray with baking paper and start to scoop the cashew mix into the middle of the tray. I like to pour it all out first into a pile, so that it forms a rough circular shape. Even out the top, using a spatula or the back of a spoon. Sprinkle a good pinch of salt on top and add a light dusting of extra dried herbs.

Put into the oven on the middle shelf and bake for about 30–40 minutes. The time will vary depending on your oven. The top should start to crack and be a lovely golden brown. The top will be crispy but the inside will be a little softer. Once cooked, remove from the oven and allow to cool and harden slightly.

Eat as you desire, warm with an extra drizzle of olive oil, or cold, crumbled slightly on salad or even in a wedge as a side. Store in an airtight container in the fridge. Keeps for around 7–10 days (if you can resist it).

—

NUT PARMESAN

Makes 120g or one small jar
—

60g raw cashews

35g raw sunflower seeds

1 tsp salt

3 heaped tbsp nutritional yeast

¼ tsp garlic powder

¼ tsp ground turmeric

Place the cashews, sunflower seeds, salt, nutritional yeast, garlic powder and turmeric in a blender or processor and blitz until you have a fine crumb-like mix. Be careful not to over-blend.

Place in a jar or container with an airtight lid. Store in the fridge for up to 3 weeks.

—

BAKED ALMOND FETA

Makes one large round (you may have extra)
—

115g almonds (soaked for at least 2 hours, and ideally overnight)

1 lemon, juiced, plus a dash of zest

1 heaped tsp salt

1 tsp miso (preferably yellow or light-coloured)

2 tsp dried oregano

2 cloves of garlic, crushed or finely chopped

1 tsp apple cider vinegar

a pinch of pepper

125ml plant-based milk

2–3 heaped tbsp nutritional yeast

100–125ml water (or more, to loosen)

Drain and rinse the almonds. Ideally, use a high-speed blender for this next process. Put the almonds into a blender along with the lemon juice and zest, salt, miso, oregano, garlic, apple cider vinegar, pepper, plant-based milk, nutritional yeast and water. Blitz in the blender until the mix starts to reach a smooth consistency. You can add more water as you go for a smoother texture. This isn't super smooth, there is some texture or 'bittiness' to it, helping to replicate a feta-like cheese.

Transfer to a baking tray, greased with a dash of oil or lined with baking paper. You want it relatively thick and even – the shape doesn't matter. Sprinkle on some extra salt, then bake in the oven for around 30–40 minutes. It will start to brown and crisp on top and be slightly firm to touch. Remove and allow to cool.

Eat as you desire, warm with an extra drizzle of olive oil, or cold, crumbled slightly on salad or even in a wedge as a side. Store in an airtight container in the fridge. Keeps for around 7–10 days (if you can resist it).

—

GRANOLA

This go-to granola base gives you something to follow initially, then you can jazz it up with different flavours and/or textures. This recipe can easily be made in a bigger batch, while this serving size allows you to make different variations each week, rather than risk getting bored with the combination and leaving it to go to waste. My top tip when it comes to making granola is to make sure you salt it. It's just as important in a granola recipe as for any other dish. You can add more or less of the given spices based on how much you like each one. This base has a great balance of fats, fibre, protein, carbohydrates and sweetness, but you can of course go fruitier, or more nut heavy, and you'll see some of my favourite variation ideas below.

Makes 500g
—

The base

180g oats (I like a mix of jumbo and regular oats)

150g buckwheat groats

70g chopped nuts (almonds, cashews, walnuts)

35g sesame seeds (white or black)

35g sunflower seeds, pumpkin seeds, coconut, or a combination

4 tsp mixed spice (either ready-made as a combination, or mix cinnamon, cardamom, nutmeg to your own ratio)

a pinch of salt (approx. ½ tsp)

4–6 tbsp sweetener of choice (maple syrup, honey, date syrup, agave)

1–2 tbsp melted coconut oil

a medium handful of dried fruit (chopped dates, chopped figs, sultanas, raisins, goji berries, etc.)

Preheat your oven to approx. 180°C fan. In a large bowl combine the oats, buckwheat groats, chopped nuts, sesame seeds and your other chosen seeds/coconut. Loosely mix.

Add the spices and salt, mixing again to coat and combine. Make a small well or hole in the mixture, ready for your liquids to be poured in.

Pour in your sweetener of choice and the melted coconut oil, starting with the lower amount of each first. Mix well to combine. I always use my hands for this part – that way I can automatically check to see if the mix is sticking well. If not, go ahead and add more of your sweetener and coconut oil. You want the mixture to stick to your hands just the right amount, not too much, not too little, and to form clumps easily when pressed together between your fingers.

Spread your granola mix out on a baking tray. Pat the granola down carefully but quite firmly, almost as if you were making a flapjack. Place in the oven on a middle shelf and bake for roughly 10 minutes. Check every so often to prevent burning.

Remove from the oven and allow to cool slightly, then add the dried fruit. Again, carefully mix as evenly as possible, using your fingers to form clumps, as well as patting the rest down. Put back into the oven and bake for a further 5–8 minutes. The time will vary depending on the dried fruit you have chosen. Keep an eye on it once again to prevent any burning.

Remove from the oven and allow to cool, then store in a jar or airtight container for up to 2 months.

Variations:

I mentioned salt already, and the base recipe calls for ½ teaspoon; however, for a saltier granola (a real favourite of mine), you can add more salt – ideally flaked – as an addition afterwards. That way it's easier to taste the ratios, starting small, then going in for more if you want it even saltier.

Often, I like my granola fruit-heavy, so sometimes I'll omit the extra seeds and replace them with sultanas, then put dried dates in there too. Another favourite of mine is dried fig, cardamom and tahini. When using tahini as the liquid fat, start with 2 tablespoons of tahini (preferably the runny type) and less of the sweetener first, then adjust accordingly.

Lastly, not to be missed . . . cacao. For the granola quantity given, add 2 tablespoons of pure cacao powder, then the higher proportions of sweetener and coconut oil to balance out the additional dry ingredient. You can then adjust as you mix. For an extra chocolatey hit, you could add broken-up dark chocolate; this of course is a little bit 'extra' but is well and truly worth it. It feels a little like a dessert and you could use it in that way, perhaps on top of some baked fruit like a crumble topping, or as a little post-supper treat with some coconut yoghurt.

Tips:

Once you've mixed your granola, it's important to test if it is wet enough – it should stick to your hands. The stickier or wetter it is, the more clusters you'll get when baking. If the mixture is too dry or loose, you'll achieve the same taste but not texture. Use your fingers to press together some clumps and if they stay together, you're on to a winner on the cluster front! When it comes to the cooking time of granola, this can vary depending on your oven. You want it to be a sexy golden colour. It can burn fast, especially once the dried fruit has been added. Store it in an airtight container/jar for up to 2 months.

NUT-PULP GRANOLA

Makes 1 large batch/large Kilner jarful

—

- 220–250g leftover nut or seed pulp
- 2 tbsp orange zest
- 1 tbsp lemon zest
- 3 tbsp fresh orange juice or 1 tbsp pure orange extract
- 1 knob of fresh ginger, finely grated or chopped
- 1 tbsp ground cinnamon
- 1 tbsp pure vanilla extract
- 4–6 tbsp date syrup (sweet tooth dependent, and also depends on the texture of the granola)
- 30–35g pumpkin seeds, lightly blitzed or crushed
- 2 tbsp sesame seeds
- 15–25g desiccated coconut
- ½ tsp salt
- 2–4 tbsp coconut oil
- optional add-ins: dried fruit, e.g. raisins, mulberries, goji berries, cranberries, any other seeds, e.g. hemp, flax or chia, coconut flakes

Preheat your oven to 180°C fan, and line a large baking tray with baking paper.

In a large bowl, mix all the ingredients. This is where you can test how much date syrup to put in, depending on how many clusters you'd like.

Spread the mixture on the paper and bake for around 30 minutes. It can burn easily, so do check every so often. About halfway through, give the granola a little mix to ensure everything cooks. Do this gently so that you can retain some of the clusters.

Remove from the oven and allow to cool. You could add the dried fruit here if you don't want to bake it, and any other additional add-ins.

—

PANCAKES

BUCKWHEAT FLOUR BASE (SWEET)

**Serves 2: makes approx.
6 thin pancakes, depending on size**
—

60g buckwheat flour

40g oats, plus 1 tbsp

½ tsp baking powder

a pinch of salt

1–2 tsp ground
 cinnamon

1 tbsp maple syrup

125–185ml
 unsweetened
 plant-based milk

coconut oil (optional,
 for frying)

Topping suggestions

fresh seasonal fruit

granola

nuts/seeds/coconut
 flakes

compote

yoghurt

maple syrup

lemon juice

For the pancakes, put the buckwheat flour, oats, baking powder, salt, cinnamon, maple syrup and milk into a blender. You could also use a hand whisk/blender. Blend until thick and creamy. It'll be quite smooth, but don't worry if you have a few 'oaty' bits left.

If you are using a good non-stick pan, you won't need the coconut oil, but feel free to go ahead and melt some in the pan.

Pour the batter into the pan, creating four smaller pancakes or two larger ones. Cook for about 3–4 minutes, until bubbles begin to form on the top of the pancake and the edges start to brown. Flip and repeat on the other side.

Serve warm, with toppings of choice.

Variations:

You can easily make this sweet batter into a savoury version. Omit the maple syrup, replace the cinnamon with turmeric and add a teaspoon or so of dried oregano. You can also add other ground spices if you wish. Follow the same method in order to cook. A cacao version of this is incredibly easy and is another favourite of mine. Replace the extra tablespoon of jumbo oats with cacao powder and add another tablespoon, both heaped. You may need to add a little more liquid, but test as you go.

Tips:

If you're making a bigger batch, you could pop the oven on to keep them warm while you make your way through all the batter. Go as big or small, thick or thin as you wish.
—

CHICKPEA FLOUR BASE (SAVOURY)

Makes 4
—

100g chickpea flour,
 sifted

300ml water, at room
 temperature

a pinch of salt

2 large handfuls of a
 fresh herb of choice,
 finely chopped
 (parsley, coriander,
 basil, or a
 combination of
 all three)

coconut oil, for frying

Optional toppings

fresh seasonal greens
 of choice

herbs, spring onions

coconut yoghurt

sesame seeds

Either in a bowl or a blender, combine the chickpea flour, water, salt and herbs. Leave to sit for about 10 minutes to thicken. You may notice some bubbles forming – this is natural.

Put a drizzle of coconut oil into a large flat pan and heat it up. Once hot, add a thin layer of the batter (either a quarter of your mixture or an eighth depending on how many pancakes you'd like each), making sure it's evenly distributed. After about 30 seconds or so, the batter should start to bubble and solidify slightly.

Carefully loosen with a spatula and flip the pancake. Once browned on both sides (roughly 60 seconds or so) you can slide it on to a plate while you make the rest of the pancakes.

Serve warm, with any toppings or sides of choice.

Tips:

These chickpea-based pancakes are similar to a traditional 'socca' recipe. You could leave the mixture to sit a bit longer if you want more of a 'ferment' to happen.

Variations:

You can easily add dried spices to the base recipe, ground or seeds. A combination of cumin seeds, caraway and fennel seeds is a favourite of mine. You could also add onion or garlic to the batter when mixing, or halfway through flipping. I quite often do this with spring onions. You could have these as a savoury breakfast or brunch, or as a side to another dish, mopping up any sauce with the pancakes – perfect as a side for curries too!

THE BEST BASIC COOKIES

Makes 10–12 cookies

—

1 tbsp ground flax

3 tbsp plant-based milk of choice

65ml nut butter (smooth or crunchy), plus 2 tbsp

approx. 50g coconut sugar/palm sugar/any other natural sugar

1 tsp vanilla extract

2 tbsp maple syrup

60g spelt flour (buckwheat, wholemeal, other 'grainier' flours are all also great)

60g oat flour/ground oats

22g whole oats (normal, jumbo – your choice)

a hefty pinch of salt

1 tsp baking powder

45g crunch of choice (chopped nuts, seeds, chocolate)

Preheat your oven to 180°C fan. In a small bowl, combine the ground flax and plant-based milk. You want these to form a thicker mixture (which will act as the 'egg'). Set aside to thicken.

In a separate bowl, combine the nut butter, sugar, vanilla and maple syrup. Add the flax mixture and carefully stir until combined.

Add the spelt flour, oat flour, whole oats, salt and baking powder, carefully folding in until combined.

Add your crunch of choice, stirring it into the mixture until a dough forms and the pieces are evenly distributed.

Divide the dough into equal sized balls, about 10–12, rolling them a little and placing them on a baking tray lined with baking paper.

Once you have made all the balls, pat them down a little with your hand or a fork – this will help them to cook evenly.

Bake for around 12–14 minutes, or until golden brown on top. They will be hard on the outside and soft in the middle. Keep an eye on them to prevent burning. You'll notice they will start to spread slightly as they cook, becoming a traditional cookie size.

Tips:

Pecans are my favourite nuts for this recipe, along with almond butter, but you can use any types you like. For a more traditional cookie, adding chopped chocolate is great. You could also add a pinch more salt for a salted cookie, or even sprinkle salt flakes on top about 3 minutes before the baking is done.

TACOS-MEET-TORTILLAS-MEET-FLATBREADS

Makes approx. 8–10 smallish tacos, 4–6 tortillas, 4–5 flatbreads

----

300g plain flour, plus extra for rolling

½ heaped tsp salt

2 tbsp extra virgin olive oil, plus extra for cooking

approx. 190–210ml water

Put the flour into a bowl, add the salt and stir. Add the oil, then slowly add the water. Knead into a dough, adding more water when needed and a little extra flour if your mixture is too wet. Allow to rest for about 8 minutes.

Flour a work surface, your hands and a rolling pin. Split the dough into equal parts and roll into balls. The number you make will vary depending on what style of bread you are going for.

Using a rolling pin on the floured surface, roll out the dough balls. You can roll them as thick and wide as you desire – the cooking time will just vary slightly. They may not be perfectly circular but that's OK.

Once you have your flattened dough, lightly brush a pan with olive oil. Heat it until it's nice and hot. Add your flattened dough (however many pieces you can fit at a time) and allow to cook for about 2 minutes or so. You'll notice they start to puff/rise ever so slightly and brown underneath – at this point, flip them to cook the other side. Repeat until you've used all your dough.

Serve warm, keeping them warm under a tea towel until you've used all the dough.

Tip:

You want to make sure your pan is really hot before frying, wiping it every now and again if you don't have a non-stick pan, then replacing with another brush of olive oil in between.

Variations:

This recipe is a go-to in my house. If I don't have any bread in, these are easy to whip up for adding more to a dish, especially if the rest of the meal is pretty light. You could use other flours such as wholemeal or spelt, for a great, slightly nuttier variation. You could add other ground spices to the mix, or some oregano for a twist. These light airy breads also make amazing chapatis. You need to get them super thin, and if you can find 'atta' flour, then your chapati dreams are about to come true. It's essentially wheat flour but the milling process is slightly different. The quantities, however, are exactly the same as above. Lots of places sell it online and I've started to see it in one of my local shops in a rustic-looking paper bag . . . tied with string, might I add, very authentic!

BERRY COMPOTE

Makes approx. 500–750g compote

—

approx. 500–750g fresh or frozen berries (strawberries, pitted cherries, blueberries, raspberries, etc., or a combination)

1 lemon, juiced, plus a dash of zest

a pinch of salt

Optional additions: ginger (finely grated), orange juice/zest, other sweeteners of choice, chia seeds (for a super thick compote), ground mixed spices, ground cloves

Pour about 2cm of water into a saucepan, add the fruit, along with the lemon juice and zest, and place over a medium heat. Add a pinch of salt and stir. Bring to the boil, then reduce the heat to a simmer.

Every now and again stir the compote, mashing the fruit gently as you go. Stir in any optional additions here.

Continue to simmer for about 12–15 minutes, or until thick and combined. Be careful not to burn the bottom of the pan – the stirring is quite important.

Remove from the heat and transfer to a jar, container or bowl. Allow to cool to room temperature before putting the lid on. Place in the fridge to thicken and set.

Serve as is, or warm up again gently should you wish to serve it hot with another dish.

——

SILKEN TOFU MAYONNAISE

Makes one small jar (approx. 580ml)

—

300g silken tofu

1½ tsp apple cider vinegar

1 heaped tbsp Dijon mustard

1 clove of garlic, crushed or finely chopped

1 small lemon, juiced, plus a dash of zest

2 tbsp water (plus more to loosen)

salt and pepper

Put all the ingredients into a blender and blitz until the mix has a thick creamy consistency. Loosen with extra water if necessary.

Variations:

Dried herbs such as oregano, thyme and rosemary are great for making more of a ranch-style variation of this dressing. Smoked paprika is also a favourite addition, as is a dollop of pesto for a creamy pesto dip. Using silken tofu keeps it thick and creamy, so it's a great mayonnaise-style dressing. For an Asian twist, you could add miso paste, a dash of soy and chilli sauce and you've a real winner.

——

QUICK PICKLES

I am a huge pickle fan. I could eat them all day every day as I love anything salty and vinegary. I really do have to have a word with myself sometimes, because it's polite to leave some for others. Their acidic hit adds a lovely balance to many dishes, often blending flavours together without needing to physically add an 'acid' to a dish, which at times could totally ruin it, so pickles are my go-to for sprucing up a meal. You can pickle pretty much anything, so it's perfect for leftover, dejected-looking veg.

These quick and easy pickles keep in the fridge for a couple of weeks, the vegetables becoming softer and starting to ferment slightly. It's important to use a clean utensil to remove them each time, to help keep the fermenting process going and make them last a little longer. The recipes here are a few of my favourites, but you can get creative with the flavours, herbs, spices, even the vinegar and sweeteners, to use what you've got in. You'll be pickling left, right and centre before you know it. You don't have to heat the mixture for these, unless you want to try it (but leave to cool down before placing in the fridge).

Some rules:

Naturally, you'll be left with some brine/vinegar at the bottom of a jar after fishing out the vegetables. If you've been strict with the clean utensil rule, you can save this liquid for a new batch of pickles, as the fermenting process will have begun. You could also use this liquid for dressings or have a swig for a bit of gut-loving stuff.

RED ONION PICKLES

A personal favourite, the colour of these is pretty special and I'm not normally a pink kinda gal. You can use any onion, or a variety, adding dried herbs if you fancy or even whole garlic cloves, similar to the cucumber pickle, or a pinch of chilli flakes for an additional kick. Pickled onion is great for adding to curries, or even Thai-style dishes. Use in sandwiches for a little sexy addition. If you know you'll get through this amount very quickly, simply use as many more onions as you desire, storing the pickle in the fridge for a couple of weeks.

Makes 1 small–medium jar

—

approx. 1 large red onion, thinly sliced (you may have room in the jar for more than 1 onion, depending on how much liquid you are left with, so feel free to use more if you like)

250ml water

approx. 125ml apple cider vinegar

2–4 tbsp rice vinegar

1 heaped tbsp sugar of choice

1 heaped tsp salt (high quality if possible)

In a small bowl, bash the onion a little, using the end of a spoon or fork, separating the rings. Pop into a jar ready for the liquid.

In a separate bowl combine the water, apple cider and rice vinegars, sugar and salt. Stir a little and wait for the sugar and salt to dissolve.

Pour the vinegar liquid over the onions in the jar and leave to stand for about an hour at room temperature without a lid/cover.

Either use/serve straight away or place in the fridge, covered, to cool further and use as and when you desire.

—

CARROT AND GINGER PICKLES

This one is quite 'Korean style', so vegetables like radishes work well in place of or as well as the carrots. Other hard vegetables such as beetroots are also great in this pickle. I like to chuck in coriander seeds when using beetroot, to balance out the earthy flavour.

Makes 1 medium–large jar

—

approx. 450g carrots, julienned/thinly sliced

250ml water

200–250ml apple cider vinegar (or rice vinegar)

1–2 tbsp pure maple syrup

½ tbsp salt (high-quality sea salt if possible)

1 small knob of ginger, thinly sliced

1 clove of garlic, thinly sliced

Wash your carrots well before julienning. When you can't go any further with a julienne peeler, you can simply thinly slice these so as not to waste any of the carrots. You'll also have a nice variety of sizes in the jar.

Combine the water, vinegar, maple syrup, salt, ginger and garlic. Stir and wait a few minutes for the salt to dissolve.

Put the carrots into an appropriately sized jar or airtight container, and pour over the liquid. You want the liquid to cover the carrots, so add more water or vinegar as needed.

Put into the fridge for about 24 hours, then open up and enjoy. The longer you leave them, the softer the carrots and the 'zingier' the taste.

—

CUCUMBER AND HERB PICKLES

These pickles are pretty ready from the get-go. You can leave them to sit for around 10 minutes or make them before you start the prep for another dish. I like mine cold, so once made, I put into the fridge straight away, then bring them back out again when I'm ready to dine. I love to add smashed whole garlic cloves to this cucumber pickle. The longer you then leave them, the softer the garlic goes. Dill is a go-to in this pickle in the summertime. I could live off them, a true reminder of my time spent in LA a few years back.

Makes 1 medium–large jar

—

2 small cucumbers or 1 large

apple cider vinegar or white wine vinegar (or a combination), enough to submerge the cucumber

approx. 1 tsp sugar of choice (coconut, palm, raw, etc.)

approx. 1 tsp coriander seeds

approx. 1 tsp cumin seeds

approx. ½ tbsp salt

a small handful of fresh herbs of choice (dill, coriander, parsley, or a combination)

Peel your cucumbers until you reach the core. Finely chop your peels/ribbons, then chop the core and place in a bowl.

Add the vinegar, sugar, coriander seeds, cumin seeds, salt and fresh herbs, then mix, coating everything and submerging the cucumbers in the liquid. You want to use enough vinegar to cover the cucumbers entirely.

Either serve straight away, or put immediately in a jar/airtight container and store in the fridge.

—

thanks

Writing and curating a cookbook was something I thought I'd only ever dream of. I'm so grateful and thankful to everybody involved. Creating this book hasn't been a solo journey, and without so many amazing people, it wouldn't have happened. This book has brought many memories which I will always treasure.

To my Mum and Dad for encouraging me from the earliest age that life exists outside of salt and vinegar crisps or Philadelphia and grape bagels (but which, I might add, are still pretty special). Dad, you always knew how to rustle up a dish out of nothing, I'm still in awe; and Mum, your bulgur wheat bake is still my favourite. Thank you for believing in and supporting me on my many culinary journeys and teaching me the ways of proper home cooking. To the rest of my family, your support means the world.

To my brother, Elliot, wordsmith extraordinare, who I'm pretty sure will be glad of no more calls from me simply reading out five-word sentences to see if they make sense, or asking him to describe a vegetable in a 'different' way. Thank you for never getting tired of my 'book chat'.

To Paul, who has confessed that he is well and truly over pumpkin, even after a year, and politely told me that celeriac is still not allowed back in the house. Thank you for being there through my many manic and dramatic book moments, for eating everything I cook, with not a scrap left on the plate, supporting my every move.

To Deb and Andy, who made my time in Australia what it was, led me down the vegetable path and encouraged me to go for what I believed in most. Deb, I will always daydream of your tofu dressings, noodle salad and parsnip nut roast. And Andy, I will always remember to put sriracha on those crispy potatoes, no matter the cuisine.

To my best friends (you know who you are) for supporting me on this amazing ride, for trying all my food, for giving constant feedback, for cooking me tempeh bolognaise when the last thing I wanted to do was cook, for buying me 3 different types of mustard just because, and for letting me sleep on your sofa when I'd probably overstayed my welcome . . . for being the greatest friends.

To my agent, Rachel, who really did make a dream become a reality, believing in me and my work from the very beginning, supporting me through at every step and explaining things I never thought I'd understand.

To the absolutely incredible team at Michael Joseph, every single person involved, if it wasn't for you, I wouldn't be writing these very words. Ione, thank you for trusting in my book before we met, helping bring my vision to life; the amazing team that led to such a beautiful book which I will never not be in love with.

To Issy, my dream photographer, thanks to the world of social media – somebody I always said 'if I ever publish a book, she'd be the girl'. Thank you for many a giggle on the shoot, encouraging me to step out of my comfort zone and making lettuce look the part. Emily, your prop and food styling skills are beyond me. Thank you sharing some of the greatest styling tips I'll ever learn and never failing to be honest when it came to the amount of ingredients in that Moroccan salad. Thank you Clare, Liam, Ben and Octavia, your cooking, tasting and garlic-chopping skills were second to none. Thank you for being the greatest assistants and for making the shoot days even more special.

And lastly, to everyone else, every single retreat guest, supper club attendee, client etc . . . and you the reader. Without your support and taste buds, this book wouldn't be what it is. Thank you.

index

a

aïoli **86–7**

almonds

baked almond feta **365**

chestnut nut roast **278–9**

courgette 'lasagne' **92–4**

parsnip nut roast **207–9**

quartered and roasted tomatoes with crumbled vegan feta **173**

savoury granola **211**

shredded cauliflower, asparagus and broccoli salad with crumbled almond feta **44–5**

stuffed courgettes with vegan ricotta **98**

apples **306**

any-day Brussels sprout kimchi **326**

apple and sprout slaw **312**

apple and walnut any-flour Danish buns **309–11**

grilled vegetable skewers **183–5**

shaved Brussels sprouts and buckwheat **327–8**

spiced apple **180–2**

spiced apple crumble **308**

apricots **74**

apricot and grain salad **77**

maple and cardamom apricots **76**

roasted apricots **79**

sourdough panzanella salad **104**

summer pasta salad **82**

artichokes

creamy garlic white beans **95**

see also Jerusalem artichokes

asparagus **62**

coconut black rice salad **66–7**

potato, white bean and mustard mash **68**

shredded cauliflower, asparagus and broccoli salad **44–5**

spring Balinese soup **64–5**

aubergines **80**

babaganoush **85**

ginger, parsley and miso aubergine **84**

ras el hanout baked aubergine **88–9**

roasted and smoked whole aubergine **86–7**

summer pasta salad **82**

b

babaganoush **85**

Balinese soup **64–5**

balsamic vinegar

balsamic cherry salsa **132–3**

balsamic vinaigrette **354**

barley

massaged kale salad **215**

basil

basil and spinach hummus **358**

Jerusalem artichoke, peanut and coconut curry **334–6**

pesto **359**

slow-cooked, smoked tomatoes **164–5**

bay leaves

chunky Polish-style cabbage **266**

beans

chunky beetroot and white bean tacos **195–7**

chunky pumpkin tacos **228–9**

coconut, white bean and celery soup **316–18**

courgette 'lasagne' **92–4**

creamy garlic white beans **95**

loaded leaf salad **156–7**

Moroccan-spiced sweet potato salad **345**

potato, white bean and mustard mash **68**

spring Balinese soup **64–5**

sweet potato and cannellini bean quesadillas **346–7**

see also broad beans; butter beans; green beans

beetroot **188**

beet green and caper chimichurri **195–7**

beet-top and millet chopped salad **190–2**

beetroot and cumin hummus **358**

beetroot gnocchi **198–200**

beetroot and gram flour flatbreads **193–4**

chunky beetroot and white bean tacos **195–7**

grilled vegetable skewers **183–5**

roasted beetroot, caraway and shallot hummus **201–3**

berry compote **371**

Bircher muesli **58–9**

biscuits

tahini orange biscuits **128–31**

black beans

chunky pumpkin tacos **228–9**

blackberries **178**

blackberry coulis 180–2
creamy lemon linguine
186–7
massaged kale salad 215
smoked blackberry
chimichurri 183–5
blood oranges
shaved Brussels sprouts and
buckwheat 327–8
breakfast crumble 126–7
broad beans 46
broad bean and mint hummus
52
broad bean bruschetta 49
cauliflower Caesar salad
42–3
green risotto 28–9
herby garlic cauliflower
couscous 53
slow-cooked broad bean
fregola 50–1
spring Balinese soup 64–5
broccoli 26
broccoli chop salad 30–1
broccoli pesto 360
charred cauliflower and
broccolini 34–5
everyday roasted veggies 210
green risotto 28–9
Jerusalem artichoke, peanut
and coconut curry 334–6
potato, white bean and
mustard mash 68
shredded cauliflower,
asparagus and broccoli
salad 44–5
bruschetta
broad bean bruschetta 49
salted pear and cauliflower
pâté bruschetta 38
Brussels sprouts 324
any-day Brussels sprout
kimchi 326
apple and sprout slaw 312
shaved Brussels sprouts and
buckwheat 327–8

warm winter vegetable and
grain slaw 267
buckwheat flour
multigrain pancakes 76
pancakes 368
upside-down pear cake
282–3
buckwheat groats
granola 366–7
shaved Brussels sprouts and
buckwheat 327–8
bulgur wheat
celery, chicory, walnut and
bulgur salad 319
buns
apple and walnut any-flour
Danish buns 309–11
butter beans
Mum's best butter beans 167
root vegetable, celery, thyme
and butter bean chowder
322–3
slow-cooked, smoked
tomatoes 164–5
butternut squash
root vegetable, celery, thyme
and butter bean chowder
322–3
see also pumpkin

——

C

cabbage 258
any-day Brussels sprout
kimchi 326
cabbage ramen 262–5
chunky Polish-style cabbage
266
Jerusalem artichoke, peanut
and coconut curry 334–6
maple-roasted cabbage
260–1
Polish-style stuffed cabbage
leaves 269–70
shaved Brussels sprouts and
buckwheat 327–8
spelt pizza 105–6

warm winter vegetable and
grain slaw 267
za'atar spiced pear and
cabbage 288–9
Caesar salad
cauliflower Caesar salad
42–3
charred lettuce and tahini
Caesar 152–3
cannellini beans
creamy garlic white beans 95
sweet potato and cannellini
bean quesadillas 346–7
capers
beet green and caper
chimichurri 195–7
caper and parsley chimichurri
256–7
charred lettuce and tahini
Caesar 152–3
chimichurri 361
tomato salad with fennel and
capers 168–9
caraway seeds
roasted apricots 79
roasted beetroot, caraway and
shallot hummus 201–3
carbonara
cauliflower carbonara 36
cardamom
maple and cardamom apricots
76
carrots 134
'buttery' spiced carrot mash
139
carrot and ginger pickles 373
carrot top pesto 360
everyday roasted veggies 210
Moroccan-spiced sweet potato
salad 345
quick pickles 193
roasted carrot, ginger and
chickpea dip 140
whole roasted carrots 136–8
cashews
aïoli 86–7

baked cashew cheese **364–5**

baked cashew cheese, balsamic cherry salsa **132**

chestnut nut roast **278–9**

green bean salad with nut Parmesan **146–7**

herbed cashew sauce **344**

nut Parmesan **365**

parsnip nut roast **207–9**

rhubarb cashew cheesecake **56–7**

slow-cooked broad bean fregola with nut Parmesan **50–1**

smoked baked cashew cheese **285–6**

cauliflower **32**

cauliflower Caesar salad **42–3**

cauliflower carbonara **36**

cauliflower pâté **37**

charred cauliflower and broccolini **34–5**

everyday roasted veggies **210**

herby garlic cauliflower couscous **53**

Jerusalem artichoke, peanut and coconut curry **334–6**

root vegetable, celery, thyme and butter bean chowder **322–3**

salted pear and cauliflower pâté bruschetta **38**

shredded cauliflower, asparagus and broccoli salad **44–5**

warm winter vegetable and grain slaw **267**

whole baked harissa cauliflower **40–1**

celeriac **244**

celeriac and chestnut risotto **250–1**

celeriac ribbon salad **253**

celeriac steaks **256–7**

garlicky parsnip, potato and celeriac mash **211**

griddled celeriac **254–5**

whole roasted celeriac **246–9**

celery **314**

celery, chicory, walnut and bulgur salad **319**

coconut, white bean and celery soup **316–18**

creamy celery and chickpeas **320–1**

Moroccan-spiced sweet potato salad **345**

root vegetable, celery, thyme and butter bean chowder **322–3**

cheese

baked cashew cheese **364–5**

baked cashew cheese, balsamic cherry salsa **132**

smoked baked cashew cheese **285–6**

see also feta; Parmesan; ricotta

cheesecake

rhubarb cashew cheesecake **56–7**

cherries **124**

baked cashew cheese, balsamic cherry salsa **132–3**

cherry breakfast crumble **126–7**

slow-cooked, smoked tomatoes **164–5**

sumac roasted cherries **128–31**

whole roasted carrots with cherry salsa **136–8**

chestnuts **272**

celeriac and chestnut risotto **250–1**

chestnut nut roast **278–9**

creamed chestnut and sage pasta **276**

twice-cooked 'buttery' garlic chestnuts **275**

chickpea flour

pancakes **368**

chickpeas

baked sweet potato, crispy chickpeas **348–9**

chickpea dosa **288–9**

chive and chickpea sandwiches **154–5**

creamy celery and chickpeas **320–1**

hummus **357–8**

and maple-roasted cabbage **260–1**

Moroccan-spiced sweet potato salad **345**

pumpkin and kale falafels **222–4**

roasted carrot, ginger and chickpea dip **140**

see also gram flour

chicory

celery, chicory, walnut and bulgur salad **319**

chimichurri **361**

beet green and caper chimichurri **195–7**

caper and parsley chimichurri **256–7**

smoked blackberry chimichurri **183–5**

chive and chickpea sandwiches **154–5**

chowder

root vegetable, celery, thyme and butter bean chowder **322–3**

chutney

stock cupboard pear and onion chutney **285–6**

coconut

coconut black rice salad **66–7**

coconut, white bean and celery soup **316–18**

Jerusalem artichoke, peanut and coconut curry **334–6**
pumpkin pie parfait **230–1**
toasted coconut milk **126–7**
compote
berry compote **371**
cherry compote **124**
cookies **369–70**
coriander
Jerusalem artichoke, peanut and coconut curry **334–6**
lemon and coriander hummus **358**
coulis
blackberry coulis **180–2**
courgettes **90**
courgette 'lasagne' **92–4**
courgette ribbon salad **97**
creamy garlic white beans **95**
stuffed courgettes **98**
twice-baked potatoes **118–19**
couscous
herby garlic cauliflower couscous **53**
croutons
cauliflower Caesar salad **42–3**
charred lettuce and tahini Caesar **152–3**
coconut, white bean and celery soup **316–18**
crumble
cherry breakfast crumble **126–7**
spiced apple crumble **308**
cucumber
cucumber dill pickles **114–15**
cucumber and herb pickles **373**
quick pickles **193**
cumin
beetroot and cumin hummus **358**

d
daikon radishes
quick pickles **193**
dal
creamy curried pumpkin split pea dal **234–6**
Danish buns **309–11**
Dijon and maple syrup vinaigrette **354**
dill
cucumber dill pickles **114–15**
loaded leaf salad **156–7**
dosa
chickpea dosa **288–9**
dressings **353**
creamy dressings **356–7**
vinaigrettes **354**

f
falafels
pumpkin and kale falafels **222–4**
fennel **100**
fennel and kohlrabi salad **103**
roast fennel, pesto gnocchi **108–9**
sourdough panzanella salad **104**
spelt pizza **105–6**
summer pasta salad **82**
fennel seeds
tomato salad with fennel and capers **168–9**
feta
baked almond feta **365**
quartered and roasted tomatoes with crumbled vegan feta **173**
shredded cauliflower, asparagus and broccoli salad with crumbled almond feta **44–5**
flatbreads **370**

beetroot and gram flour flatbreads **193–4**
freekeh
warm winter vegetable and grain slaw **267**
fregola
slow-cooked broad bean fregola **50–1**
fridge dinner salad **60–1**

g
garlic
chunky Polish-style cabbage **266**
courgette ribbon salad **97**
creamy garlic white beans **95**
garlic rice **300**
herby garlic cauliflower couscous **53**
Jersey Royal potatoes **112**
lazy day pasta and garlic kale sauce **216**
lemon and garlic vinaigrette **354**
roasted artichokes and potatoes **337**
sweet potato, greens and garlic mash **344**
twice-cooked 'buttery' garlic chestnuts **275**
whole roasted pumpkin **237–9**
ginger
carrot and ginger pickles **373**
ginger, parsley and miso aubergine **84**
roasted carrot, ginger and chickpea dip **140**
tahini, ginger, miso dressing **356**
gnocchi
beetroot gnocchi **198–200**
roast fennel, pesto gnocchi **108–9**
gram flour

beetroot and gram flour flatbreads **193–4**

granola **366–7**

    nut-pulp granola **367**

    pumpkin seed and nut granola **220–1**

    savoury granola **211**

gravy

    mushroom gravy **293**

    whole roasted celeriac with mushroom gravy **246–9**

Greek-style tomatoes **170–3**

green beans **142**

    green bean salad **146–7**

    loaded leaf salad **156–7**

    pan-fried Sri Lankan green beans and shallots **144–5**

    tahini Thai noodles **148–9**

green risotto **28–9**

greens

    apricot and grain salad **77**

    celeriac ribbon salad **253**

    roasted and smoked whole aubergine **86–7**

    spring Balinese soup **64–5**

    sweet potato, greens and garlic mash **344**

    tomato salad with orzo and crispy greens **170**

    see also kale; spinach

grilled vegetable skewers **183–5**

h

harissa **361–2**

    chunky pumpkin tacos with harissa and black bean purée **228–9**

    smashed Jerusalem artichokes with homemade harissa **338–9**

    whole baked harissa cauliflower **40–1**

    wild mushrooms, millet and green harissa **294–5**

hazelnuts

chestnut nut roast **278–9**

parsnip nut roast **207–9**

herbs

    cucumber and herb pickles **373**

    everyday roasted veggies **210**

    herbed cashew sauce **344**

    see also individual herbs

hummus **357–8**

    broad bean and mint hummus **52**

    roasted beetroot, caraway and shallot hummus **201–3**

j

jam

    apricot jam **74**

Jersey Royal potatoes **110**

    crushed potato salad **114–15**

    savoury millet porridge **116–17**

    straight up, parsley, garlic, tarragon **112**

Jerusalem artichokes **330**

    Jerusalem artichoke, peanut and coconut curry **334–6**

    risotto with Jerusalem artichokes **332–3**

    roasted artichokes and potatoes **337**

    smashed Jerusalem artichokes **338–9**

k

kale **212**

    apple and sprout slaw **312**

    apricot and grain salad **77**

    kale pesto **359**

    kale pesto with beetroot gnocchi **198–200**

    kale pesto with roasted parsnips **206**

    lazy day pasta and garlic kale sauce **216**

    massaged kale salad **215**

noodles with crispy kale, miso mushrooms **298–9**

pumpkin and kale falafels **222–4**

roasted and smoked whole aubergine **86–7**

sweet potato, greens and garlic mash **344**

warm winter vegetable and grain slaw **267**

kansui **262, 264**

kimchi

    any-day Brussels sprout kimchi **326**

kohlrabi

    fennel and kohlrabi salad **103**

l

lasagne

    courgette 'lasagne' **92–4**

latte

    pumpkin spiced latte **233**

leeks

    'buttered' leeks **332–3**

    Moroccan-spiced sweet potato salad **345**

lemons

    celeriac and chestnut risotto **250–1**

    courgette ribbon salad **97**

    creamy lemon linguine **186–7**

    lemon and coriander hummus **358**

    lemon and garlic vinaigrette **354**

    slow-cooked broad bean fregola **50**

lettuce **150**

    charred lettuce and tahini Caesar **152–3**

    chive and chickpea sandwiches **154–5**

    loaded leaf salad **156–7**

linguine
    creamy lemon linguine
        186–7

——

m

maple syrup
    Dijon and maple syrup
        vinaigrette **354**
    maple and cardamom apricots
        76
    maple and thyme roasted
        pears **284**
    maple-roasted cabbage
        260–1
marinara
    mushroom 'meatballs'
        marinara **296–7**
mash
    'buttery' spiced carrot mash
        139
    garlicky parsnip, potato and
        celeriac mash **211**
    potato, white bean and
        mustard mash **68**
    sweet potato, greens and
        garlic mash **344**
mayonnaise
    silken tofu mayonnaise **371**
'meatballs'
    mushroom 'meatballs'
        marinara **296–7**
millet
    beet-top and millet chopped
        salad **190–2**
    Moroccan-spiced sweet potato
        salad **345**
    savoury millet porridge
        116–17
    wild mushrooms, millet and
        green harissa **294–5**
mint
    broad bean and mint hummus
        52
miso
    ginger, parsley and miso
        aubergine **84**

noodles with crispy kale, miso
    mushrooms **298–9**
savoury millet porridge
    116–17
tahini, ginger, miso dressing
    356
Moroccan-spiced sweet potato
    salad **345**
muesli
    three-grain Bircher muesli
        58–9
mushrooms **290**
    baked split pea, sweet potato
        and rosemary stew **342–3**
    everyday roasted veggies **210**
    garlic rice **300**
    grilled vegetable skewers
        183–5
    mushroom and tarragon
        risotto **292**
    mushroom gravy **293**
    mushroom 'meatballs'
        marinara **296–7**
    noodles with crispy kale, miso
        mushrooms **298–9**
    roasted beetroot, caraway and
        shallot hummus **201–3**
    whole roasted celeriac with
        mushroom gravy **246–9**
    wild mushrooms, millet and
        green harissa **294–5**
mustard
    Dijon and maple syrup
        vinaigrette **354**
    potato, white bean and
        mustard mash **68**
mustards seeds
    twice-cooked 'buttery' garlic
        chestnuts **275**

——

n

noodles
    cabbage ramen **262–5**
    noodles with crispy kale, miso
        mushrooms **298–9**
    tahini Thai noodles **148–9**

nut butter **362**
    cookies **369–70**
    nut butter dressing **357**
    see also peanut butter
nut roast
    chestnut nut roast **278–9**
    parsnip nut roast **207–9**
nuts
    everyday roasted veggies **210**
    nut milk **363–4**
    nut-based cheese **364–5**
    nut-pulp granola **367**
    pumpkin seed and nut
        granola **220–1**
    see also individual nuts

——

o

oats
    cherry breakfast crumble
        126–7
    cookies **369–70**
    granola **366–7**
    multigrain pancakes **76**
    pumpkin seed and nut
        granola **220–1**
    savoury granola **211**
    spiced apple crumble **308**
    three-grain Bircher muesli
        58–9
olives
    tahini tapenade **88–9**
onions
    garlic rice **300**
    grilled vegetable skewers
        183–5
    red onion pickles **372**
    stock cupboard pear and
        onion chutney **285–6**
    see also shallots
oranges
    shaved Brussels sprouts and
        buckwheat **327–8**
    tahini orange biscuits
        128–31

orecchiette pasta
  creamed chestnut and sage
    pasta **276**
orzo
  tomato salad with orzo and
    crispy greens **170**

——

p

pancakes
  buckwheat flour base **368**
  chickpea flour base **368–9**
  multigrain pancakes **76**
  turmeric pancakes **180–2**
panzanella salad **104**
Parmesan
  green bean salad with nut
    Parmesan **146–7**
  nut Parmesan **365**
  slow-cooked broad bean
    fregola with nut Parmesan
    50–1
parsley
  celeriac steaks with caper and
    parsley chimichurri **256–7**
  chimichurri **361**
  ginger, parsley and miso
    aubergine **84**
  Jersey Royal potatoes **112**
parsnips **204**
  chestnut nut roast **278–9**
  everyday roasted veggies **210**
  garlicky parsnip, potato and
    celeriac mash **211**
  parsnip nut roast **207–9**
  roasted parsnips **206**
  root vegetable, celery, thyme
    and butter bean chowder
    322–3
pasta
  cauliflower carbonara **36**
  creamed chestnut and sage
    pasta **276**
  creamy lemon linguine
    186–7

Dad's any-vegetable-goes,
  creamy, roasted tomato
  pasta bake **160–3**
lazy day pasta and garlic kale
  sauce **216**
slow-cooked broad bean
  fregola **50–1**
summer pasta salad **82**
tomato salad with orzo and
  crispy greens **170**
pâté
  cauliflower pâté **37**
  salted pear and cauliflower
    pâté bruschetta **38**
pea shoots
  herby garlic cauliflower
    couscous **53**
peanut butter
  griddled celeriac with peanut
    satay **254–5**
  Jerusalem artichoke, peanut
    and coconut curry **334–6**
pears **280**
  maple and thyme roasted
    pears **284**
  pickled pear **254–5**
  salted pear and cauliflower
    pâté bruschetta **38**
  stock cupboard pear and
    onion chutney **285–6**
  upside-down pear cake
    282–3
  za'atar spiced pear and
    cabbage **288–9**
peas
  loaded leaf salad **156–7**
  see also split peas
pesto **359**
  beetroot gnocchi with kale
    pesto **198–200**
  broccoli pesto **360**
  carrot top pesto **360**
  cauliflower carbonara with
    leftover pesto **36**
  courgette 'lasagne' **92–4**

green risotto **28–9**
kale pesto **359**
roast fennel, pesto gnocchi
  108–9
roasted parsnips with kale
  pesto **206**
stuffed courgettes with walnut
  pesto **98**
whole roasted carrots with
  carrot top pesto **136–8**
pickles **372**
  with beetroot and gram flour
    flatbreads **193–4**
  carrot and ginger pickles **373**
  cucumber dill pickles
    114–15
  cucumber and herb pickles
    373
  pickled pear **254–5**
  red onion pickles **372**
pistachios
  green bean salad **146–7**
pizza
  spelt pizza **105–6**
plums
  summer pasta salad **82**
Polish-style cabbage **266**
Polish-style stuffed cabbage leaves
  269–70
porridge
  savoury millet porridge
    116–17
potatoes
  everyday roasted veggies **210**
  garlicky parsnip, potato and
    celeriac mash **211**
  potato, white bean and
    mustard mash **68**
  roast fennel, pesto gnocchi
    108–9
  roasted artichokes and
    potatoes **337**
  twice-baked potatoes **118–19**
  see also Jersey Royal potatoes
pumpkin **218**

black rice stuffed pumpkin 225–7

chunky pumpkin tacos 228–9

creamy curried pumpkin split pea dal 234–6

everyday roasted veggies 210

grilled vegetable skewers 183–5

mashed pumpkin with beetroot and gram flour flatbreads 193–4

pumpkin and kale falafels 222–4

pumpkin hummus 358

pumpkin pie parfait 230–1

pumpkin spiced latte 233

whole roasted pumpkin 237–9

see also squash

pumpkin seeds

celeriac ribbon salad 253

pumpkin seed and nut granola 220–1

savoury granola 211

q

quesadillas

sweet potato and cannellini bean quesadillas 346–7

quinoa

roasted apricots 79

r

ramen

cabbage ramen 262–5

ras el hanout baked aubergine 88–9

rhubarb 54

fridge dinner salad 60–1

rhubarb cashew cheesecake 56–7

three-grain Bircher muesli 58–9

rice

coconut black rice salad 66–7

garlic rice 300

green bean salad 146–7

green risotto 28–9

mushroom and tarragon risotto 292

rice-stuffed tomatoes 170–2

risotto with Jerusalem artichokes 332–3

ricotta

courgette 'lasagne' 92–4

stuffed courgettes 98

stuffed courgettes with vegan ricotta 98

risotto

celeriac and chestnut risotto 250–1

green risotto 28–9

mushroom and tarragon risotto 292

risotto with Jerusalem artichokes 332–3

rosemary

baked split pea, sweet potato and rosemary stew 342–3

whole roasted pumpkin 237–9

rye

three-grain Bircher muesli 58–9

s

sage

creamed chestnut and sage pasta 276

roasted artichokes and potatoes 337

salsa

balsamic cherry salsa 132–3

cherry salsa 136–8

sandwiches

chive and chickpea sandwiches 154–5

satay sauce 254–5

seeds

seed milk 363–4

seed-pulp granola 367

see also individual seeds

sesame seeds

celeriac ribbon salad 253

charred cauliflower and broccolini 34–5

savoury granola 211

shallots

creamy lemon linguine 186–7

pan-fried Sri Lankan green beans and shallots 144–5

roasted beetroot, caraway and shallot hummus 201–3

skewers

grilled vegetable skewers 183–5

slaw

apple and sprout slaw 312

warm winter vegetable and grain slaw 267

sourdough panzanella salad 104

spelt

apricot and grain salad 77

spelt pizza 105–6

three-grain Bircher muesli 58–9

spinach

basil and spinach hummus 358

green risotto 28–9

split peas

baked split pea, sweet potato and rosemary stew 342–3

creamy curried pumpkin split pea dal 234–6

sprouts see Brussels sprouts

squash

everyday roasted veggies 210

root vegetable, celery, thyme and butter bean chowder 322–3

squash hummus 358

see also pumpkin
Sri Lankan green beans and
  shallots 144–5
stock 352
stone fruit
  green bean salad 146–7
  summer pasta salad 82
  see also apricots
sumac roasted cherries 128–31
sweet potatoes 340
  baked split pea, sweet potato
    and rosemary stew 342–3
  baked sweet potato, crispy
    chickpeas 348–9
  Moroccan-spiced sweet potato
    salad 345
  sweet potato and cannellini
    bean quesadillas 346–7
sweet potato, greens and garlic
  mash 344

t

tacos 370
  with cabbage leaves 258
  chunky beetroot and white
    bean tacos 195–7
  chunky pumpkin tacos
    228–9
tahini
  basic tahini dressing 356
  cauliflower Caesar salad
    42–3
  charred lettuce and tahini
    Caesar 152–3
  loaded leaf salad 156–7
  tahini dressing 348–9
  tahini dressing and then some
    356
  tahini, ginger, miso dressing
    356
  tahini orange biscuits
    128–31
  tahini sauce 288–9
  tahini tapenade 88–9
  tahini Thai noodles 148–9

tapenade
  tahini tapenade 88–9
tarragon
  Jersey Royal potatoes 112
  mushroom and tarragon
    risotto 292
tea
  fennel tea 100
Tenderstem broccoli
  potato, white bean and
    mustard mash 68
Thai noodles 148–9
thyme
  maple and thyme roasted
    pears 284
  root vegetable, celery, thyme
    and butter bean chowder
    322–3
tofu
  charred cauliflower and
    broccolini with tofu cream
    34–5
  silken tofu mayonnaise 371
  spelt pizza with tofu cream
    105–6
tomatoes 158
  courgette 'lasagne' 92–4
  Dad's any-vegetable-goes,
    creamy, roasted tomato
    pasta bake 160–3
  mushroom 'meatballs'
    marinara 296–7
  quartered and roasted
    tomatoes 173
  rice-stuffed tomatoes 170–2
  slow-cooked, smoked
    tomatoes 164–5
  spelt pizza 105–6
  stuffed cabbage leaves 269–
    70
  tomato salad 168–9
  tomato salad with fennel and
    capers 168–9
  tomato salad with orzo and
    crispy greens 170
tortillas 370

sweet potato and cannellini
  bean quesadillas 346–7
turmeric pancakes 180–2

V

vinaigrettes 354

W

walnuts
  apple and walnut any-flour
    Danish buns 309–11
  apricot and grain salad 77
  beetroot gnocchi with kale
    pesto 198–200
  broccoli pesto 360
  carrot top pesto 360
  celery, chicory, walnut and
    bulgur salad 319
  courgette 'lasagne' 92–4
  kale pesto 359
  massaged kale salad 215
  pesto 359
  roasted fennel, pesto gnocchi
    108–9
  roasted parsnips with kale
    pesto 206
  stuffed courgettes with walnut
    pesto 98

Z

za'atar
  za'atar spiced pear and
    cabbage 288–9

MICHAEL JOSEPH

UK | USA | Canada | Ireland | Australia
India | New Zealand | South Africa

Michael Joseph is part of the Penguin Random House group of companies
whose addresses can be found at global.penguinrandomhouse.com

First published by Michael Joseph, 2022
002

Copyright © Sophie Gordon, 2022
Food photography © Issy Croker, 2022
Illustrations © Holly Ovenden, 2022

The moral right of the author has been asserted

Set in Caslon, Geometr415, Bell, Gill Sans
Design by Sarah Fraser
Colour reproduction by Altaimage Ltd
Printed in Latvia by Livonia Print

The authorized representative in the EEA is Penguin Random House Ireland,
Morrison Chambers, 32 Nassau Street, Dublin D02 YH68

A CIP catalogue record for this book is available from the British Library

ISBN: 978–0–241–46513–4

www.greenpenguin.co.uk

Penguin Random House is committed to a
sustainable future for our business, our readers
and our planet. This book is made from Forest
Stewardship Council® certified paper.